Sins of Our
FATHERS

Sins of Our
FATHERS

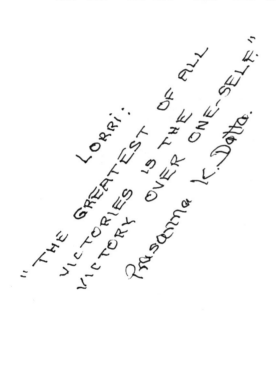

LORRI:

"THE GREATEST OF ALL
VICTORIES IS THE
VICTORY OVER ONE-SELF"

Prasanna K. Datta

PRASANNA K. DATTA

Library of Congress Control Number:		2009900030
ISBN:	Hardcover	978-1-4415-0049-6
	Softcover	978-1-4415-0048-9

This book was printed in the United States of America.

To order additional copies of this book, contact:
Xlibris Corporation
1-888-795-4274
www.Xlibris.com
Orders@Xlibris.com
54793

CONTENTS

DEDICATION

To the memory of my parents, Komoleswar Datta and Ikon Datta.

PART A

Potter's Son

IF YOU VISIT the Himalayan mountains, you will find their foothills covered with rain forests. Various types of hardwoods, bamboos, banana plants, ferns, vines, and grass grow in these jungles. The inhabitants of these woodlands are mostly tigers, elephants, panthers, antelopes, rhinos, monkeys, snakes, and long-horned buffalos.

Villages and paddy fields adjoin these jungles. On clear, sunny mornings, villagers like Manu, the young son of a potter, can see these mountains twenty to twenty-five miles away from their houses. The snow-covered peaks glitter and display alluring colors that entice adventurers, hunters, and mystics. The highest of them pierce the sky where, some believe, spirits dwell.

The Himalayas were formed forty to fifty million years ago due to the plate-tectonic forces to become the world's highest mountains. They tower more than five and a half miles above sea level and still elevate half inch a year. Captivated by their loftiness, poets of yesterday named them the "Abode of Snow."

From these majestic mountains that separate the Indian subcontinent from the Tibetan plateau, mighty rivers flow south through plains and valleys to the Indian Ocean. During the hot, dry seasons, melting snow feeds them gently. During monsoons, they sometimes become torrential and flood the low-lying villages that have spotted these valleys over hundreds of years. Generations have come and gone, leaving behind countless stories, few told, and many forgotten.

This story, however, refused to die. It's the story of Manu, Gregory Gambino, and Bir Dharma and how their paths crossed.

Manu's bamboo hut was at a lower level, next to the raised, unpaved road that passed through his village of twenty-eight households. It led east to the Ledo airfield built by the American forces and south to the market and train station.

The road was near the banks of a tributary of the longer and wider river Brahmaputra that flows west through the long valley, then south to the Ganges, and then together they meander through the alluvial soil of the fertile plains to the Bay of Bengal. The tributary's embankment had thick green tropical undergrowth and rows of tall betel nut plants.

It was late afternoon that day during the rainy season of 1943 when the Flying Tigers of the American air force flew regular missions over the Himalayas from remote airfields in northeast India to supply the Chinese fighting the invading Japanese. Manu sat quietly on his father's clay mound in front of his house, readying himself the best he could. As he waited, he smelt the humid air and listened to the crickets trilling. *They always sing before it rains*, he thought.

By nature, he was gentle and patient, sometimes contemplative, sometimes inquisitive. He didn't speak much, even to his friend Gopal, probably because as a child, he didn't hear much spoken language. He was short and thin, unlike his teenage older sister who was tall and slender. Rumi was always active and cheerful. She was strong and confident and took good care of him and their father when their mother died. Of course, Manu didn't remember her. His father told him she died giving birth to him.

Rumi was perfecting the dance steps of the spring festival and was developing into a beautiful woman with soft, feminine curves when she drowned. It had rained heavily the previous year, and the nearby tributary was suddenly filled with torrents of muddy floodwater that carried her away.

Manu missed her dearly and couldn't understand or accept the finality of her death. *Somehow*, he thought, *she would return, the same way she left—suddenly—and the three of them would live together again, happy and secure.*

His father noticed his mood changes after the drowning. He sought more solitude now. He didn't even want to play or go fishing with his friends.

Once, after the drowning, when his father was squatting on the ground besides his spinning wheel in front of their windowless hut, shaping beautiful earthenware with his sensitive and skilled fingers, Manu approached him. He held a few pink orchids in his hand, the type his sister loved. They still grew wild in their backyard.

"Father, why did she die?" he asked with tearful eyes. "Why did she have to drown? She loved these orchids so much, and now she is not here to smell or wear them. Father, can I die temporarily so that I can see her for a moment?"

This question confused and frightened his father.

"I don't know, my son, but someday you will. You will know more, much more than I do," he said. "Why don't you ask Guru Dev? People say he is the temple's most learned."

Early one morning after bathing and fasting, Manu visited the temple. He found Guru Dev in the temple yard, sitting cross-legged on a raised wooden stool, teaching the scriptures to his dozen or so teenage boys who sat on bamboo mats. He was teaching, in beautiful speech, the elaborate ritualistic portion of the *Vedas*. Such rituals are said to bring power to those who perform them in certain prescribed ways. They were listening and learning and perhaps even longing. Will such rituals enable them to develop concentration that leads to total absorption in God?

The Vedic hymns were music to Manu's ears although he didn't understand Sanskrit. He, therefore, stood there silently, with palms together in front of his heart, as is the custom.

"So what brings the potter's son to the temple yard today?" Guru Dev finally said.

"Guru Dev, my father told me that you are most learned. You know more than all of us put together. So I humbly come to you with a question that bothers me, one that my father doesn't answer."

"Ask then, boy, and always remember that wisdom belongs to seekers only," Guru commanded with the voice of priestly authority.

"My sister, Rumi, who was young, loving, and beautiful, drowned in the flood of last year. She didn't get to experience a full life. She was kind and good. I miss her. Guru, why did she have to die?"

"Your question is wise indeed, very wise for someone like you. So I'll let my pupils answer," the haughty priest replied.

The boys looked at one another and hesitated until Bonu, the brightest of them all, said, "In the sphere of duality where we now exist, the cycle of birth and death is experienced until self-realization is achieved."

"Very good answer," Guru said, proud for bestowing such profound knowledge to his pupils. "Did you understand, potter's son?"

"No, Guru Dev, I didn't."

"Then you aren't ready to understand," Koli, the dullest and most arrogant of them, said.

"You shouldn't ask such questions. Your time hasn't come for such inquiries," another said.

"Such questions are for the twice-born," one with pimples said, implying his superior birth.

"If the otter can live and survive for seven generations by eating raw fish, why should he learn to fry fish now?" a squint-eyed youth jeered, while his fellow students filled the air with mocking laughter.

The ridicule of the learned Hindus wounded Manu. He visited the temple with hope, seeking an answer for a question that tormented him. Perhaps a few kind words would have comforted him and make him feel that he belonged to the community. Instead, he found callousness and rebuke that made him feel like a stranger in the land of his birth.

Why, he thought, *would God, who lives in the temple, do things that only the learned and the wise can understand? Why must the Vedas be secret? Why can't they be simple for all?* When he didn't find answers, he decided not to tell his father of his temple experience.

Today, as he waited for the bearded man, he recalled the events of the previous days. He remembered sitting on this very same mound, frightened and weeping. His father was dying of smallpox—a highly contagious disease that frequented, frightened, and terrorized everyone in his village, for they didn't understand what it was or how to cure it. They prayed and hoped for a cure, and when nothing happened, they decided to quarantine his family, expecting that somehow it would go away.

Tradition taught them that if an insoluble problem arises, the best way to deal with it is to just ignore it or deny its existence. He remembered how the villagers prevented him from going out of his yard and shouting that when the old man dies, they would torch his body in his hut. "He deserves his fate. He has bad karma," they cried. Manu hoped his dying father didn't hear these angry and cruel cries.

When he was growing up, his education consisted of listening to *Ramayana* and *Mahabharata* stories recited by the village elders under the mangrove. He remembered his father telling him to be brave in a crisis. "Lord Rama was a young boy when he was banished to the forest with his wife, Sita, and brother Lakshman. Yet Rama slew the evil king who had abducted Sita," his father used to say. "So you must always be brave."

But he couldn't be brave when he saw his father become weaker and weaker every day. The large red spots were now all over his body, face, and mouth.

Why does my father suffer such pain when Gopal's father doesn't? Manu thought. *What is karma?*

He remembered that he didn't know what to do or where to turn. The rice bin was almost empty, but he felt like doing nothing in the hot sun—not even bathe. He recalled villagers hastening their pace on the elevated road in front of their hut. He remembered thinking that if Rumi were to be alive, he wouldn't have felt the stomach pain that only hunger can make you experience. Then something happened, something very unusual and unexpected. Through his tearful eyes, he saw a bearded man in a white robe get off his bicycle and approach him.

"Why are you crying, boy?" the sunburned man wearing a white hat asked.

"My father is alone and dying in the house."

Without any hesitation, the stranger entered the hut. Years of God's work in the hot sun gave him the uncanny ability to pick up the slightest whiff of misery in the air. Manu followed. After the stranger's eyes adjusted to the dark room, he looked around but found no bed. He then noticed on the clay floor a body of a man on a thin straw mat scantly clothed.

"How long has he been like this?"

"Many days."

"Do you have anyone to feed him, to take care of him? He is dehydrated and malnourished. Where is your mother?"

"Dead! I have no one! The villagers are afraid of smallpox. No one comes to help. They are angry and will burn our house and my father."

He remembered the stranger kneeling at the head of the mat on which the body lay, touching the cross hung on his chest, looking up at the dark straw ceiling and reciting a prayer. He then looked at Manu's tearful eyes. "Don't be frightened. I'll help. I'm Bicycle Padre. Fetch some clean water for your father."

As he sprinkled a few drops on his father's dry mouth from his trembling hands, he heard the stranger say, "Son, your father has left this world for a better place. He is with God now."

Manu sank to his knees besides his father's body, too exhausted to realize what happened.

"Stay here with your father. We'll be back soon. Don't let others see you."

As the sun set for another day at the distant horizon, and as the road became dark and quiet, two robed figures arrived with a bullock-drawn cart and a wooden box. Without uttering a word, they handed him a small bag of rice, then wrapped the body in a white cotton sheet and put it in the box. They then disappeared into the night. Strangely, he didn't feel sad nor did he understand what happened. He just sat on the floor, his head between his bony knees, and tried to find rest and comfort in the blanket of darkness.

Today, however, was a new day—though uncertain. What else could he do besides go to the orphanage with Bicycle Padre? He then remembered how his father wanted him to be brave in a crisis.

I'll go, my father, and I'll be brave, Manu promised.

PART B

Great Commission

MORE THAN FORTY-FIVE years before, and four thousand miles west of Manu's valley, in 1892, five years before Queen Victoria celebrated her diamond jubilee as the ruler of a quarter of the world's population, the third son was born to the Gambino family in Milan, Italy. His parents named him Gregory after Pope Gregory the Great, of the sixth century, who, with the assistance of Thomas Aquinas and Dante, cataloged the seven deadly sins—pride, gluttony, melancholy, lust, greed, envy, and anger.

The Gambinos were devout Catholics. They wanted their sons to join the priesthood. Their eldest son, however, was more interested in growing grapes and having a family while the second immigrated to America with his uncle. Gregory's father, Dino, therefore, decided that his youngest would be a priest and spread the Gospels (Good News) to pagans of distant lands.

Gregory forgot when he was baptized but remembered his grandmother taking him regularly to the churches in and around Milan. Like most of its women, she always wore black, from head to toe, and the rosary never left her hand. Before Gregory was ten, everyone knew that he would be a priest someday.

Dino taught him everything he knew about the Bible and Catholicism. He told him of St. Paul's beheading and martyrdom, of St. Peter's wish to be crucified head down in Rome, and about building the domed cathedral.

The parish priest told him about great St. Augustine, that he was born in 354 in Tagaste, and how he, after being baptized in 387, founded a monastery in Tagaste and devoted his life to God. "I desire to know God and my soul. Nothing else; nothing whatever," he wrote.

The story of Father Damien, who was the first missionary to serve the leprosy colony in the Hawaiian island of Molokai in the last quarter of the nineteenth century moved Gregory to tears. He learned that when Damien was thirty-two, he went there to establish a parish when others ignored the islanders because they were infected by a dangerously communicable disease that caused physical mutilation. Later, Father Damien himself died of leprosy.

Such tales excited him and filled his youthful mind with spiritual adventure. *Someday,* he thought, *he would visit Rome and pray at the holy site where St. Peter's bones are buried.* He dreamed that he would have an audience with the pope, kneel before him, and kiss the ring on his right hand. The Holy Father would bless him and entrust him with St. Matthew's Great Commission: "Therefore go and make disciples of all nations, baptizing them in the name of the Father and of the Son and of the Holy Spirit and teaching them to obey everything I have commended you."

Young Gambino heard his calling and the holy command. By the time he entered his teens, he became more and more convinced that his commission was to be a healer of both body and soul.

Dozens of missionaries came to Milan on home leave with exotic stories of ancient lands. From them he learnt that host countries lacked expertise in many fields, particularly health and literacy.

As he grew older, he believed more and more that the love of Jesus is the best gift to humanity, and sharing it can bring salvation to many in lands where cure is a stranger. He wanted to be like St. Augustine, to find a mission in a pagan land where people have not yet heard of the Gospels or of Jesus Christ and of his eventual return. He promised himself that he will be a totally dedicated missionary of the Cross and gladly leave home with all its comforts and freely choose a life of poverty and obedience to spread Christianity.

In the following years, Gambino devoted all his time to study medicine, particularly infectious diseases. The Milan seminary provided orthodox theology training, while the local churches and libraries provided excitement and stimulant for his curious mind. The books on cholera and smallpox described the deaths of hundreds of poor and simple people in India because they didn't know how to contain and treat such ailments.

The future priest visited the sick in their homes and hospitals. He met regularly with physicians who welcomed his boundless enthusiasm and shared with him their knowledge on the treatment of tropical diseases. He also studied local customs and their ways of bereavement.

He visited mortuaries and cemeteries and taught himself to control his emotions in facing the unexpected. Above all, he learnt not to be a stranger to suffering and sacrifice.

He also studied the languages and dialects of his adopted land to translate the New Testament and stories of the Old Testament. He planned to teach the local people to read and write so that they would be able to understand and remember the Gospels and build their own churches to practice the teachings of the Catholic Church. A Milan parishioner taught him carpentry, plumbing, septic systems, and how to situate and frame a house.

On the day of his departure, his parents, relatives, and friends came to wish him success. They were proud of his mission. What can be a greater undertaking than spreading the Bible?

"You are going to a land farther away than the land of Abraham and Moses. I may not see you again in this life. So take this rosary, and when you preach to the Indic people, keep it with you," his hunched grandaunt said, giving him her mother's rosary.

Armed with his deep faith in the Second Coming and in the goodness of his heart, the strongly built man of twenty-eight and medium height, with light brown eyes and jet-black hair, boarded a ship bound for the Orient, a month following his ordainment to the Christian ministry.

Changing Winds

The end of World War I in 1918 ushered in political and economic changes throughout the world. The victors of the war, particularly United States of America and Great Britain, agreed to free the smaller nations that were under German rule and give the right to determine their own forms of government.

India contributed greatly to the war efforts. It provided soldiers to fight under British command in various theaters in Europe, Africa, and Asia. Therefore, they demanded the same privileges for home rule. Mass support for the movement was soon gaining momentum.

One significant maritime change, though sometimes overlooked, was the conversion of battleships to passenger carriers. The HMS *Manchester* was such a ship. Its first two decks were splendidly refurbished and extravagantly decorated to pay tribute to the victors of the war, the dignitaries, and senior military personnel. Decks C and D, with basic conveniences, were mostly for lesser colonial subjects and poor Europeans traveling or immigrating to countries of the British Empire over which the sun never set.

On Deck C, Gambino felt the change in weather as his ship passed the Suez Canal. The mild breezes of the temperate Mediterranean regions were giving way to hot, dry desert winds of Arabia and the Sahara. The *Manchester* steamed its course through the Red Sea and the Arabian Sea on its way to Aden and Bombay—the gateway to India.

While docked at Port Aden for fresh supplies, Gambino couldn't help overhearing the discussion of four British petty officers on their way to join their regiments in India. They were greatly agitated as they discussed the possibility of renewed military operations on the Indo-Afghan border. They discussed the previous year's treaty that recognized the independence of Afghanistan.

The passengers on Deck A were the first to disembark when they docked at Bombay harbor. Gambino, in his white robe, stood on Deck C and waited anxiously for his turn along with other passengers.

"Guide me, Jesus, to bring to this land of nonbelievers the true God of Abraham. Bless me to spread your light and enlighten their souls," he prayed.

"Welcome to India, Father Gambino," a uniformed British officer said in the Customs Office after examining and stamping his documents. "You are advised to take a buggy to Bombay Railway Station. The stationmaster Brian Sullivan is an Irishman. He will assist you with your ticket to Ikonpur."

"How long will it take, Officer Preston?"

"The railway station is about an hour from here," the officer replied, pointing to the exit. "Please be advised not to pay the tongawalla more than a rupee. He may plead for more."

A sea of humanity waited him outside the Customs House as he looked for a pony-drawn cart. Before he could decide, a tongawalla tugged at his only piece of luggage that he held tightly in his right hand.

"Train station, sahib?" the man said and looked toward the row of pony carts.

"English?" Gambino asked as he glanced at his translation book.

"No English. One rupee," the man said and held up his index finger.

"How you know where I go?" he tried in Hindi.

The turbaned man in a bright orange shirt didn't answer. He led him quickly to his cart and, after Gambino was comfortably seated, guided his pony through the market clogged with shoppers, hawkers, and paddlers. Small linen stores with colorful displays lined the road. Loud chatter, laughter, and the smell of spicy, cooked food filled the noon air.

To his utter amazement, Gambino saw abandoned cattle with long sharp horns roam the market, sometimes helping themselves to vegetables stalls. Buggies, bicycles, and rickshaws zigzagged their way through the crowd. Children of all ages shouted at one another. They laughed and talked and wondered aimlessly without a care in the world. Slender and graceful women in colorful saris walked tall, with large woven cane baskets balanced on their heads. Some had large red dots on their foreheads. Some chewed betel nut and leaves that made their mouths red.

These sights filled him with excitement and intense missionary zeal. He wanted to feel what he thought St. Thomas the Apostle must have felt when he first preached in India after the Crucifixion nearly nineteen hundred years ago. He wanted to walk the same path that the apostle did and search for clues of his teachings. He wanted to witness how the Bible influences the lives of these people.

"You know St. Thomas?" he asked.

The man didn't answer. *Possibly he didn't hear me,* he thought.

As the pony clip-clopped its way, he saw and felt what he wanted to see and feel. The apparent chaos of the marketplace made him anxious. He wondered if the hidden order in disorder was due to the never-ending mercy and love of Christ for the ordinary man.

"How far train station from here?"

"Very far," the man replied.

Though he prepared himself nearly all his life to live and preach in a country like India, this noonday experience drained him emotionally. He reassured himself, however, that his labor in the Lord's name wouldn't be in vain.

At the station, Sullivan greeted him warmly and, after a glass of lemonade in his office, led him to an empty Europeans Only compartment. It was very comfortable with soft-leathered chairs fixed to the carpeted floor, not at all crowded like the other compartments where overflowing, clamorous passengers hung from door handles.

The train stopped briefly at Ikonpur as the new priest disembarked to discover the new world that awaited him.

Mission Ikonpur

"You have arrived at the best time of the year, Father Gambino," Father Julius said as he welcomed him to Mission Ikonpur after a silent supper.

Gambino smiled and nodded. He was tired. It was a long and unusual day.

"The monsoons have ended," the kindly gray-haired priest said. "Heat and humidity will lessen. The evenings and nights will be pleasant for prayers, study, and meditation. There will be plenty of vegetables and fruits at the bazaar. We are grateful to the Heavenly Father for the good rains of the last three months."

"Yes, yes. Very true," Father Angelo said. The turmeric-stained white robe that he wore couldn't conceal his fondness for food. "These past weeks have been exciting. You see, Father, many of our priests from all over the country spend their sabbaticals with us. They discuss their experiences, and we record them for learning and historical purposes. We become something like a small theology college with a Vedic flavor," he laughed and looked at the other priests seated around the dinning table in the largest room of the mission.

Gambino listened. He was uncomfortable on the old squeaky wooden chair.

"Father Angelo and I have been permanent members here for many years," Julius said. "We serve this parish with a few hundred members. They contribute labor to clear the woods to grow vegetables. Farmers donate portions of their crops for spiritual guidance. We receive free medicine from a local pharmacist. A few Hindu merchants sometimes donate cash to create good karma.

"We orientate new priests and introduce them to Eastern beliefs and practices," Julius continued, unaware of Gambino's stiffness. "This is why you are here today. India is vast and ancient. We have much to learn, and we share what we learn. For instance, the idea of choosing the rainy season for sabbatical is twenty-five hundred years old. Gautama, the Buddha, used the rainy months to teach dharma to his monks. Then when the monsoons end, and traveling becomes easier, these monks would spread all over the countryside, teaching the populace the Buddhist path to enlightenment. The concept of monkism originated during his time."

He listened quietly to the wisdom and experience of the two monks. As he sat around the multipurpose mahogany table, he stared at the two lit candles and wondered why he just couldn't teach the Gospels his own way without learning pagan ways.

He noticed a few of his compadres weren't wearing the traditional white or black robes. In fact, three of the eight who sat around the table were wearing unstitched clothes—like sheets wrapped around their bodies. He also noticed that he was the youngest and was surprised and disappointed when no one inquired about his training or voyage. Therefore, he decided to introduce himself.

"Reverent Fathers, I'm indeed blessed to be here today, to be able to meet and hear you. No doubt I have much to learn about this land that I come to serve in our Lord's name. But since I'm not familiar with the protocol of such an orientation,

I would like to know if I may ask questions during the information sharing, or should I wait until it ends?"

Before Julius or Angelo could answer, as Gambino had expected, Father Basco, in his unstitched clothes, said that the only protocol they follow is respect for truth, wisdom, and service in God's name. Barrel-chested as he was, with a black beard that covered his chest, he personified a storehouse of energy and physical strength. Moreover, from the tone of his voice and brevity of his answer, Gambino realized that he isn't someone to trifle with.

Angelo noticed Gambino's apprehension. "Yes, yes. You can ask questions at any time."

"Thank you, Father," he said. "Please tell me what 'dharma' means."

Dharma and Father Basco

"Many years ago," Father Basco said, "when I first came to India as a young priest, I found its oppressive heat to be simply unbearable. To protect myself from sunburn, I wore a European straw hat. But much to my dismay, my hat drew unsolicited attention, making me more of a sahib than a Catholic priest.

"One day, I walked to a village to find a parishioner. On the way, two old men approached me for alms. The midday sun must have affected my thinking, for my response was unnecessarily unkind.

"'Where is your dharma, sahib?' one asked, surprised at my rudeness. To my utter amazement, my mind went blank at the question about my dharma!" He paused and appeared thoughtful.

"'Dharma' is a Sanskrit word. It has many meanings. From the esoteric point of view, dharma can have connotations of universal law. For instance, the sun shines. It's the dharma of the sun to shine. Grass grows. It's the dharma of the grass to grow.

"Related to people, dharma can imply duty to the family, to the community, to the surrounding. For instance, it's the dharma of the well to care for the ill. It's the dharma of the strong to protect the weak. It's the dharma of the homemaker to cook for the family. It's the dharma of the Catholic priest to perform rites. It's the dharma of the Buddhist monk to spread the teachings of Lord Buddha."

They listened to his in-depth knowledge of Eastern philosophy.

"Dharma can also be described as a path," he went on. "For instance, when the Buddha preached his dharma, he taught his own experience under the Bodhi tree where he attained enlightenment."

"Tell him what 'enlightenment' means," Angelo suggested.

"Enlightenment means the discovery of Nirvana—the end of sorrow or rebirth."

"Does the word 'Buddha' have a meaning?"

"It means 'one who is awake.' You see, he didn't claim to have guidance from superior beings. His path isn't a system of philosophical or intellectual thought. Nor is it based on religious authority. It's simply a way of life. He asked his followers not to accept his dharma without examining it. He said his teachings constitute the dharma and asked his disciples to work diligently for their own salvation. He also asked them not to worship him."

Basco adjusted the loose sheet wrapped around his body and looked at Gambino.

"To the old men seeking alms, I personified good Western values and beliefs. Since generosity is considered the basis of morality in all religions, alms expectations are inevitable.

"My experience with the old men led me to explore the significance of generosity or charity as it relates to a way of life.

"It's said that after Gautama attained enlightenment, his father, the king, invited him to teach at the palace. Gautama and his disciples accepted. Early the following morning after their arrival, he went to the villages to beg for food. When he returned to the palace after collecting alms, his father asked why a prince should beg.

"'It teaches humility, Father, to the one who begs and causes a meritorious opportunity for a donor with good intention to create good karma,' he replied."

Gambino shifted his tired body uncomfortably on his high-backed chair.

"I have listened to you, Father Basco. I thank you for explaining dharma. Now you mention another new word—'karma.' But before we divulge into its meaning, please tell me why I, a Catholic priest, whose spiritual knowledge is derived from the Bible, should learn new terminologies and stories of pagan faiths?"

Father Savvio, the other priest in unstitched clothes, who was quiet and almost asleep throughout the discussion, suddenly came alive. "Did you say 'pagan'? Father Gambino, perhaps you could tell us how you prepared for this land."

"The core, the very essence of my preparedness, is the Bible," he said. "I read it every day, and I try to be Jesus conscious every moment of my life."

"Then you will recall St. Paul in the 'Rights of Apostles' of 1 Corinthians that to win the Jews, he became like the Jews, to win the weak, he became weak," Savvio said.

"Father Gambino needs rest. He had a long day," Angelo said, picking up a lit candle from the table. "Let me show you to your room, Father. Tomorrow, after breakfast, I'll take you to the bazaar and introduce you to India's diverse people of many beliefs."

When the discussion ended, a few priests went to the chapel for evening prayers while others retired. Gambino's room was small and spartanly furnished. He tried to kneel by the side of the bed, but before he could end his prayers, he fell asleep on its thin mattress.

Bazaar

"I used to get upset stomach before, but now I love spices," Angelo said as they walked to the local market. "In fact, I mixed puffed rice with curried cabbage for breakfast today."

Although the sun rose just an hour before, Gambino felt the heat.

"Isn't the market a beehive, Father?" Angelo said as they made their way through the narrow lanes, often stepping aside to let buggies and rickshaws pass. "The mornings are the best time to buy fresh vegetables. Otherwise, the afternoon sun withers them. So I shop in the mornings," he said with insight into local customs. "They are a superstitious bunch, you know. They believe that if they can't sell to their very first customer, sales will be less for the entire day. So they are anxious to sell."

Gambino nodded his head as he studied the shops and customers. They passed a few flower vendors selling cannas, dahlias, roses, and marigolds. No one seemed to notice them in their white habits.

"Let me introduce you to Om Prakash, our pharmacist. He speaks and writes English. He is also a student of spoken Sanskrit. He's the one who gives us medicine he receives from America. Father Julius and I have known him for years. When you get to know him, you will find him wise. He's our window to the local people," Angelo said, excited to orient the new priest.

"He doesn't see major differences between the core teachings of the Buddha and Lord Krishna. Buddha was a great teacher, born around 560 BC south of the Himalayas. Hindus consider Krishna and Buddha to be avatars, or incarnations of Vishnu, the Preserver in the Hindu Trinity. He even sees commonalities between these faiths and Christ's teachings."

"How on earth can he see commonalities with our Lord's teachings?" Gambino asked in disbelief. "Somehow I don't like the very idea of finding commonalities between Christ's teachings and Eastern religions. When I was in Milan, I once read a book on Buddhism by a German author. I learned that Buddhism is an atheistic philosophy. They don't even recognize the existence of God while the core of Christianity is belief in one God and his son Jesus as the savior." He paused and looked at the people around him. "Hindus, on the other hand, believe in many gods, like the ancient Greeks. So where are the commonalities, Father?"

Angelo shrugged his shoulders. "All I know is that Hindus and Buddhists consider God to be unknowable. They believe human consciousness is at various individual levels of development. The speed of development towards enlightenment depends upon individual effort."

They reached the pharmacy. "Now, let's see how Prakash is."

"It's good to see you, Father," the graying slender pharmacist stood and greeted them as they climbed the three concrete steps. He was wearing a knee-length white jacket and tight dark trousers and sitting on a quilt that covered the raised part of the clinic floor, talking with a patient. He motioned to Angelo and Gambino to sit on chairs next to the medicine cabinets. He bowed slightly to the patient, then turned to Dadaji, his assistant, and requested hot tea for his guests.

"This is Father Gambino, fresh from Italy," Angelo said. "He studied medicine in Milan. He's interested in the medicines villagers use. He will be with us for a while. He plans to open a primary school."

"Primary school! This is a noble undertaking indeed. And I feel complimented that you think I can share with Padre what I know about medicine. But please remember, I'm just a compounder."

"A compounder?" Gambino raised his eyebrows and looked at the faces around him.

"I fill prescriptions by mixing drugs," he said. "I specialize in a few that the villagers need most. I learned this trade working for Dr. Currie, an American Baptist missionary. His wife, Karen, was a nurse. They came from Bombay. They opened this Christian Charity Clinic and built a Baptist church in their compound. They provided free medical care and medicine to their church members."

Prakash was eager to share what he knew of medicine.

"They opened this clinic years ago." He pointed to the polished wooden cabinets with glass doors. "When Dr. Currie saw that I know the names and properties of these drugs, he let me run the clinic. Padre, you attended college in Italy. So you can teach me."

Gambino looked inside the cabinets. He felt the gaze of the customers. *They know I'm new,* he thought.

"You live here, Prakash. You know more about the villagers," Gambino said, finding him unassuming. "Besides, I didn't attend medical college. I attended a Catholic seminary before I was ordained. I only read medical books. I worked with doctors who treated Italian soldiers suffering from tropical diseases. I learned about diarrhea, dysentery, cholera, malaria, diphtheria, tuberculosis, and the various poxes. I visited hospitals and saw the sick suffer. I learned what I could to lessen their pain in the name of Jesus Christ. Love conquers pain, and Christ is love."

"Ah, my friend, I too have learnt about Jesus Christ. Dr. Currie often talked about the Bible. Jesus was an avatar, a manifestation of the Supreme Power, a divine being like Krishna and the Buddha. He told me why Jesus chose to suffer on the cross."

Gambino didn't know what to think of his knowledge of Christianity.

"You want to lessen suffering in God's name. Padre, with time, you'll see that ignorance causes suffering. Ignorance is not realizing who we really are. Until we learn this, there will be suffering."

Gambino sat on his chair, crossed his legs, and folded his arms.

"If you look around, what do you see? You see change. Everything changes with time. Change, or impermanence, causes sorrow. Desire causes sorrow, incorrect understanding causes sorrow, wrong thinking causes sorrow, bad action causes sorrow. There is, however, a way out of suffering and sorrow. Gautama, who became the Buddha, taught the Middle Way. I try to live by his dharma."

"I live by Christ's teachings," Gambino said. "'Christ' means 'the Anointed,' 'the Messiah.' Jesus is the only Son of God."

Gambino didn't see any change in Prakash's facial expressions at being told that Christ's way is the only way. So he checked his depth of religious knowledge.

"What does 'Buddha' mean, and who was he?"

"'The Buddha' means 'one who is awake.' Through meditation, he saw the depths of human consciousness and the end of sorrow or 'Nirvana.' When he was young, he probably was like you, concerned with the suffering and sorrow that he saw outside his palace. He saw sickness, old age, and death. He realized the impermanence of himself and of everything. This made him unhappy. He, therefore, made up his mind to find release from sorrow and to conquer death itself.

"At twenty-eight, he left his regal life, his wife, and child, and became an ascetic as was the practice then for ones who thirst for spirituality. Thus began his search for the path that would lead to the end of sorrow."

He paused, sipped some hot tea, and gestured to his guests to do the same. The other customers listened, although most didn't understand English.

"He soon discovered that the country was full of diverse beliefs, for Hinduism isn't based on the teachings of a single sage or text.

"Some taught that followers should avoid unfavorable karma by making their bodies suffer. Others sought release from rebirth through mental discipline. Some performed 'Yagna' and other rituals and ceremonies. Many prayed to a god to save them from their sins and take them to temporal heaven."

The two priests looked at each other. Don't they themselves pray to be taken to heaven?

"Gautama didn't know which path to follow, for in them he saw believers desperately and frantically clinging blindly to something that is impermanent. His quest was for something more, something that is unchanging, a sphere that has no sorrow, death, or rebirth. His quest was for the bliss of Nirvana. However, he didn't know how to begin.

"He visited Vaisali where a learned ascetic, Arada Kalama, taught him one-pointed concentration and meditation to attain the Sphere of Nothingness. This, however, didn't lead him to passionless tranquility, higher knowledge, and Nirvana.

"He then visited Rajagrha. Here another learned sage, Rudraka Ramaputra, taught him to pass the Sphere of Nothingness to the Sphere of Neither Perception nor Nonperception.

"His sharp intellect quickly mastered this difficult doctrine and won him deep admiration of Ramaputra who then wanted Gautama to be his teacher, which he humbly declined. He realized that he hadn't yet found anyone who could teach him the path to Nirvana."

Gambino listened, but Prakash felt he didn't understand.

"Perhaps we should continue this discussion some other time," he said with the kindness of a grandfather. "I'm sure there will be other occasions."

"Yes, perhaps. But I don't understand the Sphere of Nothingness or Sphere of Nonperception."

"These spheres or dimensions of existence can only be experienced by practice. They are beyond description. Dr. Currie once told me that faith in Jesus Christ is something one has to experience. 'Only then one would know his calling,' he said.

"Regarding myself, I can only say that I try to calm my mind through meditation and find balance between the positive and the negative without denying negative reality. When you calm the mind and make it clean of bad thoughts, bliss enters. Someday you may meet a sage who will tell you more."

"Besides infections and diseases, is there something special you would like to tell Padre today, Prakash?" Angelo said.

"We have many snakebite cases."

"Snakebites?"

"Yes, snakebites. You see, the monsoons flood low-lying areas. Rising rainwater fills snake burrows and carries them to villages at higher levels. When floods subside, these snakes try to return to their natural habitat. Sometimes they get frightened and bite those who cross their paths. Since the monsoons have just ended, there will be cases."

"Aren't these snakes mostly cobras?" Angelo said. "I know they are extremely poisonous and can be ten feet long. Besides, their legends fascinate me."

Prakash noticed Gambino's surprise. "In India, sentient beings like snakes are considered to be manifestations of energy," he said. "Dr. Currie said that snakes are snakes and should be shot. He told me about the evil serpent of the Genesis whose deceit led to the fall of Adam and Eve. But here we let them live their lives. I live mine. Why should I kill them?"

He then told them the story of a stranded serpent.

Serpent and Father Balawan

"Father Balawan found Mission Ikonpur more than thirty years ago," Prakash said. "Now, he was a priest who learned to see snakes through the Hindu-Buddhist eye.

"Years ago, after a flood, villagers found a fifteen-foot python stranded in a nearby swamp. It was swallowing ducks and kids once a week and wouldn't leave the village. So the villagers approached the subdivisional police sahib.

"He was a hunter, famous for shooting tigers and deer. He wanted to shoot the python and display its skull in his police station and send the skin to England to make shoes and handbags. But the villagers didn't want the python killed. They just wanted it caught and taken to distant, low-lying areas and then released.

"The police sahib wanted the excitement of a hunt. But how long does excitement last? Excitement is temporary. It only inflames passion and doesn't create happiness. Besides, no one becomes truly happy by inflicting pain on sentient beings."

"But a snake? What's wrong in killing a snake?" Gambino asked.

"Because life is to be lived, and it's our duty to protect it. When Buddha was a young boy, he used to play with his cousin Devadatta. One day, a flock of wild geese flew over the palace garden. Devadatta shot an arrow, and a bird fell to the ground with the arrow in its breast. Gautama removed the arrow and tended its wound. After a few days, Devadatta wanted the bird. It was his for he had shot it from the sky. But Gautama said it belonged to him for he saved its life. Finally, they sought the judgment of the prime minister. Gautama insisted that he had greater rights to the bird since he saved its life. The verdict was that life belongs to one who gives it and not to the one who takes it."

The Ten Commandments by God to Moses flashed through Gambino's mind, but he let Prakash continue.

"But the sahib didn't want any part in trapping the python and then releasing it. So the villagers approached Father Balawan at the mission.

"You see, Padre, people from the West like to dominate nature. They like to subdue it, rule over the fish of the sea and the birds of the air and over every living creature that moves on the ground. This is what your scriptures teach. Eastern people, on the other hand, choose to live in harmony with nature.

"Balawan agreed the snake's life should be saved. He then approached the police sahib who finally assigned three sturdy and eager constables to the case. The four went to the village early one morning and studied the swamp.

"He was a student of zoology before joining the priesthood. He, therefore, approached the python as a skilled trapper. He knew that the best way to find it in the tall green grass was to drain the swamp where it lived. He had a few villagers dig drains to let some of the water flow into their lower-level paddy fields.

"There was a lot of excitement. News soon spread to the neighboring villages, and many came to witness the trapping.

"By early afternoon, when the cows and water buffalos sought shade beneath trees, the water drained enough to reveal the shiny, slivery python. Most of its body was wrapped around a stump of a dead tree three to four feet in diameter. The tip of the tail was visible above the water. The head lay submerged in the muddy water, but Balawan knew where it was.

"Pythons grow very long and large. Due to their size, they are slow in their movements and aren't like fast-moving king cobras. They are strong, and though they are nonvenomous, they can easily crush their prey in their folds. The plan was to grab it by its neck while it rested in the hot sun, cover its head with a black gunnysack, tie the sack to the base of the head, and put it in a rice-storage basket of woven bamboo that can hold two hundred pounds of paddy, then cover it with its woven lid and have the secured basket carried in a bullock cart to a swamp far from the villages.

"A muscular Rajput constable had the most dangerous part of the assignment. He was young, agile, and ready to prove his warrior valor. His task was to approach the snake from behind, grab it by its neck just below the head while Balawan distracted it with a long bamboo pole from the front. Another was to hold the tail, while the third would untangle the wrapped body from the stump and hold it, while Balawan would put the gunnysack over its head and eyes. The villagers were ready with their basket and lid.

"The plan worked. The discipline and strength of the policemen and their synchronized action were more than enough to catch and transport the python. More than six hundred pounds of human muscle easily overpowered the python that was less than hundred and fifty pounds.

"From then on, Father Balawan became a hero to the villagers."

"That's amazing, truly amazing. Are snakes holy in India?" Gambino asked.

"Not all snakes, just the cobra when it's used as a symbol. The king cobra has played a mysterious role in Eastern mythology because it's the most poisonous snake in the world. Prehistoric people worshipped it. Some authorities claim that snake worship is the earliest form of worship. It's still used in religious functions in other cultures."

"In other cultures?" Gambino asked.

"Yes. Dr. Currie told me that in many churches in the Appalachian Mountains of America, parishioners prove their faith in Jesus Christ by ceremoniously handling venomous snakes and passing them from one to another."

"Really? That's hard to believe!"

"The cobra's power and stealth have also been introduced in tales of spiritual teachers. For instance, cobras shielded Sri Sankaradeva, the great Vaisnavite saint of the fifteenth century, and Guru Nanak, the founder of Sikhism. The cobras dilated their necks into broad hoods when they found the youths dozing in the sunny countryside. In religious art, Lord Shiva is shown wearing a cobra around his neck as a symbol of mysterious and potent power over evil."

Prakash looked at Gambino. For some unexplained reason, he liked him.

"Padre, you are new to this land, but soon you will learn that Hindus practice many beliefs. Many of them are similar to Christianity and other religions. One has to be confident and open-minded to find commonalities between them. For instance, the Hindus believe in the Trinity, just like you. You call it the Father, the Son, and the Holy Spirit. Hindus call it the Creator, the Preserver, and the Dissolver."

After a few more cups of tea, it was time to leave. On the way back, Gambino was thoughtful and perplexed.

"How is it possible," he finally said, "for a simple shopkeeper, who has never been far from his village, to talk about the Genesis, about renunciation, about the divinity of our Lord, about the Trinity, about coexistence and love and compassion for all God's creatures with so much faith? How did he gain this wisdom? Did he derive it from pagan beliefs?"

"That's difficult to say," Angelo said. "Though faith is a moral guiding force to them, knowing and realizing the truth play a great part in their lives. Salvation through faith is just one way, one path.

"To Christians, salvation is available only by faith in the Son of God, Jesus Christ. Only through the perfect Jesus can we become righteous. Justification is by faith and not by good work, as Paul the Apostle tells us in the Romans. Through Christ we receive grace. But Hindus believe that God has already given us grace. All we have to do is realize it to be within us."

As they approached Mission Ikonpur, they heard the church bells as if urging them on. *Someday,* Gambino thought, *he would like all nonbelievers of this land to hear the bells ring and come to churches to pray.*

That evening, he decided to keep a journal. Life for a new missionary in the land of many faiths is too perplexing. So he recorded what he remembered about dharma and of his first day at the market where he learned about the Buddha and sanctity of all creatures.

Time for acclimatization passed. After the sabbaticals of the visiting priests ended, they left for their respective missions. Gambino settled down to his task of building the primary school. Julius told him that his challenge would be to raise funds for the construction of the one-room school in the adjoining acre of wooded land. The villagers will provide the labor for clearing the site, but he'll have to find ways to build the school.

Secret Journal

Gambino soon discovered that keeping a journal takes more time and effort than he had anticipated. He wondered if writing a monthly letter to Milan would be easier and serve the same purpose. But he realized such a letter-journal won't be confidential as he wanted his to be.

The neighboring Hindu villagers, after offering *puja* to the spirits of the wooded land, cleared the area for the school. They offered free labor in exchange for the wood. Gambino found overseeing the work interesting. It gave him an opportunity to practice the vernacular he was learning.

The trees on the east were fallen because the mild morning sun makes you energetic and cheerful. Besides, the school's entry door would face east as is the local custom. The trees on the west remained to provide shade. One of these, a magnificent fig-bearing banyan, whose branches send down roots that develop into new trunks and thus produce a thick and shady grove, was hundreds of years old.

Gambino often visited the site. For reasons unknown to him, he felt tranquil in the shade of this old fig. Sometimes he wondered if he was there before, in some previous lives, living in harmony with nature. But he quickly suppressed such thoughts.

A father and his two sons soon caught his attention. They worked quietly and diligently, chopped the most wood, and never missed a workday. Every afternoon, when they broke for lunch, a teenage girl with the face of an angel brought them food. She gracefully balanced three food containers, one above the other, on her head and carried an earthenware water jar on her narrow waist. She often dressed in a bright blue sari, with a short thin red blouse that hardly covered her developed bosoms. Sometimes she covered her head with the tip of her sari to protect her face from the burning sun. Sometimes she wore silver bangles on her wrists and ankles that jangled when she walked.

She was tall and slender like most of the other women. Her lips were full, and when she chewed pan and smiled, she was a delightful sight.

Now when Gambino was growing up in Milan, all he could see of women were their faces. Most dressed in black, from head to toe, particularly when they attended church. They seemed to have an exaggerated sense of modesty and shame. Orthodoxy taught them that the human body and sensuality are sinful. Therefore, they hid their bodies. Since the Milan women have been doing this for hundreds of years, this discipline came easily and naturally.

One afternoon when the young woman was carrying food to the three men resting under the shady banyan, he happened to be there, inspecting the site. He noticed the girl looking at him, and when their eyes met, she smiled her captivating smile. Her large chestnut brown eyes sparkled mischievously.

She is so carefree, thought Gambino, *so unafraid, so natural and alive. Is she a fairy drunk with the wine of her own beauty?* His youthful mind drifted restlessly as he stared at her and felt the pulsating beat of his heart.

"What are you looking at, sahib?" he heard a voice from behind him.

Startled, he shifted on his feet and briefly held his breath. "How can she do that? How can she balance three containers on her head so well?" he blurted.

"It's not difficult, sahib," said the simple but proud father with a smile. "Those food baskets are light. But you should see her mother if you want to see balance. My wife can balance three pots of water on her head and walk long distances."

"He has come to inspect our work," his son said. "We will have this lot cleared in a few days, sahib."

But Sita knew better. Her feminine intuition told her that the sahib wasn't looking at her balance only.

He couldn't get her out of his mind for the remainder of the day. Like a musical tune, once attached and engraved in the brain, she lingered in his mind.

Late into that evening, and well after his repeated midnight prayers, he remained awake, struggling desperately not to think of her. Finally, just before the home pigeons announced the arrival of a new day, he fell asleep. He dreamt he was in the shade of the banyan, waiting patiently for his beloved to bring him bread and sweet wine. Finally, she arrived. She sat close to him, her full breasts gently touching his broad shoulders as she poured a cup of red wine. She moved closer, held her moist lips close to his, almost touching, to taste the wine of union together.

Suddenly he woke. He felt the intense, almost unbearable pleasure and wetness of his dream. He sat up in his bed, dismayed at what he just experienced.

"Good God! Good God! What has happened?" Collecting himself, he knelt besides his bed and prayed, "Father, forgive me, for I have sinned."

After much deliberation, he decided not to enter this intensely pleasurable experience in his journal.

Sita's Hope

The number of journal entries grew with time. The ones about raising funds for the school were short. Others were long, detailing history in the making. Though he was apolitical, he saw similarities between what was happening in British India with what happened in Galilee, Judea, Syria, and Asia Minor during the time of the Roman Empire and Jesus.

The villagers didn't have money for the school, and although they used barter for their needs, the war still affected their lives. The tax collectors visited more frequently. The British rulers needed more money so that the new provincial governor could invite Viceroy Lord Chelmsford to a tiger hunt. Those who couldn't pay were beaten. Many lost their land.

The villagers knew their country was changing. Unrest, insecurity, and fear were replacing the usual village calm. The number of British troops deployed grew while Mahatma Gandhi enunciated his famous doctrine of "nonviolent noncooperation." Accordingly, the people of India would boycott the British government in all possible ways. They would boycott the new Legislative Assemblies, the court system, government schools and colleges, and ultimately refuse to pay taxes.

"Self-rule will be attained peacefully," Gandhi declared. People joined him in masses and chose poverty and imprisonment for the cause. During 1920, Gambino's first year in India, there was more than two hundred strikes.

Gandhi's followers crisscrossed the land, spreading his nonviolent teachings. One of them, Maulana Azad, was visiting a town close to Ikonpur to speak about freedom and end of British Raj. Many villagers including Sita and her brother Jai Kumar attended.

As they walked to the meeting, the villagers formed rows five to seven abreast and sang Gandhi's famous song of unity: "Iswar or Allah is the same, though they are different names of God." Banners carried by women in front of the procession read, "Freedom Now" and "British Quit India." Children carried tricolor Congress flags of various sizes. The villagers were eager to participate in the movement. The march created a festive air. Excitement of such magnitude rarely occurs in village life. It became an occasion when people from different villages could gather, interact, exchange gossip, and support the country's common cause.

A news reporter from the *Rising Times* was interviewing the marchers. Sita was very excited as she and her friends carried a Freedom Now banner leading the procession. Noticing her youthful energy, confidence, and good looks, Mehta approached her.

"What does freedom mean to you?"

"It means being free," she said hastily. "It means that we can do what we want to without hurting the rights of others as Gandhiji is teaching."

"Do you know anything about Gandhiji?"

"I believe he is a great soul and will lead us to freedom," Sita replied proudly.

"What will you do when freedom is achieved?"

"I'll become a leader and build a better India," replied the fifteen-year-old, holding her head high.

More and more people joined the procession as it passed through villages. They ignored the noonday heat. They wanted to hear the Maulana speak about freedom and self-rule. As they approached the football field where he planned to speak, the marchers noticed large contingents of police. The khaki-uniformed constables carried long bamboo poles, while a few had rifles. The officers were mostly British. They wore side arms and sat in the parked police trucks fitted with loudspeakers.

When the main procession entered the field to join others seated on the grass, the police announced over the loudspeaker that the gathering is illegal.

"Disperse immediately. The Maulana is in jail for breaking the law. He won't be here."

The marchers ignored the frequent announcements. The crowd grew. Noon passed, and when Maulana Azad didn't arrive, one of the organizers went to the front of the gathering and spoke through a bullhorn, "The Maulana is on his way. Don't trust the police. We have a right to gather here peacefully and—"

Before he could complete his sentence, a policeman grabbed the bullhorn and tried to pull it away. A second organizer reached for the bullhorn, but the policeman was just too strong. He pushed the two down with his pole and pinned them to the ground. Another policeman came running, swinging his pole menacingly at the ones who stood up. A few waved their arms in the air and started shouting slogans, "Long live Gandhiji. Long live Gandhiji. Release Maulana Azad. Release Maulana Azad."

Superintendent Bull Cummings, sitting in his marked police jeep, puffed his cigarette nervously.

"Sir, we don't want to create a Jallianwala Bagh with another thousand martyrs," Inspector Larry Lansdowne advised.

"Quite right, quite right," Cummings said. "Announce another warning to disperse. If they don't, break them up with a lathi charge. No shooting, though."

"Should we first arrest the reporters, sir?"

"Yes. Get Mehta first. Lock him up for inciting violence. We will show that bastard that India is British and will remain so."

No one knows exactly what happened next. Some said they first heard rifle shots. The police reported later that there were firecrackers set off by agitators to unnerve the crowd, start a riot, and give British Raj a bad name. A constable said that someone threw orange and banana peels at the police and shouted obscenities at them for serving the British.

At the order of Lansdowne, rows of pole-swinging policemen rushed into the large gathering.

From the British point of view, the lathi charge was very effective. They arrested hundreds and crammed them into waiting lorries and transported them to detention centers. Many lay on the grass unable to move, suffering from serious bone and skull injuries. The rampaging crowd trampled four women, an old man, and a child to death as they tried to escape the merciless police charge. Since there was no provision for first aid, the villagers carried the injured to their villages. Sita was one of them.

Gambino didn't hear about the incident until the following week when he visited Prakash to discuss fund-raising.

"It's a shame," he lamented. "The villagers were unarmed. They are simple farmers. Besides, Gandhiji preaches nonviolence. Why don't Westerners understand this?"

"Why? What happened?" Gambino asked.

He told him how the British officers, without any provocation, ordered a lathi charge just to prove that Indians must obey British laws. With tearful eyes, he said he was disgusted with himself for not studying orthopedics.

"They come to me to have their broken bones and skulls treated. What am I to do? I'm a compounder. I don't know how to help nor do I know where to send them for treatment. A young man begged me to help his teenage sister. They smashed her head. She is unconscious now. Now tell me, Padre, what can I do? Can you help? Can you help? I know freedom isn't free but violence against women and children by a mighty power like Great Britain. Is this Western civilization?"

He was speechless. The seminary in Milan didn't teach him about colonial powers and empire building. He stared at the face of the disillusioned old man, but his mind was on Sita.

Forgive me for being selfish, Lord, but please spare her life, he prayed, forgetting the purpose of his visit to the market.

As he returned, he prayed continuously for her safety and wondered if he should visit her village to inquire about her family. At the mission compound, he saw Angelo working in the vegetable garden with an old man.

"A parishioner?" Gambino asked, looking at the unfamiliar face.

"No, a Hindu, but he knew Father Balawan. He comes here once every year at this time to plant a mint in his memory."

Gambino then told him what he heard and wanted to know if he could visit Sita's village.

Previous dealings with the British authorities had taught Angelo to be prudent. He didn't want to suggest anything that could jeopardize their mission.

"I suggest you talk with Father Julius. He is more familiar with the administration. Last year, he met the district commissioner regarding a building permit."

Surprised at Angelo's cautious answer, Gambino decided to wait until after supper to ask Julius. After relating what he heard, he wanted to know if they could help the injured and at the same time spread the Gospels.

"It's true that the church has a history of sending relief to poverty-stricken areas affected by natural disasters and catastrophes. A few years ago, the Catholic Church sent food to the typhoon-affected areas of the Bay of Bengal. These calamities are natural. However, this unfortunate incident is man-made. It's the result of a conflict of human rights and colonial laws. There are two sides, and we, as missionaries, mustn't choose sides."

He paused for a while and studied Gambino's sober face.

"The commissioner's office has made it clear that we are not to get involved in local politics. We may spread the Gospels but without upsetting local religious sentiments. The authorities have become very cautious after the Sepoy Mutiny of 1857."

"The Sepoy Mutiny?"

"Well, some call the uprising India's first war of independence. But the British call it mutiny to justify their cruel punishment to the soldiers. Anyway, the rumor was that the British issued Hindu and Muslim sepoys cow and pig fat to grease their rifle cartridges to pollute them and convert them to Christianity. This led to the rebellion. Therefore, if you visit Sita's village, they may see your visit as an attempt to convert by taking advantage of their present ordeal. Besides, the authorities may read your visit as sympathizing with the freedom movement. Therefore, I think it's best not to get involved."

Gambino didn't see Sita again. After two weeks, he heard Prakash say that she didn't regain consciousness and died due to the fractured skull. Strangely enough, on the day she died, she opened her eyes, smiled, and tried to utter words, perhaps to say she was getting better or to bid good-bye. Her eyes were still bright with glimpses of hope, but finally she couldn't hold on to life and surrendered it to death.

Her family cremated her and immersed her ashes in the river, thus returning to nature the five basic elements that her soul had borrowed to find physical manifestation here in its journey to the Unborn Absolute.

"Hindus believe the five basic elements are fire, water, earth, wind, and space," Prakash said. "At the time of death, the faculties and organs of the body return to their respective places in the cosmos. Vital breath returns to wind, flesh to earth, fluids to water, eye to sun, and thought to space."

"I saw Sita when she came to the mission. She was the daughter of a woodcutter. I would have liked to administer her last rites," Gambino said with sadness, his inner voice telling him that he could have saved her pagan soul from eternal hell and damnation.

"Sita was a Hindu," Prakash said. "I don't know if her father would have allowed you to participate in her funeral services."

Gambino looked at Prakash with tears in his eyes but controlled himself.

"You see, Padre, in many parts of India, missionaries forced Christianity on Hindus. For instance, when the Portuguese occupied Goa, they had legislation passed to force non-Christians either to become Christians or to emigrate. They also destroyed Hindu temples. The Protestant missions like the Danish Lutherans, the British Anglicans, the American Baptists and Methodists simply ignored India's indigenous religions. Such forced proselytizing and shepherding of Indians into different Christian churches created distrust. But let me add that ethics of the Gospels and social concern of Christians are appreciated by both Hindus and Buddhists."

"Then I would have administered the last rites as a social obligation," the priest raised his voice. "After all, it's the same God. Would the Merciful object if the soul leaving the body finds peace in a Christian rite or in a Hindu prayer? Isn't peace bliss? Does a path's name matter?"

Prakash nodded approvingly. "I see India's belief in many paths towards Truth has already influenced you. You are learning, young man. Yes, I see a great spiritual future for you."

Night of the Sufi

By the end of his first year, Gambino experienced the different seasons of tropical India. He made two detailed entries that year. The longer one was on the seasonal effects on human behavior. He liked the dry season the best, but the rainy season with its display of power, fury, and majesty made him feel closer to the Creator. He marveled at its might to quench the parched earth, giving it new life and vitality.

The flashes of lightning that briefly turn midnight darkness to noon brightness made him fall in love with nature's energy. Thunder and its reverberating echoes impressed him. To him they announced God's presence. He imagined hearing the Lord thunder to Abraham when he was about to sacrifice his son to prove his obedience and faith.

Sometimes when it rained at night, he would go out into the open and drench his body in the cool downpours. The stormy winds didn't frighten him. On the contrary, they made him feel closer to God, so close that he almost felt his kiss on his face.

In one such midnight lightning storm, when he bared himself to the elements, he felt such a high level of elation, such bliss, such calmness, that he expressed them by shouts of utter joy at the top of his voice, "Lord, Lord, you are all around me. Thank you. Thank you for making me conscious of your presence."

His shouts of ecstasy must have disturbed a shadowy figure sitting, or perhaps dozing, underneath the banyan.

"Come, sahib, come and sit with me and witness Allah's wonders," he heard a faint voice calling from the darkness.

In the frequent lightning flashes, he could see that the voice belonged to a figure of a bearded scantily clothed man. He was sitting in a lotus position, and the only visible parts of his wet body were the whites of his eyes.

Gambino was unnerved at first. He didn't expect to find anyone there.

"Who are you? What are you doing here?"

"Who am I? I'll tell you when I know. What am I doing? Seeking solitude," he said.

He didn't know what to think of this stranger. He wondered if the man was drunk, for he knew of villagers drinking moonshine made from fermented rice. He approached him cautiously.

"What is your name?"

"My name is Sufi Ali."

"And what is Sufi Ali doing here in the middle of a stormy night full of lightning and thunder?"

"Surrendering and submitting to Allah to experience his compassion, waiting for oneness with the Merciful."

Astounded by his answer, he could only stare at the stranger. He saw an unkempt skinny man with long knotted hair, his skin wrinkled and burned dark by years of exposure. The man noticed his surprise. "Aren't you doing the same, sahib?"

The priest didn't reply and, noticing no danger, sat beside him on an exposed root.

"Are you drunk? Did you fight with your wife and come here to spend the night? I promise you: I'll not have you put in jail. I just want to know."

"A Sufi doesn't drink alcohol. It makes one unclean. It interferes with the reading of the Koran."

"Sufi?"

"Yes, *Sufi*. It means 'clean.' Sufism is the mystical path of love. It leads you away from ego towards union with Allah. Pure love of God is possible only when you are free from ego. Putting me in jail will only demonstrate authority and ego. Do you understand, sahib?"

"I'm sorry. I didn't mean that to be a threat. It's just that I'm surprised at the profundity of what you say. You said that you surrender yourself, your ego, to find oneness with Allah or God. You talk of the path of love. And you live under trees, half naked, like extreme ascetics that India seems to be full of."

"Yes, you can describe me to be an ascetic. All Sufis, however, aren't ascetics and don't become recluses from worldly affairs. They can have earthly duties to perform. They can be involved with social intercourse as long as they remember God constantly by repeating one of his many names."

"Tell me, Sufi Ali. How does one conquer ego?"

Ali thought this was an opportunity for him to be charitable to a stranger.

"By constantly remembering Allah, you can enter the level of 'Contented Self.' At this level, you are at peace. Your struggles with desires and attachments are no more. You have no earthly attachments, and thus, you have no ego. Without ego, you become free. When you are free, you are unattached to the fruits of your labor. If you crave for more and more, you are always a beggar. You are never free.

"The Sufis believe that God has blown Divine Spirit into all human beings. Our main purpose, therefore, is to identify ourselves with this Divine Self, forsaking all earthly desires."

"And why do you seek solitude?"

"I seek solitude because creation began from silence. Therefore, anyone who wants to know the origin must attain inner silence in which there is no vision, no memory, no thought, and no movement. A Sufi meditates to reach a higher level of consciousness, an awakening, where the inner and the outer realities are perfectly unified or balanced. Self-knowledge enables one to see oneself clearly. And that's what I was doing when I heard your excited prayer."

The two sat under the tree and felt the rain. The broad green leaves provided some shelter. They listened to the calming sound of raindrops. They sat side by side, two complete strangers from two different cultures and lands, seeking truth in different ways, each recognizing the Lord in his own way. They were quiet until Gambino broke the silence. "Is there no fear in your heart to sit under trees during stormy nights when lightning can easily strike you?"

"My heart is completely filled with love for Allah. There is no space in it for fear, anger, or desire."

The two lonely seekers sat under the tree until early dawn. The rain clouds blew northeast, making the sky blue to reveal the crescent moon. Before the sun rose to welcome another day, the Sufi rose quietly from his meditative position and, without uttering a parting word to the dozing priest, walked away silently, remembering that charity doesn't have to be in alms only. It could be in giving good advice, encouragement, and motivation to others to remember and glorify God. He thanked Allah for this opportunity to do so.

In his first year's final entry, he noted his surprise at the similarity of the last rites between different religions. "Ashes to ashes, dust to dust, earth to earth" in Christianity and "Returning to the five basic elements" in Hinduism are very similar. He concluded this from Sita's cremation.

The Sufi's path of love for Allah and surrender of ego for God's mercy didn't seem to differ from the love and sacrifice of Jesus or right thinking of the Buddhist path.

These new observations, however, also created apprehensions in his mind. If he explored other paths, will he divert from his own faith and mission? Will his personal mission as a separate and independent God-created soul be complete without this examination? Will it hurt anyone or will it strengthen his own orthodox faith?

He remembered his pastor in Milan telling him that *orthodoxy* literally means "straight thinking." Will his curiosity encourage *heterodoxy* or "thinking otherwise"? Will his church tolerate his study and understanding of other faiths and scriptures?

After considerable thought, he finally decided by the end of his first year that he should try, in the future, to understand few of the commonalities between Orthodox Christianity and other religions practiced in his adopted country.

American Baptists *Dr Currie*

"A year has passed, and I have done nothing for the school," Gambino said as he shelved the book he was reading at their multipurpose room during their study hour.

Julius looked up from the pages of a Bible story he was writing. "Perhaps we should visit Prakash. He knows the villagers better than we do," he said.

"I hear he's not in good health," Angelo said. "But it'll be good to see him."

As they approached the market on a humid morning, Gambino saw a glazed dark-blue clay idol at the trunk of a tree by the side of the road. It was about two feet tall. Garlands of bright marigolds and jasmines adorned its neck. The idol was of a manlike figure seated on a white bull.

He smelt burnt incense and noticed lit wicks smoldering in front of the idol. A few yards away, a group of women sat on the ground and talked loudly. They carried offerings of bananas, sliced coconuts, and cups of milk on shining brass plates. *Good Lord,* Gambino thought, *isn't this idolatry from the pre-Christian era?*

Near the pharmacy entrance, a barber had set up shop with a stool and a small mirror for those who needed a quick shave. A few prospective customers stopped talking among themselves and looked at the three robed priests as they climbed the steps to the first-floor pharmacy of the two-story building.

Prakash was wearing a turban. He was unshaven and looked tired sitting behind a desk, discussing medicine with customers. His thick arched eyebrows seemed grayer that day. But this didn't prevent him from his customary courtesy. He rose when he saw them.

"You look tired, my friend," Julius said.

"Old age is subjecting me to disease and decay," he said, forcing a smile.

"Who doesn't age, Om, who doesn't?" Julius said. "I still remember the master seed story you told me long ago."

"Master seed story?" Gambino wanted episodes for his journal.

"It's about cessation," Julius said. "One day when the Buddha was teaching his dharma to his disciples, a tearful woman named Kisa Gotami, holding her dead child close to her breasts, approached Lord Buddha and wanted him to bring back its life. The Lord asked her to find him a master seed for medicine from any household that hadn't experienced death. Thinking it would be easy, she rushed from house to house, trying in vain to find such a family. Utterly exhausted by late noon, she realized the futility of her search and accepted death to be a part of life."

"So what does the story teach us besides the inevitability of death?" Gambino asked.

Julius looked at Prakash for an explanation.

"Briefly, it teaches two lessons," Prakash said. "First, it teaches us that everything in the realm of existence is transitory. Everything that becomes passes away. So if we accept death realistically, we adjust to reality. The second lesson is that there is a connection between the realistic acceptance of death and the realization of compassion for all sentient beings who are subjected to such grief."

Prakash paused and wondered if Gambino understood. "If you are totally absorbed in your own grief for the loss of a dear one," he said, "there is no way to achieve victory over your grief or sorrow. Of course, as time passes, chances are you will forget, but this is due to your accepting the sadness rather than adjusting to reality."

"How can you adjust to the reality of death?" Angelo said.

"If you identify your grief with others who experience similar grief, you will be free of your own grief. This is because of the oneness that you will create with all living beings by the compassion you generate. This oneness, this compassion, will create feelings of happiness that are higher than those of sadness."

"Why does this happen?"

"Because you can experience happier feelings by love and compassion for others and not from the hopelessness you feel trying to avoid grief. Lord Buddha asked Gotami to visit the households so that she would identify herself with others in sorrow and realize compassionate oneness with all sentient beings."

Julius looked at Gambino. "Remember, Prakash is wise. We need his advice in building the school."

"I expect many people today," he said, looking at the waiting customers. "There is an outbreak of influenza. Many are sick. So let's go upstairs to our quarters where we won't be disturbed. Dr. Currie used the upstairs as a hospital. Dadaji and I use it now."

Eleven steps up the brick stairway took them to a large rectangular room. The wall facing south had five glass windows, enabling sunlight to enter. The wall on the east had two windows of the same size besides the wide wooden entry door. Gambino noticed a few faded calendars with pictures of Jesus and Krishna hung on the wall. He saw a metallic cross nailed to the door. The walls facing west and north didn't have windows.

There were two wooden beds near the entrance. Between them were a six-foot rectangular table and five wooden chairs. The table, covered with a red cotton sheet, had a kerosene lamp and a few old books, a penholder, an ink bottle, and a few loose sheets underneath a glass paperweight. Gambino noticed a book in English. It was the Holy Bible.

A breeze blew through the windows. There was no humid smell as on the first floor. He estimated it to be about thirty by forty feet, much larger than their multipurpose room.

"Ah, yes. Those were good days when Madame Karen was here. The floor was clean, the walls painted light green, the ceiling white. The windows had curtains." Prakash paced the large room. "Next to this door were several large flowerpots. Oh, yes, she liked flowers. The hospital beds had white sheets and soft pillows. She also taught personal hygiene. And the people loved her more than him."

"Why?" Gambino asked.

"Because she cared. She had patience and respect for others. She helped women, particularly the homeless ones, the ones rejected by their husbands for not bearing sons. In fact, the woman who scrubbed the floor was such a wife. She had nowhere to go after her husband abandoned her. She couldn't return to her parents, for that would bring them shame. Karen found her one day weeping at the pharmacy steps. She took her in, gave her food and a place to sleep. So she stayed here until she died."

"And what is Dr. Currie like?"

"He is a big man, tall and strong, always in a hurry. He comes from a family of Baptist ministers. He told me how Europeans treated the Red Indians, how the Chitimacha, the Creek, the Cherokee, and Caddo tribes were uprooted and most of them killed in the early eighteenth century. He said his family was involved with Indian Affairs and that he himself is a quarter Cherokee."

"He is part Indian? I didn't know that," Julius said.

"He kept it a secret while in college but changed his mind in India. He also told me that that we lack modern organizational skills and are slow to adapt."

Just then a young boy brought cups of tea from downstairs. Prakash sat and sipped his. He then smiled—as if he remembered something.

"Sometimes I felt uncomfortable with his brusque ways," he went on. "You see, we don't go around saying bad things about other religions. We don't call others 'heathens' or 'pagans' or 'unbelievers.' But Currie sahib did. He insisted that the most satisfying spiritual experience comes from saving souls and that there is no other true faith besides his.

"He said that if the Red Indians were to be Baptists, the churches would have protected them, even saved them from eternal damnation. His ancestors tried to convert them, but the Indians were too slow in giving up their ways."

Gambino sat beside Prakash and thumbed through the Bible. He looked at the loose sheets on the table but couldn't make sense of the writing. He wasn't interested in the clinic's history; what he wanted was to discuss the school.

"Currie sahib said that the same applies here," Prakash continued. "If we accept Jesus, there will be less poverty and ignorance, for Christianity encourages common values and beliefs. He said our diversity blocks unified action. 'You are disorganized and weak,' he said. 'Compare yourselves with us. We are everywhere to help others. We have the strength of our conviction. Truth is on our side,' he used to say."

Gambino thought it was an opportune time for him to interject the simplicity of Christian faith. "Saul, who was Paul to Romans, made Christianity easy to practice after his vision of Christ. He said faith in Christ is enough in itself. The scriptures stress that salvation comes not through good work or obeying spiritual laws, but through faith in God's mercy represented in Christ."

They sat around the table in the sunny room and sipped their tea.

"Indifference or callousness to the suffering of others is sinful, don't you agree, Father Julius?" Prakash said pensively. "It's the sin of our fathers."

He glanced at the pictures of Jesus and Krishna on the wall.

"It's strange, but all religions in India encourage charity. Yet we avoid giving. Tell me, is it organization or faith that enables Christian missionaries to sail thousands of miles to preach while we don't go even a mile to help others?" His voice shook with emotions.

Was he thinking of his life, his dharma, his mortality, his right actions? Such questions rushed in and out of Gambino's mind until he blurted, "Do you fear death?"

Prakash took a deep breath and looked at the young priest. "Lord Buddha preached that fear is the cause of all evil. If you identify with your ego, you will fear the death of your ego. I try to control my ego. So I don't fear death," he said.

"Come, come," Julius said. "We have much to do before death knocks. We have to build the school. So tell us, friend, how should we begin?"

Gift

Gambino got up from his chair and walked to the windows facing south. The others joined him. They had an excellent view of the road running north and south with one- and two-storied flat-topped buildings on both sides. They could hear noisy hawkers promote their beans, cabbages, eggplants, okras, and lettuces and unhurried shoppers haggle.

A short distance away, near the fabric stores, they saw a group of people carry a brightly decorated palanquin on their shoulders. The men rang small brass bells and chanted as they approached the pharmacy. They wore garlands of jasmine, hibiscus, marigold, and tuber rose, while a few carried pink lotuses in their hands. A few in loincloths had colorful stripes on their foreheads and shoulders.

As the procession passed the pharmacy, Gambino noticed that they were carrying a white shiny clay idol of a human figure with an elephant's head. He had seen a picture of this idol before on his very first day in India. It was attached to the pony cart he was riding. "Ganesh, Shiva's son," the driver had said when he noticed Gambino looking at it.

"One in many and many in one," Prakash said, noticing Gambino's baffled look. "God is one, but it can be many. Lord Ganesh is carried ceremoniously. He is then installed on an altar, invoked and his blessings sought by his worshippers, just like American, European, and Indian Catholics carry statues of Christ and Virgin Mary on religious days to strengthen their faith."

"They aren't the same," Gambino snapped.

"How are they different?"

He didn't answer.

"This simple act of adoration awakens the dormant spiritual consciousness within us," Prakash said. "Such acts enable us to hope and better ourselves."

Gambino didn't want to listen anymore. To him, these were acts of idolatry and paganism and, as such, blasphemous.

"Take the example of ceremonial bathing," Prakash continued, unaware of his aversion. "Every Hindu will bathe before participating in temple worship. He will put on new clothes on religious days. No one enforces these customs. There is no organization to approve or disapprove such rituals.

"The Hindu way of life developed more than four thousand years ago. Enlightened sages taught at their hermitages. In those days, they didn't have to organize themselves to escape persecution from kings or emperors as early Christians. Nor did any authoritarian Rishi give structure to the teachings of sages as St. Irenaeus did to the teachings of Christianity in the second century. As you know, Irenaeus was the bishop or 'supervisor' of Lyons."

Gambino now listened. He wondered how a Hindu knew so much about early Christianity.

"In Western religions, God handed down laws that are to be learned and obeyed. Faith is everything. The clergy gives guidance in developing faith through baptisms or other ceremonies. In esoteric Hinduism and Buddhism, you aren't compelled to realize the Atman. There is no collective, structured, or organized approach to salvation as in Christianity," Prakash said.

"There is so much to do," Gambino now echoed Julius. "We can teach children to read, write, and do arithmetic. Some of them may even go on to matriculate from high school and become clerks in the British Indian Railway. The railway will crisscross the country in the future and employ many."

Gambino is right, Prakash thought. *The school will help children to matriculate and then work with modern machines, like trains and automobiles, instead of remaining ignorant and wandering the streets aimlessly as he did in his youth.*

No one would describe him to be impulsive, but this day was different. "Why don't you hold morning classes here until the school is built?" he said. "We hardly use this floor during the day. I'm sure Dadaji won't mind."

This surprised the priests. They weren't expecting such a gift.

"Oh, no! We couldn't use your living quarters," Angelo said.

But Prakash was happy with his decision.

"Wouldn't Dr. Currie object if we convert this to mission school? Didn't he use it as a Baptist clinic?" Julius said.

"Let's get his approval then," Prakash suggested. "I received a letter from him about three months ago. He was then at the Southern Baptist Church of Little Rock, Arkansas. He was rehabilitating returning soldiers from the Great War. You know, the American Baptist congregations have always supported this pharmacy. It was only during the war that their donations ceased."

"Now that the war is over, don't you think he may return?" Angelo said.

"But we need it only for a short time!" Gambino said.

Prakash nodded. "Within a few months, news of this school will spread. Boys will come eagerly. Of course, retaining them for months at a time may be difficult."

"What do you think, Father Julius?" Gambino said excitedly. "Can we begin classes here? We will move as soon as our building is constructed."

Julius knew that it would be up to him to make the final decision. Experience taught him not to dampen enthusiasm of the young. Gambino came to India to teach and spread the Bible. The establishment of the mission school was very important to him.

"Thank you, Prakash. We didn't expect this, but we thank you. True, the location of the school here will make it very visible. But before we write Dr. Currie, I have to obtain approval from the new district commissioner."

"Is he new to this province?" Prakash said.

"Yes, and I haven't met him. But I hear he is also a scholar, like his cousin Edward Gait who is a historian and an officer in the Indian Civil Service. In fact,

Edward published *A History of Assam* about fifteen years ago. Father Balawan gave me a copy. It's about a region that was never under Mughal rule. Assam was one of the few kingdoms that defeated the Mughal armies many times when they tried to annex it to their empire.

"Father Balawan told me long ago that this region could be of great interest to us because its numerous tribes haven't been drawn into the mainstream of Hindu-Buddhist influence. He called these people the 'unreached ones,' waiting to be reached by Christianity. I still have the book, and you may find it interesting, Father."

"Yes, very much," Gambino said, "but right now, couldn't we write to the commissioner for a meeting?"

"Yes, of course," Julius said. "And we have to be prepared. Gait may ask why we should have a Catholic school in a Hindu market when we have space at our mission. He may also say that the villagers may construe this to be an intrusion by another Western religion. Even the Baptist Mission may object."

But this gift is a blessing from Jesus, Gambino thought.

"Let's not forget that George Gait is a member of the Church of England," Julius said on their way back. "His duty is to maintain order and the status quo of British Raj. He may, therefore, want to keep the denominations apart."

"What amazes me is why a Hindu would let us use his living quarters for a Catholic school," Gambino asked upon their return.

British Commissioner

When World War I began in 1914, George Gait was in his final year at Cambridge University, reading Oriental history and philosophy. In order to contribute to the war efforts, he left his studies and enlisted in the Royal Infantry as an intelligence officer. His background was very suitable to study the morale of Indian soldiers who served in the Rajput, Jat, Sikh, Gurkha, and other regiments under British command.

Indian soldiers fought heroically in Europe, Africa, and Asia where thousands of them perished. In fact, the Ravi Lancers, a cavalry division, showed remarkable discipline and courage when ordered to charge a German fortification while being pounded by German field artillery. Not many of them survived to tell their tale of heroism. Gait, however, promised that someday, after the war when he joins the Indian Civil Service, he would do everything he could toward building a war memorial to honor such courage and loyalty.

When Julius's letter reached Gait's office, he was away in Delhi, serving a subcommittee to advise the building of India Gate, a memorial arch, to honor the more than a hundred thousand Indian soldiers killed. Gait's assistant, the deputy commissioner, answered Julius's letter, stating that due to the present political situation after Jallianwala Bagh in Amritsar and the home rule movement ignited by leaders like Bal Gangadhar Tilak and Mohandas K. Gandhi, approval to begin a Catholic school in a Hindu market would be unwise. This matter, however, will receive the commissioner's attention when he returns.

The hot summer months, followed by the monsoons, came and passed as Gambino waited the commissioner's return. He was now entering his third year in India and had grown a full beard to cover his youthful face, hoping to appear older and wiser.

Meanwhile, Gait took a month off to vacation in Simla to escape the oppressive heat and dust of northern India. It was a favorite hill station for British officers during the hot seasons. They came to relax and entertain the visiting ruling class from England. They played cards, golf, cricket, and soccer. Some rode horses. Others tried mountain climbing. Gait liked riding the best.

One day, accompanied by a young woman from England, he decided to ride through the wheat fields of a local farmer. Although they tried to be careful, they did trample some of the wheat.

As they galloped freely through the fields, two young men suddenly appeared from nowhere and stood in the path of the galloping horses. Startled, the horse carrying Gait neighed and stood on his hind legs, almost throwing him off his saddle, while the horse carrying the woman darted off to the right. But its skillful rider soon controlled it.

The two men grabbed the bridles of the panting, excited horses and calmed them by stroking their necks and foreheads.

"What is the meaning of this? How dare you?" demanded the frightened but gallant British officer.

"These our fields, our crops. Why you destroy them? Why you ride horses on our food?" the one with trimmed mustache said.

"Do you know who I am? I can have you arrested."

"On what charge?" challenged the other. "We Jat farmers. We grow food on our land. Few years ago, we fight in Great War. We fight for our king. Now you destroy our crops for pleasure? Who are you? Don't you have shame?"

Gait composed himself. After all, he was a disciplined British officer of the highest caliber. He realized that India was changing both socially and politically. Their involvement in the war made them more confident now. If hundreds of thousands can fight and die for a British cause, how many will be willing to die for an Indian cause? He looked at his female companion. "Come, it is getting late. Let's go back."

Upon his return to Bombay, he sent an invitation to the priests. Julius and Gambino accepted.

Cambridge Scholar

After a two-hour train ride and passing the cantonment area, they arrived at the spacious commissioner's office building. It was of white marble walls and checkered floors. A tall bearded man in a knee-length red coat, yellow cummerbund, and a fanned saffron turban saluted them smartly at the entrance. Walking with a limp and carrying a ceremonial lance in his hand, he led them through a wide hallway to an adjoining room and asked them to sit around an oval table.

Bookcases filled with hardcover books lined the walls of the room. Paintings of the king and queen hung on the walls. There were pictures of regiments and saluting generals. Flagpoles displayed a few captured German flags. Silver-coated sports trophies and skins of tigers, black bears, and deer made the room colorful and impressive. White marble busts of British war heroes on black marble pedestals stood sentry around the room.

This was Gambino's first visit to a high-ranking commissioner's office of the empire that dominated the globe. He walked around and peered at the book titles. There were books on Her Majesty Queen Victoria, her coronation, on Lord Clive, on military strategies used by Alexander and Roman generals, on histories of Great Britain and Germany, and on many other Western subjects. However, the title that interested him the most was *The White Man's Burden*. He looked to see if there were books on India, on Indian history and culture, on Hinduism and Buddhism. He saw none.

Sound of footsteps echoed the marble hallway. "Welcome, Fathers. I'm Commissioner Gait. This is Deputy Commissioner Mumford. You must be Father Gambino." Both Gait and Mumford were dressed in starched white suits and black ties. Turning to Julius, Gait extended his hand. "I have heard of your work and dedication in orienting young priests. This is marvelous." He smiled. "Now, where shall we begin?"

After Mumford explained the purpose of the meeting, Gait looked directly at the two priests and articulated as someone with authority and responsibility.

"The initiation of a Roman Catholic mission school at a Hindu market, and on American Baptist property, is interesting but can be sensitive. Therefore, we need to proceed carefully. It will be wise to look at it from the American point of view as well." Gait appeared thoughtful. He paused for a while. "I wonder if the Vatican will permit a Protestant church to build a school on its property."

The priests didn't smile. "The room at the market will be used for a short period," Gambino said. "When our school is built, we will vacate the Baptist clinic immediately."

A faint smile crossed Gait's handsome face. "Tell you what: Lord William Bentinck in 1835 declared English to be the official language of India. The British Empire needs its Indian subjects to appreciate Western culture. Our administration needs Western-educated, English-speaking Indians. They, of course, should be from all castes and socioeconomic groups. We are encouraging Indians to govern themselves under our guidance. I, therefore, see no reason not to support you. However, please remember that I'm a British officer in His Majesty's service. My primary responsibility is to maintain law and order. I take this very seriously. I also cannot allow the clergy to become a ruling class that can arbitrarily decide to alter the lives and values of the king's subjects, particularly in my province. I do not wish to see small village children indoctrinated mercilessly into Western religious values."

There was silence in the marble-walled room as Gambino wondered what Gait would decide.

"We know of the Roman Empire's influence," Gait continued. "Emperor Constantine, in the fourth century, used religious traditions and creeds to unify his vast empire of many different nationalities. Our king, on the other hand, wants to unify the British Empire by a common language and British law. This will be the greatest British gift to humanity. You see, Father Gambino, we are not just empire builders. We are a civilized people, and we rule by just law."

After a brief pause, the commissioner appeared relaxed and pleased with himself. "So the teaching of English will have my support."

His assistant nodded his head.

"Mumford here is of the opinion that fewer feathers would be ruffled if we use the word 'market' instead of 'mission' in naming the school. Besides keeping the American Baptist Mission happy, the school will sound nondenominational. Of course you may have displays of Christianity in the school, like the cross and statues of saints on holidays, but under no circumstances must we collide with local religious sentiments. I must add that we are fortunate regarding this. Many Hindus display portrays of Rama, Krishna, and the Buddha with those of Jesus in their family altars."

Gambino appeared irritated. "Why would they do that?" he demanded to know.

"The Hindus believe in what I call the 'avatars' or the 'divine incarnate' concept. In the *Bhagavad-Gita*, Lord Krishna, Himself an avatar, like Rama and Buddha, beautifully explains this concept. He says, 'When goodness grows weak, when evil increases, I make myself a body. In every age I come back to deliver the holy, to destroy the sin of the sinner, to establish righteousness.' This concept is very similar to Christ's Second Coming or the establishment of the Kingdom of God. Therefore, to them Jesus is an avatar who came to rid the Roman world of evil and establish righteousness. The Romans were living very sinful lives. They not only worshipped their emperors as gods, like Emperor Caligula who wanted to be worshipped, but their sexual practices were most uncivilized and barbaric."

The Roman Catholic priests felt uneasy but held their silence. They neither agreed nor disagreed. The main purpose of their visit was to obtain approval to open the school.

After nodding his head a few times, as if agreeing with himself, Gait continued. "You see, Fathers, while growing up as a Christian in England, I studied Hinduism and Buddhism to prepare for the Indian Civil Service. Therefore, I will not hesitate to say that these people don't see any difference between many of their beliefs and those in Christianity. In fact, an Orientalist by the name of Bir Dharma told me in Delhi that Christianity will not spread in India because it has nothing new to teach Hindus. He believes Christianity resulted like Hinduism."

"Resulted like Hinduism?"

"Yes. The core of Christianity is based on the teachings of many prophets like Abraham, Moses, Jesus, Paul, Peter, John, and so on. The core of Hinduism is on the teachings of many sages also, mostly of the Vedic period. What they taught is the same in both religions: love for one God. Seeking him and being constantly conscious or aware of him brings salvation. Yes, the paths to salvation are many, with different rituals and religious ceremonies and observations, but the destination of the soul is the same."

Before Gait could continue, Gambino interrupted. "How could this be? How dare they? How can pagans who worship many gods and idols compare their beliefs with the words of our Lord, the Son of God Jesus Christ?" His voice shook. He crossed himself. "I saw women in the market worshipping a black idol with snakes coming out of its head. I saw another god with an elephant's head!"

Gambino's youthful evangelical zeal amused Gait.

"The god with venomous snakes on his shoulders is immaculate Siva, the Great Yogi. Like the Christians, the Hindus too believe in the Trinity. Like the Father, the Son, and the Holy Spirit, the Hindu trinity consists of Brahma the Creator, Vishnu the Preserver, and Siva the Dissolver. To Christians, God the Father is the Creator, God the Son is the Redeemer, and God the Holy Spirit is the Advocate. To Hindus, the Divine Ground or God Head is Brahman. Its creating, preserving, and dissolving aspects are manifested in the Hindu Trinity. The Preserver comes as an avatar to save humanity from evil. In the past, it came as Rama, then as Krishna, and about five hundred and fifty years before Jesus, as Buddha. This is why the Hindus do not hesitate to place pictures of Christ with Rama and Krishna and Buddha on their altars."

Gambino realized he had much to learn. So he listened.

"To both Christians and Hindus, God is inaccessible to reason alone. He is beyond anything man can comprehend. He is beyond change, end, or origin. To understand these difficult concepts or 'to see the invisible, to touch the intangible, and to know the unknown,' Hinduism developed a vast mythology to assist ordinary people to develop and strengthen faith. The god with an elephant's head is Ganesh, the son of Shiva. People worship him for knowledge.

"Regarding pagans," Gait continued, "if one studies the history of Christianity, he will discover that the word 'pagan' originally referred to Romans who worshipped men as gods. Many Roman emperors wanted their subjects to worship them since they believed that metamorphosis caused this change in them from men to gods. I don't have to tell you how Pontius Pilate tried to bring images of his emperors to the temple area in Jerusalem.

"Regarding Jesus being the Son of God, the Hindus believe that Krishna is God, manifested as man. I read Eastern philosophy at Cambridge for many years. It is vast, complex, and fascinating.

"Regarding many gods, Hindus actually believe in one god, just like Christians. The Catholic Church proclaims that the Holy Trinity is one God, just as Hindus declare, 'One in many and many in one.' Even illiterate villagers say, 'The Lord is one.' Hindu theology explains this by pointing out that people with different psychological needs must satisfy them in different ways. Since Hinduism is not an organized religion, its believers can worship God in many ways based on their local needs.

"Westerners may look upon idols as objects of worship by Hindus. But idols are to improve concentration and strengthen faith. They pray through them after their invocation but not to them. Catholic churches are full of statues of saints. Asking the Virgin to pray for us sinners can explain a Hindu's method of worship.

"We must also remember that Sanskrit is like Latin to Catholics, and God has many names in Sanskrit."

Gambino listened attentively. He was impressed with Gait's knowledge and articulation. He wanted to know what books Gait would recommend on Eastern philosophy.

"I surveyed the book titles in your library. Unfortunately, I didn't see any on Hinduism and Buddhism. However, the book *White Men's Burden* interests me. Is spreading Christianity among darker races the white man's burden?"

"Oh, yes, I believe that book is mainly on administration, detailing the responsibilities of white races towards darker races. For instance, look at India and what we, the British, have done. In 1835, we abolished the barbaric Hindu custom of 'Sati,' which was the burning of widows in their husbands' funeral pyres. The same year, we completely rid the country of stranglers or the cult of 'thuggees' who terrorized with deceit and strangulations.

"We improved communication between different parts of this vast and diverse land with railway and telegram. We teach them English that has become a world language. We are giving them an administrative system patterned after the British system.

"We introduced India to modern science and medicine and to British public law and court procedures. We have appointed Indians to high judicial and executive posts. The list is long." Gait appeared pleased with himself.

"I must say that you are very knowledgeable about India. After listening to you, I admit that I have much to learn about Indian religions and history. Please tell me, Commissioner, where I can find books on Eastern philosophy."

"Difficult to say, Father. Though missionary activities in India began in 1813 in the East India Company territory, they ignored the indigenous religions and treated their followers with contempt. For instance, the first Portuguese in Goa, instead of trying to understand the local customs, had Hindu temples destroyed.

They forcefully converted Hindus to Christianity. This made them shun Westerners. To them, Christianity and Westerners appeared to be the same—aggressive and intolerant.

"No efforts were made to translate their *Sanatana Dharma* or 'eternal religion' until 1785 when the Sanskrit scholar and Indologist Charles Wilkins made the *Bhagavad-Gita* available in English. The then governor-general of Bengal Warren Hastings encouraged him to study with Brahmins in Banaras to produce this English version.

"In 1823, August von Schlegel produced a Latin translation. Wilhelm von Humboldt was so impressed with this Latin version that he declared this segment of *The Mahabharata* to be the most beautiful and only true philosophical poem in all the literature of the world. For your information, *The Bhagavad-Gita*, or the 'Song of God,' is a part of the great Indian epic *The Mahabharata*.

"The two great American philosophers Ralph Waldo Emerson and Henry David Thoreau were very interested in Indian thought, particularly in the *Vedanta*. Isaac Nordheimer offered a Sanskrit course at the City College of New York in 1836. In 1842, the prestigious American Oriental Society was established. I wish there were such associations here so that all of us could learn from them. *The Bhagavad-Gita* is a pre-Buddhist work, and I would encourage anyone to read this book to have more than just a provincial education.

"But since I don't have a copy of the *Gita* for you, the next best thing I can do is invite all of you to attend a lecture series in my office. They will be on Eastern philosophy. The Sanskrit scholar Professor Bir Dharma of Delhi University, fluent in English, will deliver them to the next batch of British Indian Civil Service officers arriving India. Lord Reading, our viceroy in Delhi, has adopted a different administrative policy, and I would like to see this new group of ICS officers implement the policy at the grassroot levels.

"Many Indian scholars say that the *Gita* is the core of Hinduism. Understanding it will help the young British officers, and perhaps even you, to serve Indians better, whether you serve them in spirituality or in education. By the way, in 1830, the Scottish missionaries opened a school in Calcutta, similar to the one you are planning. Now that you have obtained the charter for your school, we wish you success. We hope your efforts will contribute towards the welfare and education of children."

On their way back to the mission, they informed Prakash of obtaining the school charter.

"This is wonderful news! I'll have the room scrubbed, and if I can find lime, I'll have the walls whitewashed. We will need a blackboard and chalk, about thirty clay slates with wooden frames so that they don't break easily. We will need a table and a chair for the teacher. The students can sit on mats. When do we start?" Prakash said.

"Not so fast, my friend, not so fast," Julius laughed. "The commissioner advised us to attend a few seminars in his office before we enroll students." He then gave him the details of their meeting. "Would you like to attend the seminars with us?" Julius asked.

"When I was a young boy," Prakash said, "Indians weren't even allowed to walk near the cantonment area. I remember my friends and I were chased away and called 'darky savages' by the British sentries. I don't think that attitude has changed. So it's best I don't attend."

PART C

Sins of Our Fathers

SINCE ANTIQUITY, INDIA has been a land of small villages where most of its people live in mud and straw huts. They till the soil to grow their crops and borrow from nature what they need for their simple and virtuous lives. They respect nature and animal life and live in harmony without dominating them.

Hindu villages have temples that form centers of religious and social activities. Priests, who manage the temples and perform rites, provide Vedic knowledge and scriptural guidance to villagers.

Krishna Swamy, who later assumed the name of Bir Dharma, was born in one such village. His grandfather Biswa Swamy was a temple priest who made a living by performing the Hindu sacraments prescribed by the *Vedas*, like name-giving to the newborn, first feeding of solid food, marriage, funeral, etc. Hindus believe that such holy rites sanctify the body, purify this life and life after death. They also enable individuals to become full member of the socioreligious communities.

To feed his family, Biswa also practiced astrology and provided horoscopes to illiterate villagers. He discouraged them from learning to read and write Sanskrit—the language of the *Vedas*. He justified his stand by saying that if everyone reads the *Vedas*, there would be many misinterpretations. Besides, he asked, why should farmers and menial classes learn to read when they should be performing their caste duties of growing more crops and cleaning the waste of the village, like disposing carcasses for sanitation?

A few in the village went so far as to suggest that according to ancient Brahmanical laws, if Shudras or outcastes listened to the scriptures, their ears will be filled with molten lead. If they recited the *Vedas*, their tongues will be split. If they memorized any of its verses, they will be cut in two.

The menial class or "untouchables" would have to be reborn to visit temples, take part in ceremonies, and listen to the sacred teachings. They will do this in their future lives if they serve the higher castes satisfactorily in this life.

Krishna's father, Bala Swami, didn't dare to disagree with his father. He conveniently believed that the priests have a duty to preserve their ancient rituals and traditions and hand them to their sons for the benefit of future generations. Only priests should do this duty since it requires sharp memory and mental discipline, which the others didn't have. The administrative class, for instance, is full of passion and quick to anger. They are yet to master all their senses—like the priests.

Bala also shared a bothersome secret with his father. When he was a youngster, he saw his father wrap something small in dried banana leaf, then in a piece of red cloth, and put it into the hallow of a bamboo cylindrical container with a lid. He then put the closed bamboo container in a thick and sturdy gunnysack and buried it in a small hole that he dug next to the family altar in his bedroom. Biswa didn't know that his son, who pretended to be asleep in the room that late evening, was watching him.

After his father left for the temple the next morning, and when his mother and two sisters were preparing their afternoon meal of rice and vegetables, Bala quietly dug up the sack and bamboo container and found wrapped in the banana leaf two small shiny pieces of uncut gems. One was turquoise, and the other, the larger one, was light green. He stared at them and realized that they were very valuable. He had seen such precious stones in gold necklaces adorning the temple idols. But he didn't know why anyone would give his father such precious gems.

Bala realized that it would be just a matter of time before his father finds out. He, therefore, prepared himself to beg for forgiveness, for he knew he did something wrong. He was afraid of his father. His mother, Maya, once warned him long ago that his father has a violent temper when crossed. She told him of the incident of the dead calf and the two young untouchables who had come to remove the carcass.

"You were much younger then. It was very hot and humid that summer, just before the rains. The wind blowing from the south carried the cow disease. One of our calves died from it, the one that your father prized. He expected it to give a lot of milk when it matured. When it died, he was very upset.

"The untouchables, who lived outside our village, came to carry the carcass away. That day also happened to be your sister's birthday. She was very proud of the new dress she received as a present. Your father was at the temple. Jaya and I were sitting in the backyard, fanning ourselves when the two untouchable brothers arrived. They hardly wore any clothes except for their loincloth and soiled turbans. The boys first dragged it out of the cowshed and spread a mixture of lime and dry soil where the calf had bled. This reduced the foul smell.

"I could see they were just boys, although they were tall and muscular. They were perspiring profusely. They were laughing and talking loudly without any inhibitions. Their beautiful black bodies were glistening in the sunlight, their shining long black hair covering their foreheads. They tied the calf's hind legs together, passed a bamboo pole through the knot, and tried unsuccessfully to lift the heavy carcass. Then one of them looked up and saw us watching them. 'They are beautiful and strong! Mother, don't they look like the black devil in Durga Puja?' I heard Jaya cry.

"'And they look thirsty,' I replied as I got up to get the earthenware water jar from the kitchen. Jaya wanted to pour the water. She wanted to do a good deed on her birthday, but for some reason, I didn't let her.

"As I was pouring the cool water into their cupped hands, without of course touching them, your father returned from the temple. He called Jaya and wanted to know what I was doing. He then asked her to tell me to come back to the house. But instead of telling me to return, she disobeyed your father, rushed and grabbed the water jar from my hands, and poured the water over the shoulder of one of the boys. He laughed, and as his loincloth became untied, he grabbed it to prevent it from falling. But he appeared to be adjusting his genitals.

"I heard your father rushing towards us. Before we realized what happened, he picked up the bamboo pole and struck the boy repeatedly on his neck and head, yelling, 'How dare you, you pig, how dare you get sexually aroused at the sight of a Debi, a virgin Brahmin girl, you dirty dog!'

"The boy fell to the ground. The other boy, instead of taking the pole away from your father, which he could have done easily, being much bigger and stronger than your father, ran and hid behind the bushes. Your father continued beating the senseless body. Both Jaya and I screamed, asking him to stop, which he did when he saw blood gushing from the boy's neck and shoulder. He then grabbed Jaya by the hand and dragged her to the house.

"I stood there, next to the fallen boy, not knowing what to do. Should I touch him, place his bleeding head on my lap, and wipe his swollen forehead with my sari? But he was an untouchable! If I touched him, what will your father do, or what will the temple priests say?

"The other boy soon came out of hiding, frightened and trembling. He wiped his brother's bleeding neck and back with his turban, looked up at me with tearful eyes as if to ask why. Slowly the wounded boy struggled to his feet and, with help from his brother, limped off our yard. We didn't see them again."

Bala never forgot this incident of his father's rage. He became more and more afraid of him. At times, he even avoided him. And his resentment grew.

One afternoon, after a week of his gem discovery, when Biswa was teaching him Sanskrit and Vedic rituals to continue the family tradition, he asked if his mother knew. "Know what, Father?" he retorted nervously. "You know what I mean, my son." "No, she doesn't," he replied. He knew what to expect when his father called him "My son." This meant absolute control and ownership of him by his father, and he is to do anything his father commanded.

His father didn't get angry, though he noticed how stern and serious he was.

"Moni Lal, the gem merchant, gave me the two pieces. I need them for your sisters' dowry. They will soon come of age. Lal is getting old and sick. All these years of eating sweets made him fat. Now his heart beats faster and faster when he stands and walks. I want to help him die in peace. He asked me to say special prayers for him at the temple so that after death, his soul will go to Indra's heaven. I said I'll and I'm."

"You know such secrets and powerful prayers, Father?"

"We Brahmins have tremendous power over the minds of people. Over four thousand years of tradition has taught and given us this power, this right. We have used it to maintain order in society. Every villager knows his role. You must always remember this. You were born into a Brahmin family because you earned it due to the right karma of your past lives. Lal may deserve the same good fate in a future life."

"Did we do good deeds in our past lives to become Brahmins in this life, Father?"

"Yes, my son."

"Does this mean that we were of lower castes in our previous lives?"

The temple priest didn't answer.

"Does one have to be born into a Brahmin family to be a Brahmin and to read the *Vedas*?"

"Yes."

"But what will happen if I don't want to study Sanskrit and the *Vedas*? What will happen if I don't want to be a temple priest? What will happen if—"

"Then you will be a fool, unworthy of your birthrights," his father roared.

Horoscope

Years passed. Bala grew up to be a fine Sanskrit and Vedic scholar under the tutelage of his father. People came to him with donations and requests to perform elaborate ceremonies. A few even offered their daughters in marriage. But he always needed the approval of his parents, particularly his father's.

As he entered manhood, he became infatuated with a young woman whom he once saw soaked in the rains, revealing her magnificence. *Beauty has expressed itself in her form,* he thought, inflamed with desire. *No doubt she will win the smiles of even the devas.*

Her name was Prova, from the Pali household. He wanted to tell his father of his hope for her but was afraid.

"Will you read my horoscope, my father?" Bala asked one day when he thought his father was in a good mood after his afternoon nap.

"No. I don't want to know your future, but if you do, ask Saki Baba, the ascetic. He visits our village during full moons. He will sit under the pipal tree in the temple yard for three days and nights while devotees make food offerings to him. He will then return to the forest to meditate, to seek salvation from the cycle of life and death. Of course you must never reveal to anyone what he tells you about your future."

On the evening of the next full moon, Bala took his ceremonial bath and visited Saki Baba with an offering of rice pudding. He hoped his horoscope would tell him something about his wife-to-be.

"Yes, you will be married soon. Your wife will bear children. One will mar joy. Winds from different directions will blow through your house. I see someone young dying," Baba foretold.

"Is there anything I can do to create happiness and avert sorrow? Can I do penance?" he asked.

"Do your duty as a husband and a father. Crave not for the fruits of your work and grief not the inevitable."

Biswa noticed a change in his son's behavior after visiting the ascetic. He wasn't as meticulous in performing the elaborate and sacred rituals at the temple as he taught him. "This must not be, my son. Tell me what bothers you."

"I want to marry Prova of the Pali household," he blurted, surprised at the suddenness of his courage to talk so forthrightly with his autocratic father. According to Hindu customs, parents decide and arrange marriages without the knowledge or consent of sons or daughters.

"Why do you wish to marry her?"

"Because I love her!"

"Love? You love her? My son, love is nothing but a passing fancy, a fleeting feeling. It doesn't last long between a husband and a wife, except for a few days or months. Duty is more important. Tradition is more important. Knowledge is more important. They last forever. You'll receive respect and fame for your knowledge, for your wisdom, but never for your love for your wife."

"My thinking changes when I see her. I feel new and exciting emotions. These thoughts and emotions take me away to a fantasyland where pleasures abound."

"Pleasures are just bodily sensations based on passions. They are experienced even for shorter durations than love. Remember, you are the heir apparent of the temple's Goswami Brahmins. No one is of purer birth than you. Your family name goes back hundreds of years. God has blessed you to uphold the great tradition of this temple. Besides, the Palis are not good Brahmins. Just a few years ago, the Pali men were seen plowing their own fields, their women sowing seeds, instead of getting the Vaisyas to farm."

"Father, two years ago, during the drought, the Palis didn't receive enough donations to pay the farmers to plough. We shouldn't hold that against them. Prova has done nothing improper. And what's so wrong in plowing our own land?"

"We mustn't go against traditions. Brahmins don't plow. They haven't for hundreds of years. Why should they now? Besides, I don't think the Palis have enough for the dowry of three milk cows as our ancient custom dictates."

After a long pause, the young man lamented, "I'll always think of her, my father. She will always be in my mind. She will visit me in my dreams, even when she lies in the arms of another man." After a pause, he said, "What can I do to end this torture, this agony? Please tell me!"

"When you are attracted to a woman, think of her as a urine bag, filled with sweat, spit, and foul smell. Sometimes this bag will spurt diluted milk, poorer than cows' milk. Then you will revert to your good senses," the old traditionalist said.

Bride

Bala's wedding ceremony by the fire site finally ended at midnight after hours of chanting Vedic hymns. It took place under a decorated colorful tent erected in front of the bride's house. The October mist, rising from the nearby ponds, was heavy with moisture that early morning.

Hindu marriages are commonly solemnized in front of a fire of sandalwood. Fire—signifying purity and energy—bears witness to marriage vows where the groom and bride pledge loyalty and faithfulness to each other. This tradition has passed on from generation to generation for more than four thousand years.

Bala, his best man, the bride, her bridesmaid and bride's father who was going to give her away, and the priest sat close to one another on pillows placed on mats that covered the ground close to the fire. The guests, who already feasted, sat on the ground to witness the ceremony.

The father of the bride took the right hand of his young daughter and placed it gently on the extended right hand of the young man who sat beside her. His heart beat faster as he felt the warmth and softness of her palm. It was the first time he touched her. Since he had not seen her face before, he tried to but couldn't. Her sari completely hid her face.

The groom and the bride listened attentively to the priest recite the ancient vows. They repeated them without hesitation. They felt confident about their future together.

With tears in his eyes that glistened in the golden light of the wood fire, the father of the bride did his parental duty. "I give you my precious daughter, Kamala. Take her hand, Bala. Treat her well. Be gentle with her. Her years with us brought us joy. From this moment hence, for the rest of your life, she is yours. Cherish her. May God bless you."

Bala tried to understand what this moment meant. Is this really happening, or is he dreaming? Will he soon wake and discover that he is actually with his strict father teaching him the scriptures? Strange emotions filled his heart, emotions that he never experienced before. How is he to cope with them? Should he try to restrain them from overpowering him? Should he or could he control them?

Choked with emotions that were neither pleasant nor unpleasant, he could hardly hear himself utter, "I'll—for the rest of my life."

Did the father of the bride hear him? Did the priest hear him? Did Kamala hear him? Should he whisper his vows to his bride, or will she know, on her own, as life goes by?

Before he could repeat his vows once more, he felt a hand on his shoulder, urging him to stand. As he stood up, he realized that this wasn't a dream but was actually happening and very real. This lean young woman who bowed and touched his feet and called him her lord was now standing beside him. She was coming into his life to be his wife to share his life and to give herself to him and, in return, to be received by him.

The priest asked them to walk around the fire seven times. The groom led with head held high to signify dignity; the bride followed with head bowed to signify modesty. The tip of her bright blue sari was tied to the tails of his beige silken shirt. This walk around the fire symbolized their wedlock and their union.

With the giving of the bride, the tying of the knot, and the circling of the fire, the groom became the husband and the bride his wife. Like a dream, this once-in-a-lifetime event that he had taken pleasure in fantasizing many times before ended, never to be experienced again.

Tradition

It was late evening when Maya, her married daughters with their families, and neighbors greeted the newlyweds as they returned with Biswa in a decorated bullock cart. The groom's party followed. Maya waved a small basket of flowers and sweets in front of the couple's faces to signify a life of beauty and harmony. Others threw rice for fertility.

Biswa led his son and daughter-in-law through the house to the backyard to receive blessings of visitors. Maya sat beside them and gently removed the sari covering the bride's face. This created an opportunity for Bala to peep. As he did, Kamala gazed down and wondered what her husband was thinking.

The guests enjoyed refreshments of tea and sweets, while a few teased the groom. "Don't look now, Bala. Wait till tonight," a male's voice sounded for the amusement of the guests. But Biswa didn't laugh.

When darkness grew and the guests left, Biswa and Maya lit two mustard-oil lamps and led the newlyweds to the altar room. To ready himself, Bala had read the *Kama Sutra* many times before. But he was disappointed tonight. Anxiety made him unsure and hesitant. So all he did was lie beside her on the bed decorated with scented flowers. He stared at the ceiling and was falling asleep when he heard her whisper, "Don't you want me, my lord? I'm ready to do my duty."

The gentleness of her voice made his heart pound with excitement and desire. He wanted to hold her in his arms, smell her scented hair, and whisper in her ears of his longing. Slowly and without a word, he placed his head on his pillow next to hers. She lay beside him, her head resting softly, her eyes fixed on his. He looked closely at her face. He saw a young face, a girl's face. The dim light emitting from the lamps showed her lips to be full and crimson, her eyes large, bright and dark brown, her brows arched like the crescent moon, her hair long, and her neck slender. The scent of the flowers in her silky black hair filled his nostrils, enticing him to experience the sensual delights of union. He forgot what his father had told him about women.

He touched her cheeks and felt the smoothness of her olive skin, so soft, so clear. He lowered his trembling fingers to her lips, touched them gently, and felt their warmth and softness. These are the lips he would kiss for the rest of his life, the lips that will tell him that he too is loved.

He then kissed her forehead, her eyes, and her cheeks. She didn't move or protest. He chose not to kiss her lips passionately, as his married friends had suggested, for fear of upsetting her. He next touched her breasts hidden behind her sari. He was surprised at their size. They were small, almost flat and hardly developed.

"They will develop, my lord, they will grow as soon as I reach puberty," she assured him. "My mother too had small breasts when she first got married to my father. When she gave birth to me, they became much larger and were full of milk. My mother told me to tell you that," she said without any inhibition.

Bala rolled away from the pillow. Facing the other side, he exclaimed, "Oh, my god! What have I done? What has happened? A bride of less than half my age? What has my father done? He arranged my marriage with a child! I trusted you, my father. I trusted you. Now I curse you, I damn you for depriving me a woman for my bride."

Kamala started sobbing. *What future awaits me now? What will happen to me if I can't satisfy my husband? What will happen if he doesn't want me?*

Bala dug deep into his heart to find pity for his child-wife. "I'll always want you, for the rest of my life. This I promise, Kamala," he said nervously.

Too exhausted and frightened to utter another word, she nudged her body closer to his, and in the comfort and security of his words, she fell asleep. He laid awake long into the night and listened to her breath. He tried to watch the moon through the cracks of the hay roof and think of Sri Krishna and Radha and their Lila. He then thought of Prova, his lost love.

True to her word, Kamala reached puberty within the next two years. In the third year, she gave birth to twins: a boy and a girl. Their grandfather named them Krishna and Tara.

"I promised that I would give you children, my lord. And I did. Raise them well, my dear husband, for I'll not be here to see them grow. Maya Ma said that I lost a lot of blood. I'm losing strength. My eyelids get heavier."

"No, my sweet, no! You are young and strong. You have years to live. Stay, stay and see them grow. Don't leave me."

But Kamala grew weaker, and her last words were "I did my duty to my husband."

As years passed, their grandmother raised the twins with care and love. Bala devoted more and more of his time to reading the scriptures at home and ceremonies at the temple. His unexpressed anger and resentment for his father grew every day, particularly on the days when he insisted that he remarry.

"You are too young not to have a wife. Besides, I want grandsons."

One day at the temple, just before the noon meal, when Bala was performing initiation or Upanayana rites for an eleven-year Ksatriya boy, he started to stammer and lost his ability to annunciate. His whole body started to shake violently. He became unconscious and fell backward. Foam and blood appeared in his mouth as he made strange sounds. No one there knew what was happening or how to help him. Minutes passed as he gradually regained consciousness. "What happened? Why are you all staring at me?" he asked.

The twins received attention and praise from Maya as she raised them. They in turn paid close attention to their daily lessons and learned quickly all they were taught. The boy expressed great interest in Sanskrit grammar that his grandfather taught him, while Tara learned and practiced devotional songs. People came from neighboring villages to listen to her at the temple. All the attention and praise, however, spoilt her and made her want her way in everything. Once she told her father that when she grows up, she would become a songstress or an actress. Her father didn't agree or disagree. His health was deteriorating. Anger or excitement made his seizures more frequent.

One day, a group of traveling play actors came to their village to stage the story of Sri Krishna and the gopis. The villagers in that region didn't have such a group entertain them for years. They welcomed them and helped them to set up their portable stage. They asked them to perform for a week so that everyone could see the play and listen to the songs of the gopis.

The dark young man who played the role of Sri Krishna was tall and handsome. He smiled easily and played the flute melodiously. And he was clever. He knew how to attract people and make them pay to see their play. Within a few days of staging, his fame spread. Young girls from neighboring villages came in droves to see him perform and listen to his flute. They fantasized him as the perfect love, just as Sri Krishna was to Radha.

Tara was no exception. In fact, she became infatuated. She dreamed of marrying him and become his Radha. *I sing so well, and he plays sweet tunes with his flute. Together we will make a perfect couple.*

She asked her father if she could join them. Of course, she didn't tell him of her fondness for the young man. She knew Raj Kumar was not a Brahmin, and asking her father for his blessings to marry him would create unbearable excitement and more seizures.

"No granddaughter of mine will become an actress. Not in my lifetime," growled the old autocratic grandfather when he heard of Tara's ambition. However, she wasn't afraid of him as her father was. She made up her mind: if he didn't allow her to become an actress, she would elope and become one.

The play drew large audiences for five consecutive nights. Everyone liked the role of Raj Kumar. They asked the group to stay for another week. Many saw the play more than once. They believed that attending such plays strengthened their faith in the teachings of Lord Krishna. But none of them could even imagine what waited them.

On the ninth evening, just before the play began, there was commotion in the staging area. No one knew the whereabouts of Raj Kumar although they found his costume on the wooden box neatly folded. The flute and the peacock-feathered crown lay beside it.

When the news spread to the Biswa household, the old man immediately concluded what happened. He told his wife that since Tara didn't respond to their repeated calls, the actor must have kidnapped her.

"I should have seen this coming! This is why I didn't approve her public singing!"

The police constable told Bala that it didn't appear to be a kidnapping. "We need evidence. We have none. There are no signs of a struggle, no one heard cries for help. Besides, if she left voluntarily, what can we do?"

Ascetic

Bala last met Saki Baba nineteen years ago. During these years, the ascetic reduced the frequency of his visits to the village and spent more time meditating at his hermitage. Cattle herders regularly left him vegetables and wild fruits, sometimes even rice boiled in milk. Unseen passersby offered him uncooked rice wrapped in banana leaf.

As time passed, Bala's health deteriorated. His seizures became more frequent and his memory impaired. He often forgot complete stanzas of the *Vedas*, and this interfered with performing ceremonies. His father finally told him to consult Saki Baba and find the cause and cure of his misfortune.

Bala and his father had never been outside their village. They didn't know much about life beyond their world. He was hesitant at first, but when there was no alternative, he decided to find Saki Baba. Krishna accompanied him.

After two days' walk through rice fields and stretches of uninhabited woodland, they reached a jungle where the ascetic was rumored to live. They exercised caution and took utmost care not to step on the finger-long dry sharp thorns of berry bushes that littered the ground.

"Most of the ripened berries on the lower branches are gone, Father," Krishna said.

"The fruit gatherers know when to get here first before the monkeys and parrots," Bala said, pointing at a few remaining barriers left behind for the animals.

On the third day, they came across a small open space, next to a shallow pond. It had signs of human habitation. They thanked their good fortune and decided to wait. As they rested in the shade of a tree and watched the puffy clouds blow across the sky, they fell asleep. Around sunset, they woke to the sound of splashing water from the direction of the pond. At first, they couldn't see what was causing it until they saw a naked man waist-deep in water. He had a long gray beard, and his white hair was tied in a bun above his head. Oblivious to his surroundings, he immersed himself repeatedly in the water, muttering his mantra.

Finally he came out of the water and dried himself unhurriedly. He then walked toward his shade as if unaware of the two men who stood there with bowed heads and folded palms. He sat next to a died-out fire and beckoned them to sit. He offered them a few wild berries and listened to Bala's woes.

"It's time for me to retreat," he said without displaying emotions. "I meditate at night. The sky, the moon, and the stars keep me company. The wild animals don't disturb me. In the silence of my meditation, I find peace. In peace, I seek the Creator. We shall discuss tomorrow." The two bowed their heads.

When they woke the next morning, they found the old man sitting in a lotus position deep in concentration. He was facing the rising sun with eyes half closed.

Finally, he stirred and broke his silence. "Your misfortune is because you carry your past with you. Let it go. Live in the present. This will lessen your anger, fear, and hostility towards your father. Forgive him and know that anger results from fear. It destroys from within. Your fainting spells are for disharmonious thinking. It's better to think right. Let only good thoughts enter your mind. Rest your mind with deep breaths and meditation."

"How do I let go the past and think right, Saki Baba? I have read the scriptures for years. I still read them. What more can I do?" Bala implored.

"Only you can master yourself. Who can be your master from outside? Understanding right and doing what is right are more important than merely reading the scriptures. Learning and knowledge are not enough. You must understand correctly by disciplining the senses and subduing your ego. Serve the Atman for this divine spark is in all human beings. It is from Brahman and is Brahman. Serve it and good will follow."

"Whose Atman do I serve? Where do I serve? I have served all who come to me!"

"Any good or evil you do is born in yourself and is caused by you," Saki Baba replied. "So serve the people that are bullied and denied freedom. Teach the *Vedas* to the outcastes, for they too deserve release from the cycle of life and death. Deepen their faith by performing rites for them. Make them feel worthy of themselves. Remember, virtue never grows old."

Saki Baba thought for a while and then added, "The ones who deny others salvation don't deserve it themselves."

"Teach the untouchables?" Krishna cried. He was quiet until now. "My grandfather told me that their time hasn't come to learn the sacred *Vedas*! Are you a good Brahmin, Saki Baba?"

"You don't speak in that manner to a holy man, son. Speak with respect. Forgive him, Baba, for he is young."

Saki Baba looked kindly at Krishna. "When I was young and thought myself to be clever, I once asked my father if God can kill itself since it's immensely powerful. He said that such questions don't contribute towards attaining enlightenment, nor do they make sense in the sphere of unity. Concerns about birth and death are only in this sphere of duality where opposites exist, where we exist. I'm now in that part of my life where I'm beyond castes or worldly concerns. Therefore, no one asks me such questions. But tell me what you think makes a good Brahmin."

"A good Brahmin is one who reads the *Vedas* daily, one who has knowledge, one who performs ceremonies for devotees, and one who is born into a Brahmin family," Krishna said.

"I have traveled far, from Lanka to Banaras to Kashmir," Saki Baba said. "I have been to snow-covered Kailas. I met and benefited from the sacred ones who experienced different levels of consciousness in their quest to reach enlightenment. From them I have learned much.

"I then came here to meditate, to find stillness and answers to my own spiritual questions, free from worldly attachments or desires. Of course, I'm not alone with such quests. Many in the past have retreated to deserts, forests, or mountain caves to seek answers. Now, as I age, I have become convinced that birth and knowledge alone don't make you a good Brahmin. Only good conduct does. Good conduct is good dharma. No matter how well versed you are in the *Vedas*, no matter how many times you pray daily, or performs elaborate rituals, if you are the slave of bad thoughts, you are not a good Brahmin."

Krishna glanced at his father. He was deep in thought, listening attentively.

Baba noticed the son's look.

"The wise also realizes the importance of the moment of death," he said. "If the departing consciousness, conditioned by good dharma, is absorbed in God at that moment, it will reach it after its lonely journey."

That night, before the day of their return, when the ascetic meditated and Krishna slept soundly near the fire, Bala stared long into the flickering flame and wondered what he should do next.

The pure flame gives light and warmth to everyone without hesitation or judgment, he thought. *It gives the same light to all, with or without caste. Baba is right. I too should be a light and bring wisdom to all for the rest of my life. I'll do right before I die so that good dharma will accompany me in my journey after death. I'll, therefore, build a temple in the untouchables' village and perform Vedic rites for them. In serving them, I'll serve Atman and Brahman. And this I pledge today in front of this sacred fire.*

Father and son didn't speak much during their return. They were tired and engrossed in their own thoughts. The son tried to understand what good conduct entailed but didn't ask his father. He had his own illness to deal with.

I'll travel and see the world beyond my village, perhaps visit Banaras and listen to the holy ones and become wise like Saki Baba, Krishna thought as they walked in silence.

Around noon the second day, they stopped near the paddy fields to rest and boil some rice in the pot they carried with them. As he lit the fire, the son looked at his father's haggard face and wondered how long he would live or when he would have his next seizure. He knew what to do with seizures. His grandparents taught him not to pour water in his mouth or force it open, even when he bites his tongue and makes it bleed.

I don't know much about dying or death, he thought. *All I now know is that when I die, I'm no more and not here. But someday, I'll.*

He was relieved when they finally reached home that evening.

Sacrifice

A week passed before Bala decided to tell his mother of his plan to teach the *Vedas* to the outcastes. This shocked and terrified her. Not even in her wildest fantasies could she have imagined such a repulsive step. How can her only son, a learned temple priest, leave the comforts of home with his parents and friends and choose to live with the untouchables? Besides, what will her husband and the temple priests think or say?

"Mother, you gave birth to me. You raised me and my sisters. Then you raised my twins when Kamala died. You loved them all you could. You have served Father faithfully all these years. You led a dharmic life, and we will always be grateful. But my time has come." After a pause, he added, "I'll tell Father tomorrow. I wanted you to know first."

The next morning, as Biswa prepared to visit the temple after his regular prayers at the family altar, his son stood beside him, and with all the courage he could master, he described his meeting with Saki Baba and of his decision.

"I'm the cause of your seizures? Your hidden fear for me is causing them? How ridiculous!" he shouted. "And your penance will be performing Vedic rites at a temple of the outcastes? How silly! Has Saki Baba gone mad? You're of our flesh and blood! We gave you birth! We gave you life!" His eyes bulged and looked fierce. "What will the community think? What will happen to our family name? I'll never permit such nonsense!" he roared.

"It is true you gave me life, my father," he said calmly. "I came by you and through Mother. But I'm not from you. In this sphere of existence, my consciousness is of another level than yours. Besides, I can never please you or live up to your expectations. In your eyes, I'll always be less and a disappointment. So let the community think as it pleases because what I think about myself now is more important."

Biswa couldn't understand what was happening. He refused to believe his ears. *No, this can't be,* he thought.

"Father, my seizures are becoming more frequent. I have difficulty remembering. My balance is poor. I'm starting to fall. I know my end is near. So let me at least die with faith—faith that we all are from the same source, and finally, we will return to it. Bless me, Father, to perform this spiritual service in the final years of my life. Serving the unfortunate is my proper conduct. If the eternal *Vedas* have taught us how to find bliss and salvation, why can't I share this with people who don't have this knowledge?"

What he heard stunned him. Is he the same Bala that he molded to fit his image of a good son? Could seizures have such an impact on him? Did Saki Baba change his thinking? He looked into his eyes. They were no longer downcast or timid. He realized then, at that moment, that he lost his only son.

"I have to go to the temple now," he said without raising his voice. "I have a few rites to perform. We will discuss this later."

Before sunset that day, when the three men of three different generations sat on the kitchen's clay floor for their evening meal that Maya had prepared, she asked her son who would cook for him at the outcastes' village and who would take care of him during his fainting spells.

"We don't know anything about the habits or customs of those people, Bala," she said. "We haven't even seen their village. Yet you plan to walk into their lives. How do you know they want to learn rites from you?"

"I don't know what they will learn from me, but I know I'll find peace. I'll be free from worldly demands. No one will expect anything from me. I may then learn more about the Atman in me. I now think my sickness has been a blessing, for it has introduced me to a new path of service that I didn't see before. It'll be my privilege to strengthen their faith in themselves. I'll teach them that all are equal before God. This will be my path of redemption and sacrifice. All will agree that this is a noble path and truly Aryan."

"But how will the temple priests remember you? What shall I tell them?" his father asked.

"My journey is to right past wrongs, overcome bigotry and sins of injustice. My aim is to spread human dignity and rights to the oppressed. The door to salvation must be open to all. My enemy is ignorance. My weapons are faith and deed with heart fixed on the Lord. Isn't it better to light a single lamp than to curse the darkness? Father, please tell them to remember that goodness drives me, the same goodness that's in all of us."

Many, however, didn't see the goodness, particularly the priests who controlled the rites. They emphasized the sacred nature of their tradition as they saw them. They wanted to maintain them strictly and exclusively.

"How can you let your son destroy the tradition of this temple? Has he gone mad?" one asked. "If I were you, I would disown him and save the family name," another said. Others just laughed and shook their heads in disbelief.

On the day of his departure, Bala knelt, touched his mother's feet, and asked for her blessing. With quiet sobs and tears in her eyes, she kissed his wet cheeks. "God go with you," she said as she bade good-bye to her dear son.

His sisters, however, weren't there to wish him well. Nor was his father for he left the house to visit the temple long before dawn.

Krishna accompanied him to the fringes of their village. "Bless me, Father, so that I too can fulfill my destiny by serving others," his son asked for his spiritual inheritance and touched his father's feet. Choked with emotions and unable to utter a word, Bala gently touched his son's head with the palm of his right hand and tried to say, "I bless you to right past wrongs."

The son watched the lonely figure of his father gradually disappear into edge of the paddy fields as his own shadow shortened with the midday sun.

PART D

Pilgrimage

A YEAR PASSED, and the temple priests forgot their colleague. They didn't talk about him in public again. Krishna, of course, thought of his father though he didn't mention him to his grandfather.

"How quickly people forget, Grandmother. Will they forget Grandfather too when he is no more? Will they remember his fifty years of service? Are we just passers by on this planet—transitory and inconsequential? No one speaks of my father. No one seems to care or feel for him. Is this right?"

"Ancient sages described life to be an illusion, Krishna. The last incarnate of Vishnu said that everything is impermanent. Attachment to impermanence results in sorrow. Sages say that if you don't let go the past, unhappiness results. This is happening to you now. You must therefore forget the past. Remember, every new day can be the beginning of a new life."

"Then what am I to do with the new day? I have mastered all the Sanskrit grammar that Grandfather teaches. I have committed the *Bhagavad-Gita* to memory. I have studied the spirit of the *Upanishads* and the philosophy of nonduality. The older priests told me there is nothing more they can teach except mind control. They say mind control will come with practice and maturity.

"Hari Ram suggested that I should accompany him on a pilgrimage to Haridwar, a place far to the north of our village, at the confluence of the holy Ganges and Yamuna. He said thousands of pilgrims bathe in the Ganges to purify their mind and soul. The water washes away sins and frees the faithful from rebirth."

"Yes, I know of Haridwar," Maya recalled her childhood. "The Kumbh Mela is held there once every twelve years. I know about this festival because my grandfather went on a pilgrimage to Haridwar with plans to visit Banaras."

A smile crossed her tanned face with graying eyebrows. "I was about five then, but I remember my parents crying when my grandfather left. They thought they would never see him again, for the journey takes more than three years. He had to cross the Godavari River, then the Vindhya mountains, then the hot, scorching heat and desert of Rajasthan, then the Gangetic plains, pass Delhi to Haridwar. Mind you, he and his companions had to walk. Sometimes they used boats and rafts to cross wide rivers. Grandfather didn't return, and we couldn't find out what happened to him. I, of course, like to think that he died in holy Banaras."

"You may go to the Mela with Hari Ram and Govinda," his grandfather said. "They are young and strong. Traveling great distances is much faster and easier now. The sahibs have brought foreign engine trains to carry them from one part of our land to another. These also carry our people. The ones who have been to the cities to see the British have told me so. I haven't seen these engine trains, for I haven't been out of our village. Of course, there hasn't been a good reason for me to go outside our village. But someday I'll ride a train, visit a city, and even see a British sahib. Hari told me that they eat meat, particularly cows and pigs. As for now, you can go. You're seventeen, and by the time you return, you'll be ready to wed and become a temple priest."

The British started building the Indian Railway system in 1850. In early 1902, the year after the death of Queen Victoria, Krishna, Hari, and Govinda began their pilgrimage. They planned to culminate their long journey by attending the Kumbh Mela of 1905.

On the day of their departure, the three men shaved their heads to show humility and received blessings from elders. They wore their caste strings; put caste marks on their foreheads and shoulders; bundled their clothing, brass utensils, and begging bowls made of dried hallowed melons; and walked due west for a week. They spent nights at villages on the way until they reached Sholapur.

"Will this train take us to Haridwar?" Govinda asked the sleepy old man at the ticket counter.

"Haridwar? Where is that?" the man said without looking at them.

"We're going to the Kumbh Mela in Haridwar, to the north of Delhi," Krishna replied.

"Oh, so you are pilgrims, going north to bathe in the holy Ganges. To me, the river Godavari is just as holy. Why travel so far when you can bathe in the Godavari which is just a day's train ride from here?"

"Is there a Banaras on the banks of the Godavari?" Krishna said, anxious to prove his knowledge. "Banaras is the Vedic learning center for Sanskrit scholars. Its temples are thousands of years old. Some say Banaras is the oldest city in the world. It has given us tradition, culture, values, and rules to lead spiritual lives. These have survived thousands of years. Banaras has been the very heart of our great and ancient land."

"Oh, I see," the man said and yawned. "You aren't only pilgrims. You are scholars too. Where did you learn these things about tradition and culture?"

"By studying the wisdom of ancient mystics and sacred scriptures like the *Upanishads*," he replied. "Have you read the *Vedanta*, sir?"

"Can't say that I have," the ticket clerk said, wide awake by now. His interest rose in the three men in saffron robes.

"You know, pilgrims needn't buy tickets to travel by trains. So keep your money. But remember this train alone won't take you all the way to Delhi. It'll take you north as far as Nagpur. At Nagpur, get off the train and ask the man at the ticket counter which train to take towards Banaras. He may guess your destination, but tell him anyway that you three are Sanskrit scholars on a pilgrimage."

The piercing whistle of the approaching train startled them. They had dozed off in the afternoon sun, waiting for the train. None of them had seen a train before.

They watched the big black engine puff clouds of smoke as it came to a shrieking stop. They saw the line of wagons behind the engine. Some of the passengers were getting off compartments with their luggage, while others were needlessly rushing and pushing to get in. The three hesitated. Then they picked up their belongings, ran toward the train, and did what other boarding passengers were doing. Unknowingly, they climbed aboard a second-class compartment occupied by a wedding party.

"This is very auspicious, very auspicious indeed!" an elderly mustached man said. "Look, look, we have Brahmins gracing our wedding party!"

"Welcome, Brahmins, welcome," a man with a garland around his neck said. "Please sit here beside Chandra Lal and bless the newlyweds. Chandra is the father of the bride. I'm Arjun Dass, the groom's father. The rest are relatives and friends. We are very fortunate that you chose our compartment."

"How far are you traveling?" Hari Ram asked after sitting beside Chandra Lal and motioning to Govinda and Krishna to sit on the facing bench.

Krishna soon stole a glance at the bride. He saw her downcast eyes half closed, her lips pursed in a faint smile as if aware of the young man's gaze. He quickly looked away.

"We are on our way back to Nagpur from Tirupati. The wedding took place at the Balaji shrine. Have you visited this shrine, respected sirs?" Chandra Lal asked.

"No, we haven't. We are on a pilgrimage to Banaras. We plan to visit Haridwar and may attend the next Mela," Hari Ram replied.

Dust blown from the Deccan, and passengers' litter covered the floor of the compartment. A member of the wedding party leaned out of the door and got the attention of a custodian wearing a numbered black shirt. As soon as the sweeper heard the passenger's call, he eagerly came forward. Boarding the compartment, he went about his business of sweeping the floor with his two-foot-long bamboo broom. A middle-aged woman soon started ordering him where to sweep and scolded him when he missed a dusty area. As he squatted and swept, he coughed incessantly to expel the dust from his lungs he inhaled. When the train started to move, he didn't show any interest in getting off.

"What about him? How will he return?" Krishna asked the man who offered him his seat and now stood in front of him. "Oh, him, don't worry about him. He'll go from compartment to compartment, sweeping and cleaning. Some passengers will pay him, some won't. That's how he makes a living. Most of them don't have homes or families. They spend their entire lives in the railways."

Krishna noticed that no one paid the sweeper when he was done. In fact, they ignored him totally. He stood there quietly, leaning against the toilet door, with his right hand open and extended, expecting compensation for his service.

After he got used to the sways of the moving train, Krishna got up from his seat and walked over to him. He gave him a few coins from the small bundle he carried tied around his waist. The sweeper touched his forehead with the coins and, without uttering a word, was about to leave.

"Wait," Krishna said. "I have something to ask you. Do you like what you do?"

Surprised, the sweeper stopped and looked at him and, without displaying the slightest emotions, said, "Yes, sahib."

"Even when they don't pay you for your work?"

He nodded his head. "That is my kismet, my fate. What can I do? I have worked here for years. No one ever asked me about myself. So why do you?"

"I ask because I don't know. You see, this is my first train trip. We are going on a pilgrimage."

He didn't appear to understand Krishna. "That's all right, sahib. *Salam.*" With that brief exchange, he entered the adjoining compartment.

Krishna returned to his seat and looked out of the window. He watched the countryside fly by and thought he would feel happy at the good deed he just performed. But he didn't. Something wasn't right; the hopelessness of the sweeper, his fatalism, and his low self-esteem bothered him.

He knew everyone has feelings, hopes, and dreams, just as he. *Everyone should have faith,* he thought, *for it generates confidence and strength. The sweeper didn't ask for money because he lacked faith in himself. Faith, however, doesn't come easily. or naturally. It has to be taught and developed.*

He thought of his father. He wondered if he was succeeding in teaching outcastes that we are all children of God.

"You are lost in thought, pilgrim," Chandra Lal said. "Here, have some puffed rice my wife cooked. Eat. Soon it will get dark. Two of the ceiling lights didn't work last night. Let's hope they do tonight."

Krishna looked at the lightbulbs though he didn't know what they were or how they emit light.

"Charity is good," Lal continued. "The scriptures encourage charity. So when we visited the shrine to have the marriage consecrated, we donated an ounce of gold to the priests who plan to build an arch around the gold idol of the deity. It's a wonderful feeling to give to a temple. Someday, this temple will be very famous. Devotees will come from all over the world to worship."

Krishna, however, wasn't convinced. He wondered how wealthy families could donate gold to temples while ignoring the plight of the poor. He didn't believe gold generates special favors from God. He believed charity creates good karma and strengthens faith.

As the hours passed, he tried to get used to the swaying of the train and get some rest. But the incessant chatter kept him awake long into the night. Besides, the sweeper's lack of self-worth bothered him.

Modern Memsahib

"My god, this place is so crowded and noisy!" Krishna shouted as their train entered the large Nagpur Railway Station. "There are so many buildings!" Govinda agreed. He looked at the row of shops and offices. "I hope we don't get lost!"

"Be patient. All we have to do is find the ticket office," Hari Ram assured them.

"There! I see it!" Krishna cried, pointing to a black sign with a white arrow. Govinda felt relieved as they hurried toward the office. As they neared, they noticed a large waiting room with glass windows and ceiling fans filled with Europeans.

"I've never seen sahibs before, Hari Ram. Let's have a closer look," Krishna said excitedly. But much to his disappointment, the heavyset policeman standing guard at the door waved him away.

Krishna, however, walked slowly as he passed the windows. His eyes moved quickly from one white face to another as if searching for someone familiar until they were captivated by a strikingly beautiful memsahib in a floor-length bell-sleeved white gown. She had shoulder-length wavy golden hair and wore a brimmed white hat to protect her lovely face and bare shoulders from the scorching sun. She chatted cheerfully with a young man in a well-tailored blue suit, revealing her pearly white teeth with frequent smiles as she puffed cigarette smoke out of her red mouth. Besides her were other women in equally beautiful gowns. The men, with sunburned faces, kept them company. Few walked around dressed in boots, leggings, and khaki uniforms.

"She is so beautiful! She looks like an angel in a dream! Oh, please, look at me once, angel, look towards me, for I have never seen such beauty before," muttered the mesmerized Krishna, slowing his steps even more. His wish came true when she hastened a glance in his direction and then looked away. Her smile, her youth, her confidence, and the feeling of being uninhibited awed him.

"She is European, possibly British, wearing the latest fashions," said a deep voice from behind him. "Come, pilgrim, master your senses. Don't be moved by lusty sense-objects. Don't let fleeting passion deter you." The voice belonged to a spectacled balding man with large piercing eyes.

Krishna felt embarrassed for letting his stare betray his lusty thoughts and feelings. "We are from a small village on a pilgrimage to Banaras. I've never seen British women before. Are they all fair and beautiful?"

The man ignored his question. "My name is Rahul Nanda. I'm from Kandy, Ceylon, on our way to Bodh Gaya. My traveling companion Matara Lanka is at the ticket office for the necessary travel information. If you wish, we can travel together. Gaya isn't far from Banaras. In fact, Lord Buddha often walked from Gaya to Banaras to teach the Middle Way. Many pilgrims still do. Now, of course, we have trains."

As the train pulled out from Nagpur toward Jhansi and Kanpur, the five pilgrims—two Buddhists and three Hindus—made themselves as comfortable as they could in their third-class compartment. Nanda began reading the newspaper he had with him. The headline read, "Great Son of India Passes Away."

Swami Vivekananda

"He was a great man, a noble son," Nanda said, pointing to the swami's picture in the newspaper. "He was articulate, energetic, and full of love for others. I had the good fortune to attend his lectures in Colombo and Jaffna in 1897. It's very unfortunate that he died so young. He wasn't even forty. Come to think, he was fifteen years younger to me."

He noticed that his new traveling companions didn't know about the swami. So he told them of his Vedantic philosophy lecture-tour to the West nearly four years.

"He was born in Calcutta in 1863. His real name was Narendranath Datta, but after he became a disciple of Sri Ramakrishna, the saint of Dakshineshwar, he assumed the name of Swami Vivekananda."

He looked out of the window and spoke deliberately.

"I'm of Tamil decent," he said. "My ancestors came to Ceylon from South India more than two hundred years ago. They were Hindus and raised me to be one. When I taught college in Kandy, I often visited its large Buddhist temple and practiced meditation with its monks. The teachings of Lord Buddha also influenced my thinking."

By now the other passengers who heard him stopped chattering.

"In meditation, I discovered that I can observe my inner experiences as if they were happening to others. I realized that peace and bliss come from within and from how we think. They don't come from without."

They listened to Nanda as the train sped north and were surprised to learn that followers of other religions don't believe that people are at various levels of spiritual growth and that they can follow different paths to God.

"Why don't they believe that all spiritual paths lead to God?" Govinda asked.

"It could be due to misunderstanding and intolerance. People fight and kill for their own tribal gods. 'My god is true, and yours isn't' is their battle cry. I believe this is why the Portuguese and the Dutch, after deposing the Tamil kings of Jaffna, tore down Hindu temples. These invaders then tried to force their Christian religion upon them. But our ancestors clung to their old faith. Now, thank God, this persecution has lessened under British rule.

"The swami told his Indian audiences that Hindus aren't a conquering race. Military or political power has never been their mission. They never forced their way on others with fire and sword.

"India is possibly the only country that didn't invade other countries to impose their religion. The swami noticed religious persecution in every Western country he visited. But in India, Hindus build mosques and churches for Muslims and Christians. This is because Hinduism is the eternal religion. It's broad enough to include all ideals.

"He pointed out that Vedantic philosophy isn't based on persons but on principles. Most people, however, require a personality. Look at Buddhism. Although Lord Buddha didn't preach the existence of a personal god, his disciples made him into one soon after his death and began worshipping him.

"Hinduism accepts the worship of all incarnations. Hindus can worship any sage or saint from any country."

A few of the passengers nodded in agreement. They knew what Nanda was talking about.

"Yet foreigners, even the educated ones, think we are ignorant. They think and say that Hindus are superstitious idolaters. If you explain to them that idols in temples serve the same purpose as crosses and idols of saints in Protestant and Catholic churches, they show no interest in listening and understanding."

Nanda became pensive for a while.

"They simply refuse to learn the truth about another faith. The swami, of course, recognized that it's impossible for all differences to cease. Variations must exist. No religion built upon a person can be suitable to all humanity. But it's not necessary that we should hate others for this.

"He said that India has a mission to teach religion with gentleness and goodwill. The world has to know that just as different rivers beginning from different mountains, run their course—straight or crooked—to reach oceans, so do different spiritual paths that we take for our tendencies all lead to God."

Swami Vivekananda was very wise, Krishna thought. He wondered if teaching should be his life's mission.

Castes and Saint Paul

At Kanpur Railway Station, the five disembarked to take their next train, but what caught their attention was the behavior of a few passengers. They covered their nostrils and hurried away when they saw three women carry metal containers on their heads.

"Who are they? What are they carrying that smells foul?" Krishna asked.

"They are untouchables—the lowest of the lows," Lanka said. "They clean latrines and carry feces." His voice shook. "They do the dirtiest work and are treated like dogs. How disgusting! How belittling of human spirit and dignity! The caste system is the vilest scheme that human mind could have ever conceived. It stratifies Hindu society and prevents a low caste to advance and escape mistreatment."

They became silent and looked uncomfortably at one another until Nanda spoke. "My friend feels deeply for the downtrodden. Of course he doesn't hold you personally responsible for the caste system. But the sight of these women—"

"No, no! He is right!" Govinda said. "True, we can't be held individually responsible, but we are responsible morally. We are guilty if we just accept it as a part of life. But the caste system is so old that even Lord Krishna speaks of it in the *Bhagavad-Gita*. Are we to question the teachings of Lord Krishna?"

"I have memorized the *Gita*, and I can recite from it," Krishna said. "But I don't know if I truly understand the depth of Yoga of Knowledge or Yoga of Action as Lord Krishna taught. In the *Gita*, he advised Arjuna to do his caste duty as a warrior and fight the righteous war against his cousins. He told him not to hesitate to do his duty, for heaven awaits the noble warrior who falls in battle. If he doesn't do his caste duty, he brings disgrace upon himself."

"So what are you saying?" Lanka raised his voice. "Do doers of caste duties only go to heaven? Is that your interpretation of his teachings?"

Hari Ram thought it was time for him to step in and explain away the controversy.

"In the search for spiritually, there is no difference between a warrior or a priest or a lower caste," he said. "Lord Krishna, himself of the warrior caste, said the highest spiritually can be attained by anyone who follows the prescribed duty of his own caste. You can't jump to God. You have to evolve spiritually towards God.

"The caste system is a natural order," he continued. "We divide ourselves into four groups according to our capabilities and characteristics. Each group has its own duties and responsibilities, and these are to be accepted to maintain natural order in society."

"Prescribed duties? Natural order? How disgusting!" Lanka said. "How can anyone defend the mistreatment and exploitation of people because of natural order or evolutionary law without restudy and reinterpretation? How can the conservative institutions of the upper castes continue to obstruct social justice and progress of outcastes? Is carrying feces on heads and accepting abuse the prescribed duties of a caste?"

Hari Ram didn't try to answer.

"I strongly believe that a man must never sacrifice his dignity to maintain the status quo of the privileged. What happened to your belief that humans are temples of souls?" Lanka tried to calm himself. "If anyone can evolve spiritually, then anyone can also develop intellectually. Then this development should enable anyone to accept greater social responsibility—beyond prescribed caste duties."

"When I was a student at Kandy," Nanda said, trying to lessen the tension, "I met a missionary. He told me something very attractive about Christianity, something that teaches equality of all before God, whether they are saints or sinners. He told me that Christians had a saint after the Crucifixion. His name was Paul. He was a Jewish tax collector before he had a vision of Jesus.

"Since Jesus was born a Jew, many early Christians insisted that pagans first convert to Judaism before accepting Jesus as the savior. Paul changed this belief. He found it to be unnecessary. He said that a pagan could convert to Christianity directly without first becoming Jewish. This greatly contributed to the spread of Christianity."

"Paul had a vision of Christian Jesus?" Krishna's interest perked up.

"There should be similar reformations in Hindu beliefs," Nanda said. "If Hinduism is based on principles and not on persons, then revise the principles that defend the caste system. Teach them to believe that we can change our castes and duties in this very life by learning better skills. This will develop hope and self-respect."

"Are you suggesting reforming Hinduism?" Hari Ram asked. "But how can Truth change?"

"Truth doesn't change, but our understanding of Truth does, with time," Professor Nanda said. "For instance, in around 1348, Europe experienced a medical disaster. The Black Death, or plague, killed nearly half its population. People lost hope and began believing in superstitions. Some believed that it was God's curse to punish men for their evil. Groups of men, therefore, walked from village to village, from town to town. They repented by flogging their backs with chains, causing them to bleed. Frightened women collected their blood and rubbed their eyes and faces with it, expecting God's forgiveness. Some even believed the sick and weak caused the plague. So they started killing them. But these beliefs gradually changed."

"Killing or mistreating others isn't godly, while compassion is divine," Krishna said. "I now see why the caste system is a plague. I agree. Our understanding of it must change."

Hari Ram and Govinda stared vacantly. They didn't have anything more to say.

"The missionary also told me," Nanda continued, "that in countries like America, children of all economic classes have access to free elementary and secondary education. They have opportunities to improve themselves. Society, or natural order, doesn't keep anyone down. This is why even a convicted murderer, after imprisonment and repentance, can become a Christian priest, while in India, a low caste, who committed no crime, can't become a temple priest."

"Yes, yes. They must be given hope and education," Krishna agreed enthusiastically. "But tell me, sir, who was Christian Jesus that you speak of?"

PART E

To Die in Banaras

THE TRAIN FROM Kanpur to Banaras was delayed that evening at Mirzapur Railway Station, about fifty miles west of Banaras. It served as a shunting station for the Express Mail that operated from Delhi to Calcutta, the capital of India.

The passengers were dozing in their compartment when loud voices woke them. Two muscular young men were pushing a crude wooden homemade stretcher with a body into the compartment while Zia Haque, the ticket checker, was assisting them.

"Why don't a few of you go to compartment number 512 that's behind this one?" Haque asked. "It's less crowded, and you don't have to travel with a sick old man."

"We five are traveling together," Nanda said. "Who is the man on the stretcher? Is he hurt?"

"He isn't hurt. He may be sick," Haque said.

"He isn't sick. He's old, just old. He's in his sixties and wants to die in Banaras, just like our mother did three years ago. So my brother, Bihari, and I are taking him there," Manoj said as he looked at the lean face of his father and gently adjusted the white sheet over his head.

"He was very strong in his youth," Bihari said. "He was a regimental wrestler, a *Bahadur*. He proved himself in the Royal India Mountain Division, never hesitant to pursue the enemy. He fought in Afghanistan in 1878. He was in Kabul and Kandahar with the British. He received two medals for bravery." After a slight pause, he said in a whisper, "Our whole village was so proud of him. He was our decorated war hero. But look at him now, unable to stand or hear. This is what age does."

"Why die in Banaras?" a passenger asked, moved by the story.

"Because illuminated yogis say that there are right ways to die just as there are right ways to live," Manoj replied. "When Atman leaves the body, it should be pure. It must be free of all earthly senses. Your consciousness must be focused on God at the moment of your death."

"Did a temple priest teach you that?" Krishna asked.

"No, we didn't learn that at a temple. Our priest doesn't sermonize or teach us anything of the scriptures. He just prays at the altar and then distributes the sanctified food.

"Our father taught us dharma by the way he lived," Bihari said. "He taught us to avoid killing except in a righteous war. When we wanted to enlist, he told us what he experienced in the Afghan wars. He said that a noble soldier doesn't enjoy killing and does his duty without losing control of his passions—particularly anger. It confuses the mind. If a soldier is angry in battle, he isn't ready for his noble sacrifice. And this is in the scriptures."

"What is a righteous war? I think all wars are evil, for they involve killing," said a widow in a plain white sari.

"A righteous war is when you fight to defend yourselves or the weak. An unjust war is for conquest and domination," Manoj said.

"More than two thousand and three hundred years ago, Emperor Asoka attacked Kalinga, the kingdom between Mahanadi and Godavari. This was a war of annexation," Bihari said. "It was an unjust war."

"But remember that Emperor Asoka learned from his mistake and became a philosopher-king, just like Kings Janaka and Yudishthria," Manoj added.

"Philosopher-kings?" Krishna said.

"These kings weren't only able administrators, but also great spiritual teachers who use their wisdom for the betterment of mankind. They considered their kingships to be sacred and selfless vocations. They didn't use their power for personal gains. They treated their subjects as their children," Manoj said.

Haque listened attentively as did the other passengers. "Do you need anything else, my friends?"

"You did enough today. Thank you, Zia," Manoj replied. Zia glanced at the other passengers and, without another word, saluted the brothers and left the compartment.

"He is an old friend. He joined the railways while we became soldiers. He follows the path to Allah taught by Prophet Muhammad. He knows a lot about the Glorious Koran. In fact, he has memorized many of its Arabic verses. We follow the path of Bhakti to Ishwara. Our paths are different though the ultimate destination is the same. Father taught us that Ishwara and Allah are the same though sages call it by different names."

"But don't you feel sad to take your father to die in Banaras, or has soldiering made your hearts hard?" an elderly woman asked. "I wonder what my children will do when I approach death."

There was no immediate answer on the part of the brothers. Both looked at the face of their father who now opened his eyes.

"Death comes to all. It is inevitable," Manoj said. "We all have experienced death before we were born in this life. Our father will be born again in another body. His soul will continue with its spiritual journey. The soul never dies, for it always exists. And in this belief we find solace."

The passengers waited patiently until finally, around midnight, they heard the Express Mail thunder by with its large headlight shining brightly. Krishna knew that they would soon reach Banaras, the ancient city of temples and mystical learning. His heart was throbbing faster and faster the more he thought of the esoteric knowledge he will acquire from its great gurus.

"Well, Nanda and Lanka, we enjoyed meeting you. If God wills, we shall meet again. May your journey be a blessed one," Hari Ram said as the train stopped at Banaras.

"May your quest lead you to Nirvana." Lanka bade farewell as the two brothers carried the stretcher out of the compartment. The disembarking passengers didn't appear to be in the same hurry as the ones in Nagpur Railway Station. They quietly walked out of the deserted, dimly lit station and disappeared into the night.

The pilgrims decided to accompany the two soldiers carry their father to the guesthouse in Ramnagar Fort, which also housed the old palace of the raja of Banaras and his private museum. The raja, being a Kshatriya himself, always honored courage and valor and did what he could to provide comfort to old and injured soldiers who came to Banaras to die.

The three didn't know what to do next. Krishna was tired and hungry.

"Can we please rest a while, perhaps sleep until dawn?" he asked.

"As soon as we reach the bathing ghats," Govinda replied.

As they walked toward the banks of the sacred river in the wee hours of the morning, tired and hungry, they noticed rows of separate fires flicker at a distance. They couldn't help but wonder if they were all funeral pyres for the many who come to Banaras to die.

Age of Strife

"Wake up, Brahmins, wake up. The sun is rising. Go, bathe and purify yourselves in the holy Ganges. Then eat what I cooked," they heard a woman.

They rose from their deep sleep. They spent the night under the canopy of a broad-leaved tree. They were still tired, and it took them a while to collect their whereabouts. Besides, they weren't used to women waking them.

"Who are you? Why are you cooking for us?" Govinda asked the woman whose face and arms were covered with cow dung ash.

"I'm Yamuna Bai. I live under this tree," she said, pointing to her belongings. "I heard you last night. You have come to Banaras to search for the Truth. Pilgrims always do, you know. 'The best of all gifts is the gift of Truth,' they say. Many have come before you, and many will after you. And I'll live under this old tree until I die. Then they will cremate me. I'll then find final rest."

Krishna didn't know what to make of this strange philosopher. "Are you mad?" he asked.

She didn't answer but pointed to the river. "Years have gone by just as the water has flown by. If my son were to be alive today, he would have been about your age. But who knows? He may also be alive. I don't know, I'll never know. But I know one thing: he wouldn't ask me if I'm mad."

"Forgive me, Bai. I apologize for my curtness," he said, ashamed of his thoughtlessness.

They got up and walked toward the ghats.

As the sun rose, the bathing ghats came alive with people. The three bathed and took their forty-nine ceremonious dips in the cool water. They kept repeating the syllable "OM," which is the imperishable Brahman, the creator of this infinite universe.

Whatsoever existed in the past, whatever exists now or will in the future is "OM." And whatsoever transcends past, present, and future is also "OM." Krishna knew that this syllable consists of three letters—*A-U-M*. He tried to utter them the best way he could, with conviction and clarity, his eyes closed and mind free of distractions.

They felt the holy water cleanse their minds and bodies. After drying themselves, they decided to offer prayers at the temples.

"Why are there so many temples?" Krishna asked.

"I don't know, but they are ancient. A few were here when Lord Buddha delivered his sermon at Deer Park after attaining enlightenment. Deer Park is north of Banaras," Govinda said.

"As far as I know," Hari Ram said, "temples are dedicated to devas, and since there are many in the pantheon, there are many temples. Of course, this doesn't mean there are many gods. It only means many manifestations. The Supreme One can be many."

The morning proved to be good for them. The previous night was Maha Shivaratri. Many devotees came to worship Lord Shiva with offerings of morsels of sweets, fruits, milk, curd, and rice. The milk and curd were in earthenware pots. The temple priests were generous and offered them ample portions of prasad enough to last days.

When they returned, Bai wasn't there. But her bundles were, tied and nestled away between the aerial roots of the mangrove, at heights safe from stray cows and goats. Krishna was amused with her storage method. As he examined it closely, he heard her call from a distance.

"You didn't come to eat the food I cooked. So I gave it away to the urchins. They often come to tease me. They call me names and say I smell. But when I feed them, they stop teasing."

"Why do you smell?"

She came close to Krishna and looked directly into his eyes—just as a mother would while searching for her lost child. "Is that why you didn't come for the food? I can cook as well as your mother, you know."

"The temple priests gave us food," Hari Ram said. "See, we have fruits and rice. These will last days."

"So you won't eat my cooking because I'm dirty?" Bai said. "Let me tell you that once I was a beautiful girl with a melodious voice. Five girls from our village sang and danced at a palace far from here towards the setting sun. We were in our early teens then and lived at the palace. We sang and danced every evening for the raja."

"You sang and danced at a palace! Then what are you doing here covered with dung?"

She began to weep.

"She is mad. Let's leave her. We have much to do," Hari Ram said, picking his belongings.

"I can still sing. People pay to listen to me. If you hear me sing, you will believe me. I can't sing right now, for I'm very sad. I think of my baby, of holding him close to me. What happened to my son? I'll never know," she wiped her tears with the tip of her tattered sari.

"Tell us about your baby. Tell us about your life at the palace," Krishna comforted her.

"When I was thirteen, the raja's music teacher came to our village and met the parents of unmarried girls of my age. He said that the queen wanted to have graceful girls taught to sing and dance. The selected girls will live at the palace with their teacher. Besides food, they will receive beautiful dresses and jewelry to wear. All they have to do is work hard and entertain palace guests for three months before returning home. The best may stay for another three months.

"I was very excited. I wanted to live at the palace. When my parents approved, I joined the other girls.

"Can you imagine what it is like to see a palace for ones like me? Rooms filled with beautiful shining things! Paintings of kings and queens on walls! Smooth marble floors!

"The male servants wore long white tunics. The women wore clean colorful saris and studded shoes.

"We didn't see the raja or the queen for nearly two months. The teacher didn't allow us out of the palace. We bathed, dressed, and dined with proper etiquette. He taught us to smile, dance, and sing from late afternoon to midnight.

"One evening, the teacher gave us beautiful dresses and jewelry to wear. We performed in front of the queen. She smiled and looked pleased with our singing and dancing. I found out afterwards that she was planning a farewell party for her twenty-one-year son who was going abroad to study. She liked me and chose me to sing a song she composed for her son. This made me proud.

"The day for the party finally arrived. We rubbed scented water on our bodies, put jasmine in our hair, and wore jewelry and colorful silk saris.

"The male guests wore beautiful coats and turbans. The women wore precious jewelry. They sat in the Darbar room where we danced and sang well into the night. The musicians played instruments like the sitar, tabla, horn, and flute. At midnight, I sang the queen's song. My voice was sweet. It made many cry, for it was about a mother's love for her departing son.

"The guests left after midnight, and we returned to our room. When all of us were asleep and the palace was dark and quiet, a woman woke me and said the prince liked my song and wanted me to sing it again before he slept.

"I was led to his large room filled with shining furniture. In the dim light, I saw him sitting on a chair next to his bed. He was drinking something from a glass. I learned afterwards that it was alcohol. He beckoned me to sit on the bed and asked me to sing. I sang without accompaniment, and since I was very nervous, I sang terribly. But he said I sang sweetly and that I have a pretty mouth. He asked me to sing a second time. As I was singing, he got up from his chair and sat beside me. He put his mouth close to mine, and I could smell his breath.

"He then pushed me down on the bed, climbed on top of me, and started to kiss me. I tried to push him away. When I screamed, he covered my mouth with his large strong hands and told me to keep quiet. He told me that he is a prince and that all his subjects belong to him. He then ripped my clothes and violated me. I didn't know what to do but weep for the pain he inflected.

"After he was done, he told me to leave his room. He warned me not to tell anyone. Otherwise, he said, he will have my parents killed since he knew where we lived. Terrified, I quietly returned to our room. I covered the bloodstains on my dress by folding it into a ball. Naturally, I couldn't fall asleep.

"The other girls didn't know what happened. In the morning, they took their regular baths and put on fresh clothes. I then entered the indoor pool to wash away the dirt he put into me. No one saw me cry as I washed repeatedly. I then dressed and joined the other girls.

"I told myself that this would never happen again since the party was over and the prince would leave. But I was mistaken. Every three or four days, he would ask me to sing to him alone. Then he would rape me. Finally, after about two months, I told my music teacher. She told me that the prince would leave soon, and this pain will end. She also told me that no one would blame the prince, since dancing girls often seduce princes for money. Besides, she said, I shouldn't have gone to his room in the first place, unless I wanted to excite him. I was shocked at what she said. I just cried.

"I thought of stabbing myself with one of the daggers that hung on the palace walls. But I was afraid of blood. I thought of other ways to kill myself.

"Just before the prince left, my stomach started to swell. The other girls would look at me and giggle. I wondered if they knew.

"On the day the prince left, I was moved to a small house away from the palace. An old couple lived in this one-room house. They treated me kindly and told me that if the baby is born at the palace, they will kill it if it is a girl. If it is a boy, they will take it away from me and raise him to be a warrior. But if I chose to go to Banaras to give birth, I'll be able to keep my baby, and the palace will pay me.

"I wanted my baby. I wanted to raise him, be close to him. So the old couple and I came to Banaras nearly twenty years ago. The woman helped me to give birth. It was a boy, and I was happy. We lived in a small room for three months. I breast-fed the baby. In three months, he became bigger. His black silky hair grew longer. Then the old woman started feeding him cow's milk.

"Early one morning, I left my son with the couple and went to the river to bathe. I used to bathe regularly in the holy river, once or twice a day, hoping to wash away the sins I committed with the prince. I hated him, and if I were to be a man, I would have killed him.

"When I returned, my baby and the couple weren't there. Since all our belongings were in the room, I thought they had gone to the market to get milk. I waited and waited. Noon came and passed. Just before sunset, I started to get very nervous. I started to cry for crying is something I learned to do well at the palace. A passerby saw me and told me to go to the police or to the temple priest. I was afraid of the police. They may find out that the baby is of royal blood and accuse me of stealing it. So I ran to the temple. When I got there, the priest had already started his evening worship.

"As darkness fell and the temple lights were lit, I hastened to the old priest at the Sri Hanuman Temple and prostrated myself at his feet and began to cry. Through my tears, I told him that my son was missing and that the old couple was nowhere. He listened to me and told me that I should go to the police. When I told him that I couldn't, he asked me to rest for the night in the temple. He said he was a tired old priest but will help me in the morning.

"I kept awake the whole night. I was full of hate. I was angry at everything, including myself. Why do strong men treat women so cruelly?

"Before dawn, I went to the river to bathe. Only then did I feel the pangs of hunger and realize that I hadn't eaten anything for a whole day. I looked for something to eat. On the stone steps leading to the river, I saw a figure in a burgundy robe, sitting in a lotus position. I approached him for some food. He gave me a piece of bread and a banana and asked me my name. When he noticed how hungry I was, he gave me a few pieces of dried mango. He told me that his name is Sanga Rampa, that he is from Tibet, and that it takes almost a month to walk to his lamasery. I noticed that he was holding a string of beads in his right hand as he spoke.

"When I told him of my plan to drown myself that day if I couldn't find my baby, he seemed to smile. He said that everything changes with time. Nothing is permanent. Even mountains change. He said that thousands of years ago, this land around us was a dense forest with huge trees and wild animals. Great sages meditated here to find the secrets of life.

"'Look around, Bai,' he said. 'Look around and note that the forest and wild animals that lived here are now gone, and like them, we too will leave. Death will come by itself. We, therefore, don't have to hasten death. But before it comes, we can do a few good things to better ourselves spiritually. You, for instance, can forgive yourself, just as you forgive others.

"'You don't have to kill yourself just like you don't have to kill others. You needn't carry this sorrow for the rest of your life. Let go your anger and fear. Be fearless. There is nothing to fear. A great sage once said that fear is the cause of all evil.

"'Be grateful for life. It lets you think. You are very special, and you can be the light to discover yourself. Don't judge the old couple. Remember the laughter you shared with them. Be content and live each day as if it is your last day on earth.'

"Then he taught me the prayer of 'Om! Ma-ni pad-me Hum!' I asked him what it means. He said its translation is 'Hail to the Jewel in the Lotus.' I told him that I still didn't understand, to which he replied that someday I would.

"I thanked Sanga Rampa for the food and his wisdom. He did calm my anger. I left him sitting on the steps, remembering what he said: I'm special, and I could be a light to discover myself."

They listened attentively. Her plight moved them, especially Krishna. He could now understand why he reminded her of her son.

"I returned to the old priest at the Sri Hanuman Temple," she continued. "I asked him why this terrible thing happened to me, what I did to deserve this sorrow. He didn't answer but told me that I could spend the nights at his temple since I have nowhere to go. I was grateful and promised to clean and sweep the temple floor every day if he would give me food.

"I spent nearly twelve years of my life with the old priest and gradually learned to take care of myself. Since he didn't have a family of his own, he treated me like his daughter. He also taught me about the *Mahabharata*, about the Kauravas and Pandavas, about the war that lasted eighteen days. He told me about Sri Krishna's death and the beginning of Kaliyuga, the Age of Strife, and that it will last three hundred and sixty thousand years.

"When I asked him about Kaliyuga, he told me that this is the age when righteousness is replaced by unrighteousness, when courage is replaced by cowardice and when dharma is replaced by adharma. He said that in this age, the Ksatriyas would have violent temper and addiction to wickedness. Instead of defending the weak and providing safety to Brahmins and the land, the warrior caste will inflict death on women and children. Brahmins would devote themselves to acquiring wealth and influence and not to spirituality and learning, while the Vaisyas and Sudras will use falsehood and deceit to quench their insatiable earthly desires. All nations will follow these evil ways.

"He told me that at the end of this age, Kalki, a divine incarnation, would appear and destroy evil and reestablish dharma on earth."

They listened to the religious knowledge of the woman with long black knotted hair.

"You have learned much in Banaras," Govinda said. "You have learned to purify yourself by controlling your anger, hate, and fear. But please tell us why you cover yourself with ash?"

"For safety. During the twelve years that I spent at the temple, I developed into womanhood to become interesting to men. The priest noticed this and advised me to cover my body with ash. This smell provides me security, particularly when I'm away from the temple yard. After he died, I left the temple. Now I'm capable of spending nights alone under trees like these.

"Life isn't bad," she said with a weary smile. "I'm safe. Besides, I serve visitors by cooking their meals. Sometimes, I even sing the song the priest taught me about the soul and hope." She then sang a rueful tune about a hidden place in our hearts.

"Bai, Banaras has taught you to develop internal purity. We hope it will teach us also," Govinda said.

"It's important to develop personal cleanliness," Hari Ram added. "When you cook, the food must be free of impurities. Avoid defective and bad quality food, like meat and excessive amounts of garlic and onions. They create passion. Don't eat food touched by wicked people, food must always be clean."

"Do you think the food I cooked was unclean?" Bai asked.

They didn't answer. They had much to learn at Banaras.

Paths to Salvation

"Why does time pass so swiftly in Banaras? Do you realize that 1902 is over?" Hari Ram asked Govinda one day during the middle of their second year.

"Time passes quickly because we are busy and learning," he answered. "We attend many ceremonies and dharma talks. Look at Krishna. He too is busy talking and eating with strangers. I wonder why they always give him food."

"Because he is growing and looks hungry," Hari Ram said and laughed. "But seriously, I asked Advani why food plays such an important role in rituals. He said that rituals are one of the important features of Hinduism, and since the *Vedas* say food is life, one should give food. Eating, on the other hand, is considered to be the supreme sacrifice to the spirit who dwells in us."

Many visit Banaras to share their spiritual experiences. Others come to inquire and find answers to age-old questions. They gather under canopy of trees and listen to theological discussions.

The concept of plurality of equivalent paths is very important in Hinduism. It teaches two main paths: the path of works, suitable for the ones who are inclined to be active, and the path of knowledge for the contemplative type. The path of devotion, or worship, developed out of path of works. Most present-day Hindus follow the path of worship.

"What we discuss today will interest many of you," Ajit Advani said, standing at the trunk of a large broad-leaved tree. He was a middle-aged man who left his law practice in Delhi after his wife died three years ago to become a follower of Guru Devananda. During these years, he visited Banaras to share his spiritual knowledge and encourage others to find happiness through self-discovery.

"In early Vedic period, life consisted of the householder and that of the ascetic. The work of the householder provided food for all. Therefore, this important work was religion in itself as long as it was performed properly. The path of works, or *Karmamarga*, also included offering elaborates sacrifices.

"This path promises wealth and pleasure to the ones who have the rituals, or *yajna*, performed according to the scriptures. People believe the Supreme, or Brahman, dwells within rituals.

"The priests, or Brahmins, were the professionals who performed the Vedic fire sacrifice. As the importance of rituals grew with time, so did that of priests who gradually claimed exclusive rights to perform them.

"There are historical reports of some of these rituals lasting months. Rajas and other wealthy individuals invited thousands of Brahmins to offer animal sacrifice as part of dharma. The ordinary householder, who chose this path, would offer a goat or a duck for sacrifice.

"History tells us that avatars like Lord Buddha and Lord Mahavira vigorously opposed these rituals and the slaughter of animals. Gradually, worship or *puja*, replaced animal sacrifice. Vegetarian food and flower offerings replaced the partaking of sacrificed meat.

"After Lord Buddha, many sovereigns in India, like Emperor Asoka, forbade animal butchery. In later part of our history, a few Muslim rulers did the same. In Europe, even the 'barbarians' invading the 'civilized' Roman Empire put a stop to the slaughter of animals at the coliseum.

"This path encourages you to perform your duty without any attachment to the results of your work. You dedicate the results of your work to God. This frees you from ego. Duty done in this spirit leads you to salvation."

Advani then described the second path.

"The path of knowledge, or *Jnanamarga*, leads you to the knowledge of Brahman," he said. "Followers of this path aren't interested in things on earth or heaven. They only seek insight into the ultimate, the no-thing. This is the final reality. This path shows the way to self-discovery, which in itself is the ultimate. If you know yourself, you know reality."

"How do we seek insight?" someone asked.

"You attain insight by freeing your mind of worldly desires. This is done through introspection or meditation."

"Is it like cleaning your house before inviting an important guest for dinner?" a woman asked.

"Good analogy," Advani said and smiled. "The path of knowledge has four stages," he continued. "The first state is wakefulness or awareness of rational thought. Your spirit is limited to time and space and the physical laws of the universe.

"The second is the dreaming state that you create yourself. This that you create is not limited to physical laws. It is of whatever your mind conceives. Your spirit is free of the limitations of the physical world.

"The third state is dreamless. It's higher than your dreaming state. It's blissful. It's a state of unification where your spirit is free of yourself. The spirit, however, is not aware of bliss or unification.

"The fourth state is beyond and can't be described. It's awareness of consciousness. It is freedom and bliss. It is knowledge of self. It's not knowledge of something but knowledge of nothing particular. It is enlightenment."

Krishna became excited at the mention of enlightenment. "What is enlightenment?" he asked.

"Enlightenment is discovering who we are. The path of knowledge needs strict discipline. It takes many years of *tapas*—the training and meditation to sharpen your intellect. No one can describe or teach reality. You must find the self yourself."

A hush fell over the crowd. Advani didn't know if it was due to the complexity of the topic or the intellectual level of the listeners.

"It's difficult to interpret and communicate the awareness of consciousness. Objective knowledge can't identify 'no-thing' or the ultimate reality."

He paused for a while and said, "This reminds me of the sage from Lahore who spoke here last year. He asked how imperfect words could describe something perfect."

A couple sitting in the front nodded their heads. They knew what Advani meant.

"The path of knowledge has not only interested people in India, but also many in America and Europe. The Christian saint Augustine spent his life with the sole goal to know God. We too can begin this adventure today, this blissful journey of self-discovery."

No one made comments or ask questions. Phrases like "spirit free of one's self" and "state of awareness of consciousness" were just too difficult to fathom.

Advani then introduced Bhupen Das, professor of Eastern philosophy at Calcutta University, to discuss the path of worship or *Bhaktimarga*.

"The religions of the world differ in their forms of worship," Das began. He was visiting Banaras to discuss this path of loving devotion that he himself practiced.

"I'm one of the fortunate few who had the opportunity to attend lectures by Swami Vivekananda. I like to discuss his teachings in sunlight. It reminds me of his open mind, his courage to explore different paths, and his willingness to share his knowledge.

"He said that Bhakti is the love of God with a pure heart. Anyone can practice love of God at any time, anywhere, and in many ways. For example, some may build temples to worship in, while others may worship symbols and idols out in the open. Some worship fire, others worship seers as if they were gods, while others don't choose images at all.

"This path is easier to practice than the path of knowledge. But the end is the same. He said that the great quality of Bhakti is that it cleanses and purifies the mind.

"A mind defiled by hate can't reach God. We shouldn't hate or harm people of other faiths. We should do what we can to increase our faith. The wise can always help us to advance spiritually.

"True devotees, or *bhaktas*, want nothing. They are contented in loving God. They take refuge in God. They surrender themselves completely to it and believe in its protection. Devotees seek the company of the truly pious and avoid the ones who don't love God. They control their passions and bear grief without complains.

"The *Gita* teaches devotion. The Ultimate is unreachable through insight, learning, or explanation alone. But fixing your mind on Lord Krishna and worshipping him can reach the Ultimate. 'Taking the name' is most essential in becoming a devotee.

"We are all born with distinctive tendencies. These remain with us and make our nature differ from others. Remember, we are at different levels of spiritual development.

"Violence arises when one religious group thinks theirs is the only way to salvation. But one religion can't meet the needs of all on this planet. Variety is necessary.

"All civilized religions are based on morality. All religions have produced good and able men and women. All teach external and internal purity. External purity is easier to attain while internal purity is more abstract. It involves truthfulness, service to others, and charity to the needy.

"We shouldn't love God from fear or greed. It's not devotion if I love God for the sake of a son, a beautiful wife, or other earthly desires. When we help others, we should remember God because we can attain perfect devotion if we see God in everything.

"Devotion can be the salvation for everyone, irrespective of castes. Many great devotees are Hindus, Muslims, or Sikhs. Even Christians in India have accepted Bhakti as theirs.

"Love of God has inspired thousands of Indian poets and singer-saints. For instance, the great Hindi poet of mediaeval India Kabir was a Muslim weaver. In his songs, he tells us that we all seek God and that Hindus and Muslims have equally realized God. Through his songs, he said that those who are kind and righteous, who avoid world's entanglements, who consider all creatures on earth as their own self, who are devoid of pride and self-deceit attain the immortal."

A few in the group nodded in silence as did Govinda. But he wanted to learn more. "Why do some use idols and images to worship?" he asked.

"They help us to concentrate. They help ordinary people conceptualize a personal God. Worshipping God is natural and human. It brings religion from the highest levels to ordinary levels for common people to practice. Remember, an impersonal God is difficult to visualize, conceptualize, or explain."

"But some look upon the use of idols as a lower form of worship," Krishna said.

"That's because Bhakti is worship through matter. Man is mostly a material being now. It takes time and effort to evolve spirituality. When a man worships through idols, he conjures by incantation until he reaches his spiritual goal. Then he doesn't need material help anymore."

"Do other religions use idols?"

"They do to strengthen faith of the faithful. I've seen images of saints and angels in churches. In fact, some angels are depicted to be tall and handsome. They even have wings. Your question reminds me of a beautiful Christian prayer: 'Hail Mary, full of grace, pray for us sinners.' Worshippers ask Mary, mother of Christ, to pray for them."

"Is Christianity a form of Bhakti then?" Krishna asked.

"I've attended Christian services in Calcutta. I think it's a form of devotional worship. When I read their scriptures, I found Krishna's teachings to be similar to the teachings of Jesus and his to Krishna's. The rituals are different, but both teach love and worship of God and salvation through faith. Both teach forgiveness and self-control of body's desire. Both teach devotion for welfare of humanity."

After a brief pause, he added, "Of course I have more to learn about Christ's teachings."

"How can I learn about Christ?" Krishna asked, anxious to learn about another path.

"Have you studied English?" Das asked. "If you have, you can read their scriptures. I've read the Holy Bible, King James Version. It's in English. If you are interested, visit Calcutta. It's not only the capital, but also a learning and intellectual center. Since 1857, Calcutta University has attracted many bright people. You can study various subjects there—even English and the Bible. Evangelists are eager to teach their scriptures."

As time passed, Krishna became more convinced that he should study Christianity. He had heard about the Glorious Koran during his trip, but he knew nothing about the Bible. *To be wise, I must know other faiths and paths,* he thought.

"I'm going to Calcutta to study," he told his companions one day. "I don't want to visit Kumbh Mela now. I can always visit Haridwar, but I may not get another chance to learn English in Calcutta and read the Bible."

Govinda and Hari Ram, however, wouldn't hear of it. "Your grandfather holds us responsible for your safe return. What shall we tell him? Going to Calcutta will be a diversion from our pilgrimage. We are yet to visit Sarnath. It takes only half a day's walk from here, and we can do that before the monsoons."

Krishna was now torn between obedience and loyalty on one hand and his own desire to explore on the other. He questioned what constitutes a virtuous desire. He wanted to know if following his own goal, and not that of his grandfather, would lack virtue.

The professor had told him that Lord Krishna described virtue as reverence for sages, seers, and teachers. One who speaks without causing pain to others, one who is harmless, clean, pure, honest, and candid is virtuous. A virtuous desire can be an action without desire for reward—an action that seeks no advantage for the doer.

"Christians have three theological virtues," Das had said. "They are faith, hope, and love. Greek philosophers described virtue to be justice, temperance, prudence, and fortitude."

Krishna finally concluded that his desire for knowledge is utterly harmless. Desire for spirituality is virtuous for he seeks no earthly rewards for himself. And after he attains insight, he would gladly share it with others.

He became convinced that his desire to study English and Christianity is harmless, pure, just, and selfless. So he made up his mind to visit Calcutta after Sarnath.

Sarnath's Ashes

The dusty, unpaved road to Sarnath was through the flat plains of Bihar province dotted with fruit trees and old monuments. In the tall grass by the side of the road, relics of the past suddenly appear from nowhere. Foundations of ancient monasteries hide in the grass until you stand right in front of them. Sarnath was one of the first Buddhist pilgrimage sites that British archaeologists explored.

In 1798, a Briton by the name of Jonathan Duncan, a resident of Banaras, published an article about the destruction of precious relics in the region. In the eighteenth century, the Dewan of the raja of Banaras plundered Sarnath for building materials. When he found a green marble casket with reliquary ashes, he had them dumped into the Ganges without any regard for their religious significance.

In 1800s, archaeologists in Sarnath excavated evidence of a time when fire suddenly destroyed Buddhist sites. In his excavations, Major Kittoe discovered that Sarnath was sacked and burnt, its temples destroyed, and its monks killed. In some places, he unearthed many huge heaps that had bones, iron, timber, and idols. The extreme heat caused by fire fused all together.

He reported that the destructions were sudden and unexpected. He found remains of ready-made wheaten cakes in the recesses of the chambers. He also found wheat and other grains in one cell. These discoveries suggest that the fires were so sudden and rapid that monks had to abandon their very meals to escape total destruction.

The Chinese Buddhist pilgrim Hiuen Tsiang, who visited Sarnath during the mid-seventh century, described a great two hundred feet high temple. Its foundation and stairs were of stone, while its towers were of brick. There were hundreds of niches on the four sides. Each had a golden figure of the Buddha. In the middle of the enclosure was a life-size copper figure of Lord Buddha.

The traffic to Sarnath that day in May 1903 consisted of bicycle rickshaws, bullock carts, and horse-drawn buggies. There were a few elephants. The air was fresh, and many walked to celebrate Lord Buddha's birthday. Two of them were from Japan and three from Burma.

As the pilgrims approached Sarnath, they could see the tips of three tall stupas against the blue sky.

"The first one, just ahead of us, is Chaukhandi Stupa," an excited young Japanese monk said, pointing at the stupa. "The second one is Dharmarajika Stupa, and the third, on our right, is Dhamekh Stupa. Here the Compassionate One taught the Four Noble Truths and the Noble Eightfold Path."

"We two are Zen monks going to Lumbini," Muro Kyuso, his older companion walking with a staff, said with a smile. "The Lord was born in Lumbini. It's to the southeast of Kapilavastu, near the Indo-Nepali border."

The pilgrims had never met Japanese monks before, but the older monk's smile reassured them. "We are Hindu pilgrims visiting holy places," Govinda said as he introduced his companions. "How is it that you know so much about these stupas? Have you been here before?"

"Yes. Fujiwara has been here before," Kyuso said. "Three years ago, in July 1900, he accompanied Kawaguchi to this part of India. Fujiwara visited Bodh Gaya to fulfill his lifelong dream, to meditate where the Lord reached enlightenment."

"Who is Kawaguchi?" Krishna asked, trying hard to pronounce the name correctly.

"He is a Zen monk and a devout Buddhist scholar," Kyuso said. "He came to unveil the ancient wisdom preserved in Lhasa, Tibet. He speaks Tibetan fluently, and his goal was to read and collect Tibetan translations of the Mahayana Buddhist scriptures. He left Japan thirty months ago to prepare for this trip."

Kyuso then looked at Fujiwara and nodded.

"He and I spent a week here before he began his journey to forbidden and mysterious Tibet," Fujiwara said. "He crossed into Tibet from Nepal. We don't know where he is now, but young monks like me admire him."

"How did you like Banaras?" Krishna asked Fujiwara unassumingly.

"We like its history but not its air," Fujiwara answered without hesitation. "It's a dirty crowded joyless city with sullen people."

Surprised at the condescending answer, Krishna looked at Govinda.

"The city is four thousand years old!" Govinda commented.

"Do you need more time to clean it? There are millions of you Hindus. Why can't you clean up your holy city? You believe in creating good karma and in the purity of body and spirit, don't you?"

"And you, Fujiwara, you being who you are, you are to practice right understanding, right thought, and right speech as the Lord taught. Although the sun is scorching and draining, you mustn't harbor impatience. You are to be harmless and refrain from harsh speech. You must make the right effort and work diligently to prevent bad thoughts from entering your mind," Kyuso said as he defended the pilgrims.

Young Fujiwara bowed his head respectfully. He said no more.

Later that afternoon, when the temperature reached its highest, the three pilgrims and the five monks rested in the shade of the beautifully inscribed walls of Dhamekh Stupa and quietly ate their food. Govinda, sitting beside Kyuso, leaned toward him and whispered, "What Fujiwara said about Banaras isn't really untrue."

"He is inclined to be a bit impatient," Kyuso said. "The blood of samurai runs in his veins. He is a direct descendant of Shogun Iyesada, who signed the Treaty of Kanagawa with Commodore Perry in 1854."

Govinda looked perplexed. He and his companions knew nothing about the history of Japan or of other countries.

"We are just priests who study Vedic scriptures in Sanskrit," he said. "We perform temple ceremonies. This is the extent of our knowledge. We have never been out of our village before, but we are willing to learn."

His honesty impressed Kyuso. He, therefore, told them about the culture and recent history of Japan, about its first contacts with Westerners and the humiliating treaty Japan had to sign with Commodore Perry about fifty years ago.

"The samurais had grown soft. They were inactive the previous two hundred years," he said. "They were unable to defend the emperor's sovereignty. They lacked unity and didn't recognize the emperor's authority completely. Japan needed modernization. It needed exposure to the economic and military might of the West to open its eyes."

"How does a country or a man become modern?" Krishna asked.

"Modernity relates to present information and knowledge. It means keeping up with discoveries and inventions," Fujiwara answered.

Kyuso nodded in agreement. "A great American by the name of Thomas Jefferson once said that a nation could never be ignorant and free," he said. "Japan now became determined to learn from the Occidentals about their wealth-building ways and modern military methods. America and the European countries thus became Japan's teachers. They assisted Japan to Westernize and industrialize as rapidly as possible. Japan gave up its feudalism by ending the shogunate and became a democracy with its emperor as the supreme authority.

"The Japanese were amazed by the Western steamships, their powerful battleships, their telegraphs and railroads. The emperor commissioned the English to build Japan's railways, telegraphs, and the navy. He employed Germans to build hospitals and improve public health. The French were responsible to train the army.

"America sold Japan arms and battleships. It established a modern educational system so that talents from every class can be recognized and encouraged to contribute towards rapid economic development. A new class of people—merchants, manufacturers, and financiers—emerged from the very bottom classes of society. They acquired power and status that were previously kept exclusively for the nobility."

Fujiwara looked at Krishna's eager face. "Modern ideas," he said and laughed.

"And this is where I played my humble part for Japan's future," Kyuso said. "Japan sent me, with others, to Italy to study art, painting, and sculpture. I spent a year in Italy, and I tell you I have never seen anything as spectacular as the works of Leonardo da Vinci and Michelangelo. Truly, they were masters. Fujiwara's uncle was sent to England to study shipbuilding, while others went to Europe to study their industries and institutions."

They had never heard of such subjects, let alone understand industrializations and Occidentals. The more they listened, the more confused they became. Fujiwara noticed their bewilderment.

"Perhaps we should talk about your land, about your history and culture, about Hinduism and Buddhism, about the bloody Islamic conquest and British colonization," Fujiwara suggested. "A few years ago, during my first visit to study Buddhist history, I informed a civil service officer of some authority, at the deputy commissioner's office at Banaras, that the city lacks sanitation. I also told him that Sarnath and Bodh Gaya are in a state of utter decay and neglect. To my surprise, he became defensive and argumentative. He felt personally criticized and didn't recognize the woes of these places.

"His attitude reminded me of the observations made by Chinese Buddhist traveler Hiuen Tsiang," Fujiwara continued. "He wrote that Indians argue and claim that there is no country like theirs, no culture like theirs, and no philosophers like theirs. Islamic scholars, who accompanied Turkish invaders, described Indians as a people who don't appreciate the beauty of a flower garden, the soothing effects of running water, or the beauty of a spirited horse. All they have, they wrote, are gold and silver that they value.

"It may be true that no country can teach you spirituality, but others can teach you how to organize and plan," Fijuwara said with the self-assurance of a confident leader. He then mentioned the subjugation of India by aliens for more than eight hundred years.

"The price India paid for its occupation has resulted in poverty and ignorance of its masses, the loss of hope for a better life, and the dilapidated state of historical monuments. If you love your land, your culture, your temples, your riches, then learn to defend them, just like Japan."

"But what can ordinary people do?" Govinda asked.

"Learn to use modern ways. Don't cling to your past dreams of glory. Teach others the truth about your history, your tradition—though they are painful. Recognize the fact that internal divisions and weaknesses encourage external aggression, just as insects attack undernourished plants.

"Indian history tells us that for hundreds of years, Afghan, Turkish, and Mughal invaders repeatedly robbed and sacked your temples, monasteries, and killed countless numbers. Muslim fanatics—forgetting the love, tolerance, and beauty taught by the prophet—destroyed the external portion of Buddhism with sword and fire, while some Brahmanic cults belittled and destroyed the literary portion of the Buddhist path by misrepresenting its teachings.

"For instance, Lord Buddha didn't suffocate while devouring a pig's feet, nor was he an enemy of Brahmanic faith. He believed in the happiness of all beings.

"He didn't hurt anyone, either by speech or action. He held his noble silence when scholars asked irrelevant and inflammatory questions. He disagreed with some theology and cultural practices, but he didn't consider anyone his enemy. He conquered ego, and as such, he wasn't domineering or overbearing.

"Once a learned Brahmin asked him if he was a god to which the Buddha said no. He then asked if he was a spirit. He answered no. Then he asked if he was a devil to which he also said no. 'If you are not a god or a spirit or a devil, then what are you?' the irritated scholar asked. 'I am Awake,' the Lord answered.

"In another instance, an angry ascetic called Lord Buddha an imposter and said that he hadn't reached Nirvana. 'If you give me a present and I do not accept it, who owns it?' Buddha asked. 'If you don't accept the present that I give you, then, of course, the present will be mine,' the ascetic replied. 'Then the anger that you are giving me belongs to you, for I do not accept it. This anger will harm you, not others.' The ascetic understood and requested acceptance to his Sangha.

"The Buddha's compassion was boundless. For instance, the last meal he ate was poisonous. A smith, anxious to honor the Buddha who was passing through his village, cooked wild mushrooms and, not realizing that they were poisonous, offered them to the Buddha. Although Buddha perceived the danger of the poisonous meal with his Buddha eye of insight, he partook the offering out of compassion for the smith. He, however, asked the smith not to serve it to any of his monks and had it buried deep in the ground.

"He was eighty then and suffered from grievous dysentery. The poisonous mushrooms caused extreme pain and bloody flux. But he endured them calmly until his death that followed soon. Why would such a man who suffered so much to achieve perfection hurt feelings of others?"

Fujiwara became silent for a while. He then continued.

"The social harm caused by uncivilized invaders and the wounds inflected by ignorant Hindu theologians are so vast that even today, after nearly a thousand years, India suffers from internal ills of caste oppression, untouchability, treatment of widows, and use of ceremonial superstitions to keep its masses ignorant.

"Lord Buddha, like a physician, treated all people alike and made no distinction between men and women. He allowed women, for the first time in history, to become preachers and missionaries. He taught compassion. Yet he was intentionally misunderstood.

"These are the sin of your fathers. They denied you the teachings of the Noble Eightfold Path," Fujiwara said. "The time has come for India to accept modern ways to better themselves, just like Japan is doing today. If you continue to be silent about your sins, you will never turn around for a just society."

The more Krishna listened, the more convinced he became that there is more to life than being a temple priest. He realized that reciting Sanskrit verses alone doesn't make a person wise and liberated. He, therefore, concluded that there is much to see and learn about the modern world.

Story of Buddha's selection?

The Buddha Points the Way

A large crowd gathered at Sarnath's Deer Park to celebrate the Buddha's birthday that hot, humid, overcast day. It had rained lightly the previous night, announcing the arrival of the monsoons.

"They are mostly from neighboring villages," retired sepoy Ganga Bahadur whispered to Krishna as they stood in the shade, waiting for the speaker. Bahadur spent his entire adult life in the Gurkha Regiment. He was one of the seventeen Gurkha recipients of the Victoria Cross, the highest military decoration for bravery in the British Empire. "They come every year to listen to the wise lama, just like I do."

Although it was hot, the hairless lama wore a heavy burgundy robe as he limped to the shade of a fig tree where the people waited. They became quiet as he seated himself on the golden straw spread over a large concrete slab that was a remnant of a broken temple pillar. It now served as a speaker's platform. He sat in the lotus position and took deep breaths. His back was straight, eyes half closed. A young lama sat beside him.

"Do you know what he is doing?" the sepoy asked Krishna.

"No."

"He is becoming fully aware of his breathing. He knows that he is breathing in and breathing out. He is telling himself that he is feeling happy and is at peace. He is aware of his own mind and of what he is thinking. He is letting go bad thoughts and purifying his mind."

"He is doing all that?"

"Yes. Hush, they're about to speak."

"My name is Lama Dondrup," the younger man introduced himself. "My guru Lama Rampa and I have come from Tibet to celebrate Lord Buddha's birthday. Lama Rampa has visited many Buddhist places of pilgrimage in India, Tibet, and China before. He will deliver today's dharma talk. This is my first visit to India."

"Welcome, welcome to India," someone cried.

"Namaste," Rampa greeted the crowd. "May peace be with you. Today, I'll tell you the story of a warrior prince who lived in this region a long time ago. While a young man, enjoying the sensual pleasures of palace life, he noticed that everything changes on earth and that changes result in sorrow. He, therefore, wanted to find freedom or release from sorrow.

"The discussions he had with wise men of his time didn't satisfy him. So he practiced extreme asceticism, for people in those days thought that denying the body can attain wisdom. But this almost killed him. He, therefore, gave up self-mortification and began intelligent meditation with purity of life. This led him, at thirty-five, to complete bliss and enlightenment. He realized Nirvana or the absence of sorrow.

"For the following forty-five years until his death, he walked from village to village, from kingdom to kingdom, teaching the path to Nirvana to anyone who would listen to him." He then paused and touched his palms in front of his heart. He took a deep breath and bowed his head. "Lord Buddha encouraged his monks to spread his dharma to others so that they too could find liberation from sorrow.

"'Go ye now, monks, and wander for the gain of the many, for the welfare of the many, out of compassion for the world. Preach, monks, the dharma, which is lovely in the beginning, in the middle, in the end, in the spirit, and in the letter,' thus spoke the Compassionate One, here at Sarnath, two thousand and five hundred years ago, for the welfare of the many," Rampa announced.

"Like you, my friends, I'm blessed to be here today where he preached his first sermons and accepted monks into the Buddhist order."

"Did he teach anything that isn't in the *Vedas*?" a young man asked.

"He said that we are responsible for our own liberation from the circle of life and death," Rampa said and smiled. "No one can save or liberate us. Gods or prayers alone will not. Only we can, through our own effort. In fact, his last words to his disciples were 'Strive diligently for liberation.'"

A low-pitched murmur spread through the crowd. Many felt uncomfortable. A few fidgeted. They believed in an invisible force, much greater than themselves, to save them. All they needed to do was worship, believe, and offer sacrifices to please that force. Therefore, what they heard disturbed them.

"Why is he called the Compassionate One?" a woman asked.

"When we love a person or an object, we hope to find love and happiness in return. We expect our wishes to be satisfied. In compassion, there is no expectation or attachment for your love. The Buddha gave freely. His compassion flowed unhindered to all sentient beings. This free-flowing self-giving produces bliss. He is thus called the Compassionate One."

"Why should we accept his teachings?" a gray-haired man rose and asked.

"The Buddha too was posed the same question," the monk said. "The Lord asked him if he would buy gold without first examining it. When the man said that he would definitely examine it first, Buddha said that he should do the same with his teachings and never accept them to be true just because the Buddha said so. He advised him to test the teachings himself to see if they are true. If he finds them to be true and helpful, then he should practice them."

The man looked at his wife sitting near him. She beckoned him to sit and ask no further questions.

"The Buddha didn't proclaim to be a savior or a prophet, receiving revelations from a supernatural source. He was a human being who, through hard work and discipline, became the Buddha, the Awaken One. He taught a system of self-development, a process of moral evolution. He preached a dharma of action, not just belief."

He paused, took a deep breath, and looked around. He noticed that the crowd had grown.

"You may now ask how this liberation from sorrow is possible and what you can do. I'll, therefore, tell you the steps you need to know and practice. Remember, knowledge gives you strength to find salvation." He then took a sip of water from a clay cup his companion offered him.

"When Prince Siddhartha lived at his father's palace, he had all the worldly pleasures that a man could wish for. When he renounced his princely life and lived in the forest as an extreme ascetic, he almost died from starvation. This made him realized that neither hedonism nor self-mortification is the way to enlightenment. So he followed a path between the two extremes. This is called the Middle Way. It consists of Four Noble Truths and the Aryan Eightfold Path.

"The first noble truth is that everything is impermanent and that there is suffering in this world. We suffer at birth, in old age, in sickness, in death. We suffer when we separate from the pleasant, we suffer when we experience the unpleasant, and we suffer when our desires remain unsatisfied.

"The second noble truth teaches us that suffering has a cause. Cravings and attachments cause suffering.

"The third noble truth is that we can end suffering.

"The fourth noble truth is that we can end craving by practicing the Eightfold Path: right understanding, right thought, right speech, right action, right livelihood, right effort, right mindfulness, and right concentration or meditation.

"Your body and mind must be conditioned for this path. You must be physically healthy and your mind free of distractions. In other words, you need to perform good acts and clean your heart."

"Holy lama, please tell us how to clean our hearts," a woman said.

"That I will," he replied. "Hear me well."

Right Steps

"The first step in the Eightfold Path is right understanding," he began. "It means understanding the reality of suffering, where and how it originates. Suffering can end when we understand that everything is impermanent. We must understand the reality of suffering to end it, just as we have to understand the causes of sickness to cure it.

"Now, what does right thought mean? It means thoughts of harmlessness, free from ill will, cruelty and sensuality. 'We are what we think,' the Buddha had taught. 'All that we are arises with our thoughts. With our thoughts, we make the world.'

"What does right speech mean? It means speech free from deceit, malice, abuse, slander, and silliness.

"What does the fourth step—right action—mean? It means action free from killing, stealing, lying, adultery, and use of intoxicants.

"What does right livelihood mean? It means making a living by right and honorable means. It means avoiding evil trades like dealing with weapons, meat, poisons, intoxicants, usury, soothsaying, and trickery.

"What does right effort mean? It means using your own energy to incite your mind to prevent bad thoughts from rising, driving away bad thoughts that have already risen, develop good thoughts that haven't yet arisen, and maintain good thoughts that have risen and develop them fully."

Before he could describe the last two steps, a frail old man struggled to his feet with the aid of a younger man. He appeared to be in his seventies or eighties, but his eyes, under bushy white brows, were alert.

"Honorable lamas," the man said in a clear tone, "we thank you, and we appreciate you coming from distant Lasha to preach the teachings of Lord Buddha. Your presence blesses us. But based on what you say, Lord Buddha didn't really teach anything new when he said that to strive for Nirvana, you should avoid bad thoughts and entertain only good thoughts. I would like to humbly point out, holy lamas, that even my eight-year-old great-grandson could impart such wisdom."

Surprised at the articulation of the old man, Rampa smiled and remained silent. It was the young lama's turn to speak.

"It may be true that your eight-year-old great-grandson could make such statements, but let us remember, sir, that even the ones in their eighties have difficulty practicing the noble path."

The old man bowed respectfully and sat down.

"These six steps will enable a practitioner to acquire some degree of moral and physical control," Rampa said. "I'll explain the other two steps after three days.

"Friends, the path to Nirvana requires a pure heart and constant effort," he went on. "For you to experience this effort, I ask you to be aware of your speech for the next three days. Everything you say must create happiness. If your speech creates unhappiness, then avoid speech. But when you speak, create happiness only."

How difficult could this be? The old man thought as he struggled to his feet.

"When we meet again," the lama said, "let me know who succeeds. In the meantime, Lama Dondrup and I'll meditate in the pure shade of Dhamekh Stupa."

The dharma discussion thus ended.

Right Mindfulness and Right Meditation

News of the moral challenge spread to the villages. On the fourth day, a larger crowd gathered. No one knew that speech awareness is difficult. At first they thought it would be simple. So many tried but failed. A few even created anger and impatience, while others simply gave up.

"Why is something so simple so difficult?" they asked.

When the lamas seated themselves and the crowd settled, Rampa greeted them. He appeared rested and happy, at peace with himself. And he knew why no one claimed success in practicing right speech.

"Three days ago," he began, "we discussed the first six steps of the noble path. Today, we will discuss the final steps in the journey towards Nirvana.

"The seventh step is right mindfulness. It's the beginning of the final stage to control your mind and its evolution. The mind is difficult to control. By its very nature, it wonders. So you have to concentrate to control it. To do this, you put aside all sensual desire, greed, and grief and excluding everything else, focus on a single point.

"There are four basic steps to develop right mindfulness. They are contemplating on your body, on your feeling, on your mind, and finally on your phenomena. You sit in a quiet, solitary place, with legs crossed and body erect. You observe your own body at work. You observe how you breathe in and breathe out. You train yourself by observing your body, how it arises and passes away. You observe how you sit, eat, stand, walk, or any other movement. You observe your body from the soles of your feet to the tip of your head. Once you develop this discipline, you can suppress bad thoughts from arising. You will be able to conquer fear, anxiety, hunger, thirst, and heat or cold. You may also attain magical powers, like hear distant sounds, have greater insight into people, and even remember your previous births."

"Wouldn't magical powers be wonderful?" Krishna whispered to Fujiwara.

"The second step is observing your feelings. Think about the good, bad, or indifferent feelings you experience. Think about how they arise, how they pass away, and how you can be attached to them or detached from them.

"In the third step, you contemplate on your mind. You know when your mind is angry or not angry, greedy or not greedy, composed or scattered, developed or less developed, focused or unfocused, free or tied. You dwell in how the mind arises, how it passes away, and how you can be attached or detached.

"Finally, you contemplate on the phenomena. Concentrate on your lust, anger, indifference, worry, and doubt, how they arise and how you can conquer and abandon them so that they don't rise again. You contemplate on the five aggregates of existence: bodily form, feeling, perception, mental formation, and consciousness. You then look upon the sense factors the same way and become free of them."

"What are sense factors?" someone asked.

"They are the senses—seeing, hearing, smelling, touching, and tasting. Senses can produce attachments. You observe how they arise, how you can overcome them, and finally how you can get rid of them. Then you contemplate on the Four Noble Truths.

"How do I contemplate on the Four Noble Truths?" Krishna asked.

"You become aware that there is suffering, you become aware of the cause of the suffering as it arises, you become aware that this suffering can end and are aware that there is a path that leads to the end of suffering," Rampa answered.

"Right mindfulness is to look at things truthfully, their meaning and their significance rather than at their appearance and relations. Our senses give us perceptions, but they have very little value in truth. They appear to be real to the intellectual mind, but they may not be real. You are, therefore, to transcend the intellectual mind and become aware that all composites are impermanent and subject to decay."

He looked around to see if there were other questions.

"After right mindfulness," he continued, "we have right concentration or right meditation. This final step is *Dhyana* in Sanskrit. It means 'concentration of the mind.' The *Mahasatipatthana Sutra* tells us that breathing plays a very important role in regulating the mind and keeping it fixed on a single point.

"As you progress through meditation, you may experience various psychic effects—like colors, sounds, visions, raptures, etc. Ignore them. Forget them. The goal of meditation isn't delightful ecstasy. The goal is highest wisdom and blissful peace, born at the end of all thought."

"Does progression through meditation mean that there are different levels in *Dhyana*?" someone asked.

"Yes."

"Could you describe them?"

"They are difficult to describe, but you can experience them yourself," Rampa said.

Krishna and Fujiwara, however, didn't want to wait to experience them. "I'll be returning to Japan soon and it—"

"Then I must try to describe them, shouldn't I?" Rampa said and smiled.

Four Levels of Meditation

"There are four realms of mental or spiritual state," Rampa began. "The first one is of desire. Here senses rule. The second one is of form. Here there is no sensual attachment but form remains. The third state is the formless realm. There is no physical form here but a condition of utter calm, bliss, and pure spirit. In the fourth, you transcend.

"In the first level of meditation, you will be aware of physical matter and sensations within the realm of form. But you will be free of attachment, caused by desire, and this freedom will make you experience spiritual joy and physical bliss. This state of rapture is due to detachment.

"In the second level of meditation, you no longer investigate and reflect. Your mind is free from the five senses and shallow mental activities. Your mind no longer wonders. Reasoning ceases, and inner tranquility sets in. You meditate with a pure mind and experience joy and bliss of the first stage. This is the result of concentration.

"After you experience the second level, you leave behind joy and sorrow. You are completely detached from emotional response. You now enter the third level. You retain right mindfulness, bliss, and right wisdom. You remain composed and unperturbed, mindful and aware. You experience within what enlightened sages said is tranquility, characterized by physical bliss and concentration.

"In the fourth stage, you transcend bliss and suffering. Physical or mental joy or sorrow doesn't exist. The mind is free from all sensual and emotional hindrances. Now your purified mind sees clearly the true nature of all things. When you achieve this stage, you have great knowledge and supernatural power."

He paused to take a sip of water and wondered if the crowd understood his difficult topic. He thought of Lord Buddha and how he faced the challenge of putting indescribable mysteries into words during his sermons. He must have realized how language may alter his teachings. Rampa did what he could: keep the teachings simple.

"These four levels are called 'the Fine-Matter Absorption,'" he said.

"Let me now talk about the four levels of 'Immaterial Absorption.' Please remember that although these levels are difficult, we can realize Nirvana. I'll try to put into words what I heard from the wise. I haven't experienced them myself.

"After the fourth level where you transcend the Fine-Matter sphere, you attain and dwell in the Sphere of Boundless Space. After transcending the Sphere of Boundless Space, you attain the Sphere of Infinite Consciousness. After this sphere, you attain the Sphere of Nothingness. You then attain and abide in the Sphere of Neither Perception nor Nonperception."

The crowd remained seated and quiet. No one uttered a word. Finally, the monsoon clouds broke the silence with lightning and thunder. The villagers looked up as large raindrops fell on their faces and bodies. They thanked aloud the Almighty for the life-giving rain.

Fujiwara and Krishna were very impressed by what they heard. They were sitting next to each other. They rose from their lotus positions, touched their palms in front of their hearts, bowed their heads, and approached the old lama. Fujiwara was the first to speak.

"Holy lama, was Lord Buddha the greatest teacher that ever walked on earth?"

"Lord Buddha discouraged praise from anyone," he said. "In fact, when Ananda, one of his disciples, proclaimed that he was the greatest teacher that was ever born or will ever be born, the Buddha asked him if he had met all the great teachers who appeared in the world. When the disciple answered to the contrary, he asked him if he met all the teachers alive now or those that would appear in the future. When the disciple answered to the contrary again, Lord Buddha said that it is foolish to say that he is the greatest, for no one has any way of knowing if this is true.

"'I am not the only Buddha. There were many before me, and there will be many after me,' he said.

"Young men, think of the humility of this remark and the goodwill he had towards all on earth. How great must have been his victory over his own ego. The one who has mastered his ego will not say that his is the only way. Only egos will make such a claim."

"Holy lama, we are striving to master ego," Krishna said. "May we meditate with you? Will we then experience psychic effects and be on the way to perfection? Will we experience spiritual joy?"

Rampa looked into Krishna's eyes. "How can I answer questions that only you can answer?"

"How long did it take the Buddha to reach Nirvana?" asked a man standing behind Krishna.

"It took Gautama nearly seven years. It took Bodhidharma nine years," Rampa said.

As others pressed forward to pay their respect, the two young seekers rejoined their companions and discussed meditating with the lamas. They wanted to benefit from their experience. They learned that meditation disciplines the mind and that thoughts can change the brain.

The Burmese monks were very willing. They knew that meditation enables you to practice the noble path. "To be Burmese is to be Buddhist," they said.

Faith and Cosmic Symbolism

"We plan to be here next year," Rampa told Krishna as he and Dondrup prepared to return to Tibet after the monsoons quenched the thirsty land. "If you seek enlightenment in the Buddha path, you must make the right effort to have only right thoughts enter your mind."

Krishna was sad to see them leave. They had meditated together and learned that truth is the offspring of meditation. Once, for a fleeting moment, he even thought of accompanying them to mountainous Tibet to the land of great lamaseries where lamas discover meaning of life and death through meditation, where they teach mysterious relationships between duality, where telepathy, clairvoyance, and reincarnation are age-old beliefs.

When they returned to Banaras, Krishna did all he could to experience the true meaning of compassion. Rampa had told him that it results from understanding and acceptance.

The water level of the Ganges was still above the high-water mark at the end of the rainy season. But this didn't dissuade believers from bathing in its waters that always wait patiently for anyone to wash away sins. After all, she is "Mother Ganga"—ancient and accepting.

Early one morning, when the rising sun was turning the sky bright pink, forcing the moon and stars to hide, Krishna was in the river bathing. "If the sight of these majestic temples doesn't fill your heart with faith and peace, then nothing will," a stranger near him said.

He noticed Krishna's surprise. "Faith, acceptance, and devotion are sometimes more important than in-depth spiritual understanding," he continued. "See, I don't have to understand everything spiritual, for God is infinite, and I'm finite. All I do is carve stones and repair temples. I do this as my duty with devotion and nonattachment. Do you know what I mean?"

"No," Krishna replied.

"Well, we aren't the only ones who believe in 'nonattachment.' The Christians do too. They just call it 'holy indifference,'" he said. He then talked about being a temple architect.

"The temple has been a place of worship for thousands of years. It symbolizes spirituality and the abode of God. Its paintings and statues are to awaken devotion and increase our spiritual awareness."

When they left the waters and climbed the concrete steps of the bathing ghats, Krishna noticed the middle-aged man's left eye was closed, marring his depth perception. He fumbled picking his clothes from the ground. His good eye, however, quickly noticed Krishna's unconscious stare.

"Oh, this," he laughed, pointing to his left eye. "I gave it to Konarak's Sun Temple. I lost it years ago while replacing worn steps at its entrance. If you visit the temple, you may still see them. Do you know how important stones are in temple building?" Krishna shook his head.

"Anyway, I think I should have offered my eye to Mother Goddess Shakti, or any of her incarnations, like Uma or Parvati," he rambled.

"Why? Is sacrifice to a female god more of a penance than to a male god?"

"No, but I'm more inclined to worship a female form of god than a male form. You see, I'm a farmer's son. My ancestors were farmers.

"In an agricultural society, Mother Goddess is the dominant mystic form. Just as a woman gives birth to humans, the earth gives birth to nutritious plants. So woman and earth are related. Everything you can think or see is within Mother Goddess. She is time and space and beyond time and space. When I worship such a symbol, I'm actually contemplating the spirituality of the origin of life which is of energy, consciousness, and form."

Krishna tried to make sense of the stranger's spirituality.

"You probably worship Siva. You worship the lingam, the holy mystery that generates life. The very act of generating a new life is a cosmic act. It's thus holy. The pouring of life's energy into the field of time is the lingam and youni—the male and the female creative powers on earth. This is what you worship in the lingam. It isn't different from worshipping Mother Goddess, and since they are the same, I worship by repairing their temples."

As they dried themselves on the steps, the stranger introduced himself as Rishi Mondir. He said his family name was Mohan before the accident. The loss depressed him, but he was grateful for his other eye. So he decided to dedicate himself completely to God, to serve him the best way he knew. "This was my calling. I said good-bye to my past, to my family, to my name, and to what I was. Now I clothe myself entirely in God in his awareness. My work has become my prayer. When I curve stones, I think of him alone and thank him for my sight."

They entered the temple dedicated to one of the gods of the Hindu pantheon. After prayers, they ate the blessed food offered to the deities. As they were leaving, he asked Krishna what he saw.

"I saw beautifully decorated altars, curved pillars, images of gods and goddesses. I saw and understood that gods and goddesses are but names and forms of one God who is neither masculine nor feminine, who has no name or form. I saw that God is immanent in all creation and that he is not separate or above creation or nature. I saw flowers and adoration. I saw devotion of worshippers, their offerings, and felt his dwelling in their hearts and in all creatures. I noticed peace and calmness in their faces," Krishna answered thoughtfully. "I saw many things."

Mondir smiled and looked at him with his good eye.

"Did you see the temple as a symbol and appreciate the important part it plays in the religious tradition of this land? Of all the social, economic, and political institutions of our land, the temple is the most significant. Symbolism plays a very important part in temples, and these symbols that you see are manifestations of spiritual concepts. Symbolism is used to represent something holy, something divine.

"For instance, why does the temple have a square base? Because the Hindus believe the axis of the universe rises from a square base. So the temple rises from a square base. The square is the symbol of the world of gods. What symbolizes the world of man? It's the circle, and so you will not see many circles in the temple.

"Why does a temple entrance face east? It faces the auspicious direction of the rising sun—the source of energy. This allows the first rays of the rising sun to illuminate certain parts of the interior. The directions of the rays are used skillfully to lighten some areas first, then other areas."

"Are variations permitted in temple building?"

"Many religions of the West have monolithic traditions based on one single text or one way of worship. Hinduism, on the other hand, accepts the plurality of beliefs and worship. The heterogeneous Hindu tradition and philosophical systems permit Hindu temples to face south or west as well," he replied.

Krishna wanted to learn more. Mondir continued.

"If you are interested in the role of cosmic symbolism in Eastern religions, let me tell you my experience in Bodh Gaya."

By now the sun's strong rays and high humidity forced people to seek shade. The sight of a saffron-turbaned man sitting and discussing something with a priest wearing vertical caste marks drew attention of temple goers. So they joined them, expecting to acquire spiritual knowledge.

"Being a member of the Nagara and Dravida Mondir Sangha, an association of craftsmen who volunteer their time and expertise for the preservation of temples, I and a colleague of mine were asked to repair a few misaligned rocks under the large marble slab that now covers the original Vijrasana—the very site where Lord Buddha meditated to attain enlightenment. Can you imagine the good fortune, the great honor, to perform such a task? I, an unworthy one-eyed man, filled with ignorance and weaknesses, getting a chance of many lifetimes to touch and repair the rock underneath the seat where the Buddha sat more than two thousand and five hundred years ago determined to attain Nirvana?"

The visitors listened quietly. A woman wearing bangles covered her head with her new sari.

"I worried for days and couldn't sleep. What will happen if I make mistakes? What will happen if I chip the marble slab? I was unable to eat or drink regularly until I remembered that Lord Buddha was the Compassionate One. He judged no one and found fault with no one. Somehow, this thought comforted me and gave me confidence.

"When we reached Bodh Gaya, we noticed a Chinese artist painting the Buddha's spiritual birth on a silk canvas. It depicted Gautama being born from his mother's right side. When he noticed my surprise, he said that it symbolized spiritual birth. Physically, of course, Gautama wasn't born from his mother's side but symbolically he was, from the level of the heart chakra."

"What is a chakra?" Krishna asked.

Mondir hesitated. "You ask a difficult question. Perhaps a few of you can help me," he looked at the faces around him. "I'll, of course, share what little I know."

Chakras

"Chakras are wheels or fields of energy in human bodies," said a slender man with deep-seated eyes. He was the first visitor to speak.

"They are psychic centers of consciousness," another added.

"I don't have a good understanding of them, but I know they exist," a third said. "Once I concentrated on the Manipura chakra for seven weeks at the advice of my grandfather, and this cured my chronic stomach pain."

Mondir became more confident as participation grew. He felt their energy, their willingness to share

"True. Chakras are wheels of energy," he said. "But where does this energy come from?"

"From us, from our own thoughts and feelings, for wherever the mind goes, energy follows," the man with stomach pain said. "For instance, the brain requires blood to operate. So the more I think, the more blood flows to my brain. I know this from experience. When I was unhappy with life, I developed stomach problems. My stress resulted from troubled thoughts and feelings. This blocked energy flow to my navel area through the fine channels. But my concentration on the chakra dissolved this blockage."

"Why can't I feel these chakras?" Krishna asked.

"Chakras remain dormant until you use them," he replied. "You have to awaken them through meditation."

"Let me say that there are seven basic energy fields in the human body," the man with deep-seated eyes said. "The first one is Muladhara. When you transcend the seventh or final chakra, called Sahasrara chakra, you live as divine."

"How does one transcend from a lower chakra to a higher one?" Krishna asked. "Does one feel or see the chakras?"

"You transcend through meditation and visualization," the man continued. "Those who have seen the chakras described them as spinning vibratory light wheels or auras with colors. For instance, when you meditate on the fourth or heart chakra, you concentrate on a green spinning wheel. Through concentration, you can move from the lower spheres to the higher spiritual fields by developing compassion. This higher field is where spiritual man can be born out of animal man."

Mondir realized that the information was becoming confusing. So he decided to organize its presentation. His past involvement with the association of craftsmen taught him basic organizational and leadership skills.

"The study of chakras involves concentration, visualization, and colors," he said. "We know that color and light are inseparable. Different colors affect us differently. We know that pleasant colors please us more than dull colors. This is because different lights have different vibrations.

"There are seven basic human chakras. They are located in different parts of our body, rising from the rectum area to the top of the head, from the physical, emotional, and mental to the spiritual. These wheels of energy are areas of concern, consciousness, and action through which our personality is expressed. In fact, our bodies reflect the balance or imbalance of chakras."

They listened. His confidence grew.

"The first chakra, Muladhara, is at the base of our spine, between the anus and the genitals. When we meditate on this chakra, we visualize a red spinning wheel at the base of the spine. We try to feel the heat and warmth generating. This chakra deals with the basic life-sustaining earthly issues, like eating. Those who meditate on this field of energy can reduce negative issues of mind, body, and earthly attachments."

"Can we really see the color and feel the heat and warmth through meditation?" a woman asked.

"Yes," he replied. "There have been many instances of monks raising their body temperature through meditation. The mind, my friends, has more potential than we realize.

"The second psychological center, Swadhisthana, is located just above the pelvic bone. This area produces the urge to procreate and influences feelings like love and passion. The flow of energy in this area is the flow of blood necessary for sexual and creative activity. When flow of energy is unblocked, people are energetic. When blocked, they can suffer from various blood disorders, like reproductive organ dysfunctions and stiff joints. The visualized color is orange. Those who meditate on this chakra can lessen their anger and pride and increase intuitive knowledge."

"Will my wife be happy if my blood flow becomes—"

"Try and see," someone said, amusing many.

"The third chakra, Manipura, is the area above the navel and below the chest," Mondir said. "It's visualized yellow—like that of the sun. It's the center to the will, to physical and material power, to control and achieve. If your energy flows freely in this area, you are confident, intelligent, and have sense of purpose. Disciplining the ego begins here. If your energy is blocked, you will lack self-confidence. You become aggressive and try to dominate others. When you meditate on this chakra, you can improve your digestion and other physical activities related to abdominal organs."

Mondir was pleased with himself for being able to hold their attention.

"So far we discussed the first three chakras. Keep in mind that these are areas of gross or animal instinct. We will now discuss the chakra where spirituality can be born to the animal man."

"Is this the heart chakra that I mentioned before?" the man who spoke of the green spinning wheel asked.

"Yes, brother," Mondir replied. "I call you brother because we are brothers and sisters, helping one another by sharing the wisdom of ancient sages."

"I agree and I'm happy to share what little I know," the man said.

"And for that we are grateful. Wisdom is a gift, and sharing it makes it grow," another said.

"Let's now discuss the heart or Anahata chakra. It's located in the center of the chest and green in color. Due to its location, it's the wheel of love and compassion. It influences understanding and forgiveness. Meditating on this chakra enables you to love yourself. It then grows into loving others unconditionally. The vibration caused by concentrating on this chakra can improve circulatory, respiratory, and immune systems. If the flow of energy is blocked, heart conditions may result."

"Is this the chakra used to symbolize the spiritual birth of Lord Buddha?"

"That's what the Chinese artist told me."

"Can we please discuss the other charkas now? My wife and I have a train to catch this afternoon," a man said as he gently touched his wife's shoulder.

Mondir was amused. He had no idea that his dharma talk would create such interest. He liked teaching others to appreciate the deeper aspects of human lives and experiences. *How worthy is truth,* he thought, *if it doesn't serve to spread happiness?*

"Then let's discuss the fifth chakra. The Vishuddha chakra is located at the base of the throat area between the chin and the top of the sternum. Its blue color symbolizes pure consciousness and creativity. It influences communication and expression of our knowledge and wisdom. It controls the lungs, the vocal cords, and the windpipes. Concentrating on this chakra can remove resentments, increase calmness, serenity, and artistic abilities. It can enable you to seek true knowledge that is beyond time and cultures. If energy flow is obstructed in this area, communication suffers."

"I sing at a temple," an attractive young woman in a light blue sari said. "I praise God with my songs and thank him for his blessings. However, sometimes my throat gets sore and my voice hoarse. Will concentrating on this chakra reduce my hoarseness?"

"Yes, and it may also increase your cosmic consciousness," Mondir said.

"The sixth chakra, Ajna chakra, is often referred to as the third eye," he continued. "It's located in the center of your forehead, between the eyebrows. Its visualized color is indigo. It represents superior mental consciousness, extra sensory perception, and other psychic abilities. When you meditate on this chakra, you can transcend the physical sphere and experience divine bliss. When the flow of energy is obstructed, you may experience anxiety, headaches, and insomnia."

Without pausing and before anyone could discuss the sixth chakra, Mondir rushed to the seventh, the Sahasrara chakra.

"I find the seventh chakra to be most fascinating. It's located at the very top of your head. If you use this chakra for meditation, you seek connection with your spiritual nature. You explore time and space. Concentrating on this chakra causes the highest vibration. It, therefore, has the violet color. It's the final chakra, and meditation on it can lead to divine integration."

The group became quiet at the mention of divine integration. Such phrases are difficult to understand. But Krishna had questions about color and visualization.

"In chakra meditation, you visualize bathing yourself in different colors to purify yourself, just as a lotus bud blooms to receive sunlight. Of course, you don't have to begin with the first chakra. You can begin with any chakra, but first determine your level of awareness. You do this by examining your traits—like your temperament, weaknesses, desires, etc. It's better to know where you are before deciding where to go," he said. He rose from his lotus position, smiled, and bowed to the gathering as it dissolved.

"May you find bliss in your journey," someone cried a blessing, making him happy.

"How did you become so knowledgeable and such a good public speaker?" Krishna asked as they were leaving.

"I listen with an open heart and without pride or jealousy," the one-eyed man said.

Krishna was sleepless long into the night. He was confused. His thinking was unclear. Repeated surfacing of pride and envy—feelings he initially refused to recognize—were engulfing him.

He wondered how a vision-impaired man without priestly heritage impart such spiritual knowledge so extemporaneously. Why couldn't he—the grandson of a devout scholar, the defender of the eternal religious tradition, and the son of an all-sacrificing temple priest—speak thus? Shouldn't he be blessed with articulation due to his birth? After all, psychic heredity does exist. His grandfather told him that sharp memory, articulation, and other special gifts are inherited.

When he finally fell asleep, he dreamt of the old ascetic in the forest, telling him that birth and knowledge don't make him spiritual.

Lonely Is the Seeker

"How can you find death so fascinating?" Govinda snapped. "How can you attend hundreds of cremations so diligently? You have done this for three years now! This is morbid! I'm glad our visit to Banaras is over. Soon we will be on our way to Kumbh Mela."

"I'm sorry I disappoint you both," Krishna replied calmly. "But I attend cremations because I want to know what we experience at the moment of death. Do we experience emotions like fear or anger or love? Will we remember this experience of death in our next lives, or will we forget, just like we forget the experience of our birth?"

He waited for a response. There was none.

"The sages of the past knew the unknown, saw the invisible, and touched the intangible. I want to develop their insight, defeat envy, and become ego-free. No, Banaras hasn't made me mad. It has made me older and wiser."

They looked at one another nervously. They had gotten along well until now.

"The time has come for me to decide what to do with my life. Govinda, I have decided to go to Calcutta and experience the modern world. I don't want to go to the Mela."

"Not go to the Mela?" Hari Ram was annoyed. "What will we tell your grandfather? He'll be very upset. Besides, how will you maintain yourself in a large city? Here the temples feed us. Banaras is safe, and we are together. And now, you want to go alone to a strange city?"

"You two have been brothers to me, and I'm grateful. But I want to know more than temple priests do. For instance, I want to know how the beautiful queen of Chittor Padmini felt as she threw herself into a funeral pyre to protect her honor when Alauddin Khilji, the barbaric Afghan king, sacked Chittor.

"A few nights ago, when I was attending a cremation of a Sindhi at the burning ghats, the eldest son of the deceased told me that as he lit the pyre, he saw and felt a moth from nowhere land briefly on his hand before flying away into the darkness. He said dozens in his village had similar experiences at cremations. He told me that people like him believe that the human soul becomes a moth immediately after it leaves the body before entering another form of the next life.

"Tell me, brothers, how can such superstitions exist? What happened to the teachings of the *Gita* where Lord Krishna said that at death, the Atman passes into another body based on the consequences of past karma? How can anyone possibly even think that the evolved human consciousness takes the form of a moth?

"Govinda and Hari Ram, there is so much to learn, so much to share. Let people like us teach the true meaning of the eternal dharma, about love and duty, about karma and reincarnation so that superstitions don't hamper spiritual growth. And to do this, I would dedicate myself."

They could not believe what they heard. They were speechless.

After a pause, Krishna added gently, "In fact, I think you should join me. Come with me and together we will teach that faith is not the monopoly of priests, that love for God is the love for others, and that the socially rejected are capable of empowering themselves if given a chance."

"Should?" Govinda was now hysterical. "We should? Now you are going to tell your elders what they should do? Have you forgotten that traditions dictate our livelihood? Traditions shouldn't be questioned or challenged. You want to change that? For heaven's shake, look at you—one filled with lust. And your sister? She eloped with a total stranger of another caste!"

This rebuke hurt Krishna. He wasn't aware of Govinda's feelings toward his sister.

"These traditions that you speak of have been preserved and propagated by and for the benefit of the priestly caste. They have enslaved and deprived the minds of millions over hundreds of years. Doesn't the *Gita* tell us that grace is in all of us, waiting to be realized, irrespective of caste or creed? How can I then support the traditions that conceal the Lord's teachings and perpetuate ignorance?"

"How dare you? How dare you?" Govinda said.

"This is outrageous! This is blasphemy!" Hari Ram cried.

Born-Again Bir Dharma

After Govinda and Hari Ram left for Kumbh Mela, Krishna began his lonely journey to transform himself and conquer his ego. He no longer wanted the walls of a temple to confine him for the rest of his life. He now wanted to acquire the wisdom of the ancients and study the religions of the world to develop into a cosmopolitan personality and perhaps even a modern teacher.

He gave up his caste marks. He stopped shaving his head. He wore clothes of ordinary people. Above all, he assumed the name of Bir Dharma (Heroic Path)—a nonsectarian name in a caste-conscious society. He then visited Sarnath for the last time, hoping to meet Lama Rampa before venturing to Calcutta, the City of Celebrations, where learning is not only prized but also worshipped.

One day, before the monsoon winds began blowing northeast, Bir met a teacher at Sarnath. He was from Chakpori, Tibet, and the father of two unmarried daughters. Lobsang was visiting the holy places before retiring.

"Have you heard of Lama Rampa?" Bir asked.

"Lama Rampa left this sphere of existence last year. The monks who knew him say he had a good death. He can now choose to reincarnate."

"Good death to reincarnate?"

"Yes. Tibetans believe that when you reach a certain level of advance evolution, through learning and discipline, your consciousness is at peace, and you can be aware of your own death without fear. You can choose to exist in another sphere or return to help others. The holy ones with such power are called *lamas* or 'superior ones.'"

"You say that he had a 'good death.' Does it mean death without pain?"

"To manifest, we take form, and when there is form, there is suffering. The external self may experience pain, but the inner self of a lama is free of pain."

"Then what is a good death?"

"A good death means the end of rebirth. Since we die as we live, those who experience good death lead good lives. And what is a good life? It means the life in which you conquered the six earthly enemies: pride, jealousy, anger, greed, lust, and ignorance. I once heard a Christian preacher say something similar about living and dying when he said that those who live by the sword die by the sword."

"Christian preachers? Yes, I have heard of them. But tell me what happens to an evildoer at death?"

"The general belief is that an evil consciousness can descend along the path that would lead to lower forms of beings."

"And what are these lower forms of beings?"

"They are the same types of beings that the *jiba* or life had used over millions of years to emerge into the higher human being or human consciousness. When human consciousness descends, it isn't sudden. It's spiral and gradual. If you descend to a lower form of being, your consciousness loses its human nature. Your consciousness isn't human anymore.

"The human consciousness can't live in harmony in a subhuman body of a lower spiritual plane. Once consciousness achieves human level, there is no turning back. It, therefore, chooses the human body and the environment most suited to its needs, but it doesn't choose a subhuman body or environment."

"Then why do some say that a returning evil human consciousness can assume the body of a subhuman?"

"Ask them if they have seen or heard of a plant degenerating into another plant. Ask them if one species of animal suddenly deteriorate into another. In the same way, a human doesn't become an ape or a monkey for evil deeds. But his evil karma can earn him the body of a caveman to live in an unenlightened environment. Remember, his soul isn't lost for eternity. Its spiral ascend will begin again."

"I wonder what Lord Buddha said on transmigration. Ah, what I would give to hear him. How wise and wonderful he must have been."

"He didn't speak of past lives. He emphasized the importance of thinking and living correctly in the present moment. 'If an arrow is shot through your heart, do you first find out who shot it, or do you want it pulled out to lessen the pain?'" he tried to quote the Buddha.

"Lobsang, I was born into a Brahmin family and raised to be a temple priest. But I want to know and do more. For instance, I want to know what happens at the moment of death. So I attended many cremations, talked with hundreds of weeping relatives about what happens at the exact moment of death. No one could tell me. Your country is a mystical land with many ancient mysteries. Can you tell me what we experience at death?"

"Dying also interests me," he said, impressed with his earnestness. "In fact, as soon as my family duties are complete, I want to be ready to welcome death. So let me tell you about what lamas say about death and dying."

When Death Comes

"Tibetans believe that everyone living today experienced death before. Why? Because death is the reverse of birth," Lobsang began. "We are reborn because of unfulfilled worldly desires at the moment of our death."

"Why don't we remember our past death?"

"For the same reason we don't remember our birth."

"Then how do we know what happens at death?"

"You know about the existence of the subconscious. Let's describe it as the memory storehouse of the mind. It isn't consciousness. It has no 'cognitive' awareness. It's hidden, but it can be brought to the conscious level through *tapas*."

"What are they?"

"They are yogic practices and meditation. Through them, a virtuous person, or a sage, can draw from the subconscious memories of past lives. I say a virtuous person because an ordinary person without a prepared mind will be devastated with what he may discover of his past lives. So the subconscious is guarded to prevent the unprepared from recalling and harming himself."

"Do sages who practice yoga and meditation know what happens at the moment of death?"

"To know the moment of death isn't simple. Sages who know dedicate their entire lives to discipline, to spirituality, and to the practice of *tapas*."

"What do they tell us about what happens at the moment of death?"

"They tell us that our very last thought, at the moment of death, determines our next life, our next character. We are what we think. For instance, your past thinking determined your current status and what you think now will determine your future."

"Then what should I think of just before I die?"

"For this, you have to understand the three different states of death."

"Three states of death?"

"What I tell you next is simply wonderful. If you appreciate and remember what I say, you will never be afraid of death. This is why I want to lead a life that will enable me to welcome death when it arrives."

Bir stared at Lobsang's face with wonder and disbelief. How fortunate to meet him!

As his admiration grew, he saw before him a kind and gentle face, a clear face without blemishes or wrinkles. His light golden skin glowed in the sunlight. He had a full head of gray hair. His eyebrows were thin and his eyes chestnut brown, bright and lively.

"There is an intermediate period consisting of forty-nine symbolic days between death and rebirth. The actual period, however, is determined by the karma of the deceased.

"We have to remember that when we die, we take with us recollections of our past life. We don't realize that we are dead. We think we still have bodies. These are imagined bodies or dream bodies. They cast no shadow. In these bodies we experience the three states. In the first state, we see the clear light."

"Clear light?"

"Clear light is pure consciousness. It's clear, colorless light from which everything in the universe originates and returns to. The *Gita* describes it as light beyond the light of the sun, moon, and fire. It's formless and colorless. If it were to have color, it would have form. So it's not an object."

"If it is colorless and formless, how does one recognize it?"

"It's experienced within as indescribably joyful."

"Is it the same as Nirvana?"

"Lord Buddha described Nirvana as the absence of sorrow. As such, Nirvana is described relative to the world. Clear light is difficult to describe in relative terms. It can best be described as a bright and colorless light. We can recognize it at the very moment of our death if we have no earthly desires."

"What happens if we recognize the clear light?"

"We can merge with it. We are then liberated. Salvation is reached, and we are not reborn in this sphere. If we fail to recognize it or hold on to it due to our karma, we begin to realize that death has occurred. We start experiencing hallucinations caused by our own karma. We now enter the second state or the intermediate state."

"Are these hallucinations the ghosts of dead relatives coming to receive us?"

"These hallucinations are figments or reflections of our mind, how we lived, how we thought, what we believed in, how we acted, and what we visualized. These worldly experiences now appear as apparitions, as visions, some as wrathful deities, while others as peaceful deities. But keep in mind that none of them have any real individual existence. If we don't get involved with them, they will pass by harmlessly, just like clouds on a calm day.

"These experiences of the second state are delusional or psychotic, and though we may realize that death has occurred, we still think we have earthly bodies of flesh and blood. When we finally realize that we don't have bodies, we crave for one. We now enter the third state and desire rebirth.

"As our past lives become faint, we are overcome by infantile sexual fantasies. We now have visions of mating couples. Finally, we enter a womb that we have earned due to our karmic past and are reborn."

"Do I experience these three states after I die?"

"You stop breathing and appear dead, but your consciousness has not yet left. Your mind is still there near the body. Some say it floats in the air and can hear and see."

"So the mind is outside the physical body and brain?"

Lobsang smiled and nodded.

"Where does my mind go after it floats?"

"Where does a flame go after it blows out? Does it go north, south, east, or west?"

Bir Dharma was lost for words. He couldn't think of anything to ask. Has he found the secret states of dying? Are they really experienced when death comes? Finally he asked what he could do to prepare himself and others.

"You prepare by appreciating that human life is a privilege and regard every moment of life as if it were the last. While you are dying, a lama can whisper in your ears, or in those of the corpse, that you are experiencing the clear light of pure reality and that you should recognize it. He can tell you that the visions are unreal and that you should only concentrate on the clear light. On occasions, he may even recite a familiar mantra.

"Relatives and friends can quietly surround the dying or the just-dead person with good thoughts in their minds without demonstrating emotions like weeping or sobbing. Deaths should be calm and serene."

Lobsang became quiet, perhaps thinking of his own death. "Life is what we think it to be, for we are our thoughts," he said as he bade farewell.

PART F

Modern World

"I HAVE NEVER seen so many people in my life before!" Bir said as he looked out of the compartment.

"Yes. Howrah Railway Station is probably the largest in India," said a fellow passenger as they disembarked. "Well, good luck with your studies at the university, young man."

Bir wondered what to do next. He was now alone in a big city. He missed the company of his two friends. *I'll have to look after myself,* he thought. He wrapped his beige shawl tightly around his back and shoulders and grasped his small bundle of clothes. As he walked toward the exit, he found courage in the saying "It is better to travel alone than in the company of the unwise."

"If you are new to Calcutta, perhaps I can help," he heard a muffled voice behind him.

"Can you tell me how to get to Calcutta University?"

"You are a student! How wonderful!" the eager, smiling stranger said, noticing his anxious face. "Who are you going to meet there?"

"Professor Bhupen Das."

"Oh, Das Dada! Yes, indeed! I know him very well. In fact, we grew up together. But how did you come to know him?"

"I met him in Banaras when he spoke about spirituality."

"Of course, Dada is a very spiritual man. We all respect him for his goodness. Isn't he a wonderful speaker?" As they walked toward the exit, the stranger greeted and waved at others as if he knew them. However, no one seemed to recognize him.

"Forgive me. I should have introduced myself. My name is Babu Basu. I work for the railways. And you are—"

"Bir Dharma. I'm a Sanskrit scholar. I'm also a temple priest."

"I have great respect for people like you. Tell you what: I'll take you to Professor Das. I haven't seen him for weeks. It'll be good to see him again."

Bir felt relieved. He thanked God for running into this kind and helpful man.

"You wait here, Bir. I'll go and bargain with a rickshaw. Calcutta University is far. No, no! You don't have to worry about the money. I'll take care of it."

Bir was happy to be in Calcutta. He was anxious to begin his studies to be modern. He looked up at the high ceiling with various fixtures and marveled at their steel construction. And he waited. But he felt uneasy when his new friend took long to return. Finally, he showed up but didn't appear to be cheerful as before.

"The rickshaw pullers want more than I have. Now I don't know what to do!"

"I have some money. We can use that."

"No, no! I can't take your money. You are our guest!"

"I have a few rupees." Bir opened the knot that tied a small bundle securely to his waist.

Basu grabbed the bundle from his hands. "You don't have much. But this will have to do. You wait here. I'll be back shortly," he said and rushed away.

The Sanskrit scholar waited hopefully. Hours passed. Basu didn't return.

Calcutta University

"Calcutta isn't like Banaras," Professor Das said matter-of-factly. "Calcutta is a metropolis. Good and bad people from all over the world come here with various missions and goals. They come to trade, to dominate, to administer, to find cures, to teach and learn, but above all, most come to get rich quickly. Banaras, on the other hand, is a spiritual city. Its visitors have mainly spiritual interests."

Bir sat across the table in the professor's small untidy office filled with books and stacks of paper. He looked out of the window and saw students rushing back and forth from building to building. They appeared young and eager. *Someday they will change the world for the better,* he thought as he listened to Das.

"I have said this before: you don't have the requirements to be admitted to the university. You haven't even matriculated from high school!"

"Professor Das, you said that universities are learning centers, and I'm here to learn. Because of my background, I need a modern education more than your other students. They are already modern. I'm not. And I promise to work hard, I'll not fail."

Das remembered his advice to him at Banaras. He couldn't disappoint him now.

"Tomorrow I'll plead your case with Dr. Tommy Dutt. He is our provost and the one who can make an exception for admission. But don't be too optimistic. He decides everything according to the book. I'll also ask Brother Curren to speak on your behalf."

"'Tommy' Dutt?"

"Yes. He was educated in England where his cricket-playing friends called him 'Tommy.' The name stuck. He is brilliant but impatient. He expects everyone to be like him. But all of us are not Cambridge-educated or sons of landlords," he said and smiled.

"This decision will be entirely up to you, Brother Curren," Dutt declared. "If you want Bir Dharma to be one of your assistant translators, it's all right with me. But please, don't expect additional university funds."

He paced the large room and then looked at Curren. "I suppose he could assist you in translating Sage Patanjali's aphorisms if he's as good in Sanskrit as he claims to be."

"A pilgrim on a spiritual quest doesn't expect physical comforts. His other expectations will also be minimal. Besides, he's determined to learn about Christian Christ," an amused Das added.

"Christian Christ?" Dutt didn't smile. "Well, that's Brother Curren's area. And who knows? We may be initiating one who will make the world better, someone simple and unprejudiced, someone who won't have a 'holier than thou' attitude. I don't have to tell you again that I strongly believe that any religion can be dangerous when it's all attitude and opinions with very little information about other faiths." He then turned to Curren. "Reverend, my question remains unanswered: does a just father have a favorite son?"

Translations and Interpretations

"I had absolutely no idea that interpreting and translating are so time consuming and difficult," Bir complained to Curren in his office one day. "I have to study every Sanskrit word objectively to determine what the author meant at the time he wrote it. Then I have to discuss its meaning with a committee of scholars, and all must agree that we have the right understanding. Then we must find English word or words with the same or very similar meaning before deciding. And then, after all our work, our interpretations may change with time. Three years . . . what have I really accomplished?"

"A lot, I would say," Curren assured him. "You're learning English. You're studying the Holy Bible. You're learning to write critically and persuasively and developing public speaking skills. You're doing fine."

But Bir wasn't encouraged. He appeared depressed.

"Let me tell you a true story about a young man who sacrificed his life for what he believed in. He lived in England around 1529."

"Isn't that the time when the Mughals invaded India? Babar, their first emperor, died in 1530 at Agra." Bir wanted Curren to know that he was also studying Indian history.

"Yes. That was the time. Anyway, King Henry VIII occupied the English throne then. A bright young priest by the name of William Tyndale wanted to translate the Bible from Greek to English. He wanted to do this for the benefit of the English-speaking people."

"Something like what we are doing?"

"Yes, but with one big difference. The church was against the translation. The pope's personal legate Cardinal Wolsey and Sir Thomas More, his lord chancellor, opposed it. They banned and outlawed English prayers. Their laws severely punished those who said their prayers in English. They even beheaded a few. As for Tyndale, he became a fugitive in Western Europe. But he was finally captured and burnt at the stake."

"Burnt alive? How barbaric! Why were they against the translation? If Christianity is a universal religion, with a universal message, why should it be presented and practiced in Latin only?"

"There could be many reasons. The pope could have been concerned about maintaining the true meaning of the scriptures and rituals. He didn't want unauthorized translators to dilute or scar the sanctity of the Gospels.

"The second reason could be because many wanted it this way. Wouldn't you agree that in this violent and uncertain world, there is something very comforting, very soothing about rituals conducted in old languages like Sanskrit and Latin? Doesn't this give us security and stability to know that these rituals have been practiced unchanged for thousands of years?"

Bir nodded his head. He enjoyed theological discussions with him.

"Another reason could be because the church wanted to maintain control and power. Let's not forget that from the very beginning of Christianity, the church had many authoritative teachers, and they played very important roles in preserving and spreading Christianity."

"Control a religion, a faith? Isn't Truth greater than the capacity of any person, church, or tradition?"

"Perhaps it is, but let me go back about fifteen hundred years. Around 383, Ambrose of Milan, a bishop, wielded great power. He directly dealt with many rulers of the Roman Empire and succeeded in making Catholicism the only legitimate religion of the empire. He once said, 'The palaces belong to the emperors, the churches to the bishops.' He placed the church outside the jurisdiction of the state by writing that 'in matters of faith and in any problems of the ecclesiastical constitution . . . bishops can be tried only by bishops.' By doing this, he placed it outside the jurisdiction of the state."

"When was the Bible translated from Greek to Latin?"

"Come to think of it, this translation has changed the world forever. You see, Bir, Christianity has been blessed with many brilliant and dedicated personalities. One of them was Jerome. He was born around 345 near the Italian-Dalmatian border. His parents were Christians, and he received a fine classical education. In fact, he was a pupil of a distinguished grammarian and studied the works of Virgil and Cicero who influenced his life.

"Like you, he too went on a pilgrimage. He visited Antioch, learned Greek, and pursued Bible studies. The ascetic life interested him. After two years in the desert, he returned to Antioch and was ordained as a priest. In 382, he became the secretary to Pope Damasus who encouraged theological works in Latin and needed a new Latin translation of the Greek New Testament.

"Jerome was selected for the work. It took him twenty-three years to complete. He also translated the Hebrew Old Testament to Latin."

Bir became quiet. He saw the similarities of his life with those of Jerome. He realized that three years mustn't frustrate him. He needed more discipline and dedication if he wanted to be productive like Jerome.

"Translating the scriptures to Latin was very important. This made them available to people who spoke Latin—the only common language of the Western Roman Empire." Curren paused. "I wonder what India was experiencing spiritually during the first century after the Crucifixion."

"The Kushana dynasty was ruling North India at that time," Bir answered quickly. "Their greatest emperor was Kanishka. He was a patron of Buddhism. He convoked a great assembly of Buddhist monks. The famous Buddhist scholar Asvaghosha lived in his court. He also erected a magnificent tower over the relics of Buddha in Peshawar. It attracted visitors from foreign lands." Bir stopped and looked at the circular clock on the office wall.

"But please tell me more about Christianity," he said.

"I'm so glad, so glad. I have come all the way from Dublin to teach English and theology in Catholic colleges in India. I'm not here to convert anyone by force. 'Brandy and gun power in one hand and the Bible in the other' isn't my style. I just want to spread the teachings of gentle Jesus. I want Hindus and Buddhists to know that Jesus Christ preached love for all."

Catholicism and Hinduism

As time passed, Curren and Bir developed respect and fondness for each other. They enjoyed esoteric topics. Curren introduced him to the works of Western philosophers like Cicero, Seneca, Schopenhauer, and Socrates, but the one he related the most to was Michael de Montaigne of France who stipulated that a truly wise man would measure the true worth of anything by its usefulness to him.

"I'm impressed with Western philosophers, Brother Curren, but what can I do with my life? I want to be useful and valuable. Could promoting understanding between different religions be the answer?" Bir asked one day.

"In this age of uncertainty and unrest, spreading Christ's love is my answer," Curren replied.

"We can then do one thing together," Bir suggested, "We can discuss Hindu and Catholic beliefs and their influence on meaningful lives. We can compare and find commonalities between them. For instance, Hindus use symbols in their temples. Don't churches have symbols? Does the cross you wear symbolize a useful belief?"

"Before we begin, tell me why you are so interested in Catholicism? Are you thinking of converting?"

"I'm interested because I want to know. Besides, learning other religions doesn't mean I reject my own. I was born and raised as a Hindu. In my late teens and early twenties, I learned about Buddhism. Now I want to learn about Christianity, someday, Islam and Sikhism.

"As I mature, I find that studying religions helps to develop respect. I stress 'respect' and not just 'tolerance.' Respectful theological discussions can promote peace. Otherwise, we will always be ignorant of others. We will fight and kill because we are afraid of what we don't understand. World history is full of persecutions due to varying beliefs of God."

Bir's idealism reminded Curren of his own youth in Dublin. He too was full of hope for a better world. He thought of Ireland, about the historical conflicts between Catholics and Protestants.

"Yes," he said, "our hope for peace must never die. Let's discuss symbols, rituals, and their usefulness. When I first came to India, I thought people here worshiped idols. I thought they were pagans—like ancient Romans. Then I learned that idols are symbols as in Catholicism. The cross that I wear symbolizes the Crucifixion though believers didn't use it in the first century. Another is the phoenix—a mythical bird rising from its ashes, symbolizing the resurrection."

"Catholicism? Crucifixion? Resurrection?"

Curren laughed. "Yes. And let me add the 'virgin birth' to that!"

Bir seemed confused.

"Christianity is more than nineteen hundred years old. You will find its history fascinating. To begin with, the center of Christianity moved to Rome from Jerusalem in AD 70. The stories of apostles like Peter and Paul will touch your heart. To learn more about Christianity, continue studying the Bible. This holy book reveals God's wisdom. Today, I'll tell you what I can, as simply as I can. The rest will be up to you."

He paused and watched the reaction on Bir's face. It was young, fresh, and hopeful.

"It's always encouraging to remember one of the eight blessings of Jesus: 'Blessed are they who hunger and thirst for righteousness, for they will be satisfied.' This prayer can be said by anyone, particularly a spiritual seeker like you."

Bir nodded. He hoped his spiritual thirst would quench someday.

"Christians believe that Jesus is of virgin birth, that he was crucified and resurrected. The core of Christianity is faith—faith in Christ for eternal salvation. Christians have many ways to practice their faith. Some through the Catholic Church, some through the Eastern Orthodox, some through Protestant denominations—like Lutherans, Baptists, and Methodists.

"The form of Catholic worship is highly structured. For instance, Mass is in Latin. Protestant worship is less structured. They allow congregations greater degree of participation."

Bir was familiar with rituals. "Vedic rituals are performed in Sanskrit. The degree of participation varies. Priests generally perform the rituals. The all-pervading Brahman dwells within the rituals taught by the sacred scriptures. Others can pray by reciting mantras or singing devotional songs. Is it possible that Hinduism encompasses many of the rituals of Catholics and Protestants?"

"Catholics believe in the seven sacraments. They are Baptism, Confirmation, the Eucharist, Penance, the Anointing of the Sick, Matrimony, and Holy Orders."

"Seven Catholic sacraments? This is amazing! Hindus too have sacraments!" Bir was excited. "They begin with conception and end with cremation. A few of them are first feeding of solid food, shaving of the head before receiving sacred thread, marriage, name-giving, and renouncing."

"*Catholic* means 'universal.' *Scriptures* means 'divine revelations.'"

"Hindus believe in 'realization.' Its history is more than four thousand years. It's the oldest living major tradition going back to prehistoric times," Bir added.

Curren nodded. "Yes. In addition, Hindus believe in the Trinity: Creator, Preserver, and Dissolver. I learned that in Dublin. Catholics believe in the Triune God: Father, Son, and Holy Ghost. Keep in mind that Christianity is monotheistic. They believe in one God."

"Hindus too believe in one God. Lord Krishna in the *Gita* states, 'I am he who causes. No other besides me. Upon me, these worlds are held like pearls strung on a thread.' *Bhagavad-Gita* means 'Song of God.' Hinduism encompasses the teachings of divine incarnations, saints, or prophets. Hindus also believe that God is without attributes. Words can't describe it. It's nameless for we cannot name it."

Curren scratched his head lightly and took a deep breath. He wondered when he would find time to read the *Bhagavad-Gita*.

"Catholicism is an organized religion. It needed an organization to survive the persecution of pagan Roman emperors. It has a hierarchical structure. The pope is the head of the church. We believe he is infallible. I should add that the Protestants don't recognize the pope as such."

"Hinduism was never an organized religion," Bir said. "Organization wasn't necessary in its early history. Those who invaded and conquered India accepted Hinduism, except Islam, possibly because they despised and abhorred the caste system and rightly so. Many Hindus chose Islam to gain political and economic favors. The teaching of brotherhood in Islam is also very appealing.

"The sultans of Ghazni invaded India from around the end of the tenth century. Hindus should have learned to organize themselves to defend their culture and tradition—just like the early Christians. I think Hindus have much to learn about organizational skills in practical matters." Bir paused. "But let's get back to Christianity. I want to know more. For instance, who was the first pope?"

"The first head of the early church was St. Peter. Jesus himself appointed him. He was the first bishop of Rome. A bishop has a certain area under his jurisdiction called a diocese. A diocese is made of congregations ministered by priests. The members of a congregation share a common sense of belonging to the church."

"Yes. The feeling of belonging is very important," Bir said, thinking of the inhuman ways in which upper caste Hindus treat outcastes. He thought of ones like his grandfather who prevent such feelings from generating. He thought of temple priests who curtail feeling of belonging and social equality by imposing conservatism as natural laws.

"The Mass or Holy Communion is a celebration of worship. The priest presents the assembly with bread and wine that convert into the body and blood of Christ. The church teaches that Christ is present in the consecration of bread and wine during Mass. 'Transubstantiation' is transformation of bread and wine literally into the body and blood of Christ. This sacrament is the Eucharist. It has other names like the Breaking of the Bread, Holy Sacrifice, Holy Communion, and Lord's Supper."

"This is very interesting. This is like prasad, the consecrated sweets, fruits, or certain types of leaves given to devotees by temple priests. I'm very interested in the Eucharist. Can a non-Catholic attend Mass?"

"Yes, of course. Why do you think 'Catholic' means 'universal'? We are open to anyone who wants to experience Christ's love."

Bir wished he could have invited Curren to a Hindu temple. However, he remembered his experience at his village. He recalled how the priests drove off the untouchables when they came to receive prasad during Krishna's birthday celebration. He was ashamed of himself. He wondered why Christianity could be so open to all while Vedic teachings are not.

"Hindus describe their religion as *Sanatana Dharma* or 'eternal religion.' It always existed, even in previous universes when there were other moons and suns. It will exist in future universes with their own incarnations."

"In Catholicism, *incarnation* means 'made into flesh.' It means Jesus, a divine person of God, assumed a human body and condition for a brief period to redeem the world."

"In Hinduism, there have been many incarnations of the Divine. The last three in human form were Rama, Krishna, and Buddha. There will be one more in the future."

"One of the most basic doctrines in Catholicism is the belief that man can attain salvation through divine grace or God's love."

"So to go to heaven, one has to earn grace? Well, according to Hinduism, God has already given us grace. All we have to do is realize this to attain salvation."

"Jesus was both man and God. God's grace is through this dual nature. He is everywhere and in everything. Since everything comes from him, everything is sacred. This presence of God is called 'sacramentality.'"

"This is amazing!" Bir cried. "Hindus too believe that God is everywhere, in everything. This is why, for example, many Hindus go on pilgrimage to Mount Kailash, the abode of God, some twenty-two thousand feet high in the Himalayas."

"Catholics believe that Christ is the ultimate mediator. He can advocate for us and plead our case to God. His mother, the Blessed Virgin Mary, is the second advocate. Of course, others—like a saint, a holy man, or a priest—can also plead for us."

"I have heard the 'Hail Mary, full of grace, pray for us sinners, now and at the hour of our death' prayer. It's a beautiful prayer. Is this a mediation prayer?"

"Yes. You can call it that."

"I'm glad. When Hindus worship the incarnations and contemplate on their attributes, they are seeking mediation of incarnates for eternal unity of their Atman with the Ultimate. *Atman* in Sanskrit means 'God within.'"

Curren looked at his watch. "This is fascinating, but I have to leave. I have a class."

"Brother Curren, did Jesus Christ appear in vision to any of his disciples as Lord Krishna did to Arjuna as described in the *Gita*?"

"Yes. He did to his apostles. In fact, Saint Paul changed world history after Jesus appeared to him in a vision."

"Did Jesus or any of his disciples visit India?"

"Many Indian Christians claim that St. Thomas, one of the twelve apostles of Jesus, came to India in AD 52. He landed on Malabar Coast and lived in India for twenty years. During these years, he established seven churches."

"Seven churches in twenty years?"

"Yes. Does that surprise you? St. Paul the Apostle founded churches in twenty cities. He helped in establishing a network of Christian communities in the Mediterranean and covered ten thousand miles in his journeys."

"How could they do so much? Were they superhuman?"

Curren didn't answer. He was already late for his class.

Law of Love

The British Empire experienced great historic changes in 1911. Emperor Edward VII died in 1910 and his son George V succeeded him. In India, Lord Hardinge II succeeded Lord Minto II as the new viceroy. Minto's repressive policies greatly increased anti-British sentiments throughout the country. In December of 1911, Hardinge held a Darbar in Delhi to welcome the new king and queen to India. At the Darbar, the royals announced the transfer of capital from Calcutta to Delhi.

"Did you know that this universe, before it was created, existed as Brahman?" Bir said. "It first existed as a seed. Then it grew and took on names and forms."

"Where did you learn that?" asked Nongrim Hilly, the recipient of the Northeast India Catholic Award. This scholarship enabled him to leave his village in the hills of Assam and attend St. Xavier's College, an affiliate of Calcutta University where they first met.

"From the *Upanishads*," he replied. "I also learned that the universe is made up of many worlds, and they are inhabited by various beings."

"This sounds like the stories of Creation in the *Genesis*. But I really don't care. Right now, I'm more concerned about this world and about completing my studies in theology. I'll receive my degree next year. I hope this transfer of capital to Delhi doesn't delay my graduation."

"And if it does?"

"Not sure. Maybe return to my village and grow oranges and green pepper—like my forefathers."

"What will you do when you receive your degree?"

"After my ordination into the ministry, I plan to work in the Assam Mission with Monsignor Christopher Becker. He is its first apostolic prefect. Since 1904, they established several mission centers. Their headquarters are in Gwahati on the banks of the Brahmaputra."

"And then what? Convert more people to Christianity?" Bir laughed nonchalantly.

"Why shouldn't we? What have you high-thinking Hindus done throughout the centuries? You talk about big things like past and future universes but don't bother to venture a few miles from the safety of your homes to teach your dharma to others. Look at these Christian missionaries. They travel thousands of miles to remote regions of the world for their missions. Did you know that in 1626, two Jesuit priests, Father Cacella and Father Cabral, traveled through Assam to Tibet?"

"No, I didn't, but I'm sure they were brave and good men."

"They weren't only brave and good. They were blessed and inspired to make the world Christian. And I want to be a part of that mission." After a pause, he smiled. "Perhaps you should convert, become a priest and join the mission."

"That thought has entered my mind," Bir said seriously. "The teachings of Jesus Christ attract me. His message is the law of love. It rejects all forms of violence. I find this very appealing. But a few practices of Catholicism frighten me."

"What are they?"

"Organized religion frightens me for its power, authority, and control. It claims to be the absolute and the only. It simply ignores the convictions of followers of other faiths. It doesn't tolerate open debate or dissent. Look at what happened during the Spanish and Roman Inquisitions: accused heretics were condemned and punished, some burnt alive at the stakes, while others boiled in oil. Do you think God was pleased with such barbarity? People like me who try to think and understand before accepting or believing find organized religion to be too restraining and confining."

Hilly became uncomfortable. "Why are you frightened by the absolute and only?"

"I just can't accept the teaching that salvation is only through Christianity."

"Why can't you accept Christianity to be the only true faith?"

"There are other good faiths, and they are equal. All of them lead to the same Truth. God wills the salvation of all through many paths. A just God wouldn't make Truth the exclusive property of one religion."

"Why not?"

"Because exclusivity and intolerance are twins. Belief in exclusivity permitted the merciless killing of innocents in the Holy Lands during the crusades. Besides, Jesus didn't proclaim a religion called 'Christianity.' He didn't preach violence or intolerance. He preached the Kingdom of God."

Hilly was silent. He had to think for a while. "And what else did you learn during the last six years in Calcutta University, Professor Bir Dharma?"

"I learned that there are varying degrees of faith and that geography, history, and culture play roles. I know all of us can't be at the same level of spirituality at the same time, and thus, one path is not suitable to all. I also learned that good energy can create an organization that is not arrogant. I see that goodness in the likes of Brother Curren and Brother Donovan."

Nongrim grinned. "Tell you what: I'll not be like those Western missionaries who stand in street corners and spit at Hindu gods and customs. I'll never say that Lord Krishna was a womanizer. I promise to use the best in Christianity to help Hindus to live according to the religion of their forefathers. I'll be a good Christian and impart knowledge—just like your mentor Brother Curren."

"What counts is what you are, not what you call yourself," Bir said thoughtfully. "Perhaps someday, people like us, temporal global travelers of different paths searching for the same Truth, will come together in peace and promote understanding, love, and compassion to realize the spark of the Divine in all of us."

Good and Bad

"I have difficulty bidding farewell to ones I love and respect," Bir said to Curren after the publication of the first English translation of Patanjali's aphorisms. "During the past years, you made it possible for me to learn English, Christianity, Western cultures, and modernity. Although we are of different faiths, we are no longer strangers. But my tenure has ended. Today is my last day at St. Xavier's." He suppressed his emotions. "How should we say good-bye now, Brother Curren?"

"The same way we said hello, Bir, the same way. The Lord knows when we will meet again."

He handed him a package wrapped in white glossy paper and tied with a jute string.

"For me? What is it?" "The Holy Bible containing the Old and New Testaments—King James Version. The second book is catechism."

"Catechism?"

"Catechism of the Catholic Church. The word means 'instruction.' It's the summary of what Catholics believe in throughout the world. It'll have answers to the hundreds of questions you have been asking." Curren smiled. "In it you will find details on the sacraments, the Mass, lives of saints, and many other traditions."

Bir looked at the old dog-eared book held together by a hard black moth-eaten cover.

"Yes, I know. Brother Donovan used it for many years. He wishes you well."

He read the sentiment Curren and Donovan wrote on the front pages of the books. Emotions overcame him. Unable to utter a word, he almost bent to touch the feet of his beloved guru in the manner of his ancestors. But he restrained himself. He remembered reading what St. Peter said when Cornelius prostrated himself before the apostle in Caesarea: "Stand up, I too am a man."

"I have nothing to give you," Bir uttered inaudibly.

"You dedicated six years of your life studying comparative religion. You have strengthened my belief that this land will continue to give birth to sons and daughters who value spirituality. Your face is the face of hope and love. No, Bir, you have given me much." He paused and looked deeply into his tearful eyes. "You will always be in my prayers."

At the train station, he sat on a freshly painted white bench and flipped through the pages of the Bible. He was fascinated to remember that the word *Jesus* means "God saves" in Hebrew and that the angel Gabriel gave the name. He wondered if Gabriel spoke Hebrew with an accent and if all angels were tall and strong like Gabriel, or whether a few were like the baby angels he saw in the paintings while attending Mass.

As he discovered that the word *Christ* comes from the Greek translation of the Hebrew word *Messiah*, which means "anointed," he found himself suddenly hurled to the floor.

"Scram, you dirty swine! You don't belong here!"

Bir looked up from his fallen position and saw the unshaven faces of three British soldiers laughing and glaring at him. They had rifles and backpacks slung from their broad shoulders. They wore khaki uniforms and Australian brim hats. They were perspiring and had strong body odor.

"Whom did you steal these books from?" growled one as he picked up the two books that had fallen to the floor. His forearms were massive and muscular. On one were the tattooed words "Scotland For Ever."

Bir was too startled to answer. He searched for words to utter.

"You bastard! Don't you know this bench is for Europeans only?"

"Kick the dirty dog, Willie. The bugger needs a lesson."

Willie kicked him twice on his side as he lay on the floor.

"Stop, stop," shouted the other. "Don't kill the chap. See, he is reading the Bible!"

They looked at one another and started laughing.

"The darky savage, the darky savage is reading the Bible, the Bible," the three started singing. The one holding the books then hurled them at him, hitting him on his neck and shoulder.

"Go and screw yourself, pagan," he said. "Let's go, boys. We have a train to catch."

Bir lay on the floor. He felt like a mistreated dog. His pride, however, was hurt more than his ribs or shoulder. A few passengers watched the commotion from a distance. He got up slowly, picked up his books, and walked toward them, trying to understand why this happened.

"Are you hurt?" one asked.

"Not much. But why?"

"Because benches painted white are for Europeans only."

"They treat us badly because of our skin color. They think we are dirty."

"Didn't you see those English signs?" a man asked.

Bir was angry but felt utterly helpless. He then remembered what he witnessed at Nagpur long ago. He wondered if this is how untouchables feel when they are treated unjustly because of their circumstances. He thought of his village and of his grandfather's tradition. He felt guilty.

Imperial Capital

The enormous task of designing the new capital in Delhi was commissioned to Edwin Lutyens, the great British architect. He and Herbert Baker, another famous architect, incorporated various Indian architectural features into their designs. The dome of the official residence of the viceroy was to be drum-mounted, in the Buddhist tradition, while the Parliament and other office buildings were to use local red sandstone in the traditional Mughal style.

Bir was full of hope in finding employment in the construction of the new capital. It was time for him, he thought, to be an integral part of the modern world and do his part as a royal subject.

"It won't be difficult to find employment in Delhi," he had told Curren. "I have skills now. I'm fluent in English. I have learned to interact with Europeans. I can always be an intermediary between the English designers and planners and the native building contractors and laborers. This way I'll also learn more about Western administration and organization."

But he wasn't that fortunate. The greater demand was for group leaders, overseers, timekeepers, and payroll clerks to deal with hundreds of illiterate daily workers. And this is where he found employment, away from interactions with modern sahibs.

Early one morning when he first approached the makeshift employment station in a sandstone quarry, the overseer sitting behind a desk told him to put his thumbprint on a registration sheet.

"Why should I use my thumbprint when I can sign my name?"

"Because all coolies do!" the heavyset man snapped. "Besides, who knows you here? I don't. You are one of a thousand. If a falling stone kills you, we will identify your body with your thumbprint. Your signature won't be worth a damn, unless you come back from hell to identify your body."

The rudeness of his compatriot puzzled him.

"Don't mind him," the man standing behind him whispered. "He just barks. He feels superior in treating us badly. But you should see him kiss the boots of the white sahibs!"

Bir received three sticks of different lengths to measure the three dimensions of each brick cut from the quarry. He was to oversee the work of twenty stonecutters and to make sure that each brick met the required specifications. He had to pay them their daily earnings at sunset. Since most laborers could not count above ten—the number that correlates with fingers—Bir was very careful not to shortchange any of them. He obtained the correct sums from his overseer who sometimes conveniently made errors.

"You are honest, you are. I have watched you for nearly three months now," said Ispal Kaur, a stonecutter whose bearded face, turban, and shirt were always covered with red dust. They were sitting around a campfire with others, trying to keep warm in the damp cold of Delhi winter. The sky was starry and bright, making their faces visible in the soft light of dusk. Bir fed more straw to the fire. They watched the sparks fly high as he poked the fire with a twig.

"What are they?" one asked, pointing to the sky with his chin. "Do they know we are here?"

"They are stars," another replied.

"I know they are stars. But what are they?"

"They are the souls of great gurus. When gurus die, their souls become stars."

"Really?"

Bir listened quietly to the discussion on stars. He loved their simplicity. He wanted to learn how they think, how they accumulate values and beliefs. Finally, he decided to speak.

"You ask what they are. Well, they are really suns—just like our sun. Our sun is just one of many suns in the sky. There are so many suns and planets that we can't count them."

"Are there more than all our fingers put together?"

"Yes. Many, many more."

"Do beings live in such places?"

"I don't know exactly, but according to the *Upanishads*, beings of other order than us inhabit various spheres of the universe."

"What types of beings?"

"Beings of higher order than us—like devas and Gandharvas."

They were silent. A few gazed at the flame. A few looked up at the stars.

Finally, Ispal broke the silence. "Where did you learn all this, Bir Babu?"

"From the holy books of our ancestors. For instance, the story of suns—of many suns—is in the *Puranas*."

"Then tell us more about the sun."

"It's like a ball of fire. It is very, very hot. No life—as we know life—can exist there. But it gives us light and energy. Because of light, plants grow. We live on plants, directly as vegetarians or indirectly—by eating meat or fish."

He wondered if he should tell them what the *Puranas* say about the sun, the world, and the universe, that they evolve and grow, then decay and dissolve, then grow again, that this process continues endlessly, without beginning or ending, and that there were other suns, moons, and earths. He wanted to tell them that each immortal soul has passed through more than eight million lives before attaining human form and a day of Brahma or Kalpa is more than four billion years.

But he realized how silly it would be if he shares such concepts and numbers when they don't make sense even to college students. So why should he tell people who can only count up to ten? But they wanted to know more, and he wanted to teach.

"The sun is very old, very old. It's older than our world, our planet . . ."

Soon he heard snores. They were falling asleep where they sat. The warmth of the campfire relaxed their tired bodies. They had worked hard, dawn to dusk. He knew it was time to stop and sleep.

Ispal added a bundle of straw to the dwindling fire and watched the sparks rise. "Wonderful," he smiled. "You are a good teacher. Your stories are very interesting. You must visit our temple, our gurdwara."

Bir couldn't fall asleep that evening. He watched the separate groups of men and women sleep in the light of the campfires, a few hunched like bundles. He wondered who had the duty to teach them to count, to think correctly, and perhaps even to read and write. The nation that contributed the Hindu numeral system to the world has not taught its own people to count.

He thought of them. They were strong and honest, willing to do backbreaking work for a few annas a day. They knew how to use money at the market but nothing about calculating how much they earn daily. They accepted what they were paid and were always at the mercy of those who knew how to add and subtract. *Someday*, he thought, *he would become a teacher and help them to better themselves.*

Finally, he fell asleep and dreamt of modern sahibs.

The Gurdwara

"The sahibs recruit soldiers regularly from our village nowadays," Ispal said as the two approached Kannauj, a large village eight miles northeast of Delhi. "They say that there will be a big war in their lands. So they want our young men to fight for them."

"A big war? Really?" Bir said. "Is that why we see so many soldiers in Delhi?"

"I don't know."

"Do they fight well? Do they make brave soldiers?"

"What?" Ispal said, surprised at the question.

"Do they fight well?"

"Of course they do," he snapped. He remembered his years in the Sikh Regiment. "How else do you think they fight?"

Bir became quiet. He wasn't really interested in fighting nor did he know much about wars. He started to walk faster.

"You fight well when you are armed and trained well," Ispal said in a stern voice. "The Mughals committed great atrocities during their rule. They tortured and killed thousands of innocents. So the Sikhs had to arm and train themselves. They had to defend themselves."

Bir nodded his head to show that he understood. "You know we started before breakfast."

"We will get there before Langar."

"Langar?"

"It's a vegetarian meal prepared at the gurdwara. It's eaten jointly by the community without regard to status or rank. Our spiritual leader Guru Nanak taught us the equality of all men and women. He said that caste, or an exalted name, is worthless, for there is only one refuse for humanity. In fact, Guru Amar Das said that when we die, we don't carry our caste with us—only our deeds. They determine our fate."

They sat on the ground in a large circle and ate the distributed food. A tall wiry man with a full snow-white beard wearing a large light green turban and shirt and tight white trousers sat beside Ispal and Bir. The deep wrinkles around his eyes and nose told the story of his life's struggle. After studying Bir's bare head, short hair, and clean-shaven face, he casually began a conversation with him.

"Life should be lived generously and courageously," he said. "You should be industrious and honest. You should meditate upon the divine reality, not by escaping or seeking solitude from worldly affairs but by performing dharma by conquering lust, anger, materialism, and pride."

"I try to conquer them, sir," Bir said. "I don't crave fame or fortune either. All I want is to be a modern teacher. But to share a secret with you, I often dream of beautiful maidens." He hastened a look at the women sitting in front of them in the circle. His face flushed. "During the day I see these shapely women with heaving bosoms sway their hips as they carry bricks on their heads. I see their eyes sparkle with life and lust, and I fall prey to them—like a buck to a doe. Sometimes I want to give them more money than they earn."

"The young have lust in their eyes because they want to experience life's pleasures," Ispal added.

"But how do I conquer lust?" He wiped his forehead with his sleeve.

The toothless man became thoughtful. Light emitting from the holes of the blackened metal coal heaters placed at the center of the circle reflected in his eyes. "You conquer lust," he began slowly, "by keeping your senses from attaching themselves to objects of pleasure. Remember, the lust you see in their eyes could be the reflection of your own thoughts, of your own lust for them. You see, young man, the world mirrors our thoughts. We see what we want to see. We hear what we want to hear. We believe what we want to believe. To lessen lust, you have to be God conscious."

"But how can I be God conscious all the time—from dawn to dusk and then at night—with temptations all around me?"

"You become God conscious by not letting pleasure distract you from your dharma. If you crave pleasure, you experience unhappiness."

"But I like pleasurable thoughts. I like to fantasize, to imagine."

"If you play with your imagination, your wishes will become desires. Lust will take roots. Pain, fear, and sorrow will follow. So you have to uproot them and go beyond likes to free yourself."

"How can I free myself?"

"You become God conscious. You free yourself by developing a determined mind and a pure heart. Look into your heart and soul and at the world around you. You will see divine order in creation. God's message is in creation. We believe that God wills the universe. By opening our eyes, we see his nature and through it, we try to understand him and be conscious of him. Guru Nanak stressed inward spirituality for liberation. He said that this transcends all religions."

"Who was Guru Nanak?" Bir asked. "What did he teach about God?"

"Nanak was the son of Mehta and Tripta Kalu. He was born in April 1469 in Nankana Sahib. When he was about thirty, he had a spiritual experience while bathing in a river. He felt the presence of God. Since then, he traveled extensively, from the Himalayas in the north to Ceylon in the south, from Assam in the east to Mecca in the west, spreading his religious experience through hymns. Mardana, a Muslim, who played a string instrument, accompanied him.

"Guru Nanak said that we as human beings can't understand God. But we can experience him through love, worship, and contemplation. This is why Sikhs worship God in his abstract form, without using statues."

"Why can't we understand God?"

"Because our ego, pride, and materialism blind us."

"Did Guru Nanak teach the law of karma and rebirth?"

"Yes. He also taught that release from the cycle of life and death is a matter of concentrating on the total divine reality. The efforts to clean ourselves of evil must be blessed by the grace of God and Guru. He said that it's not a matter of caste or performing rituals."

"Am I bad because I experience lust?"

"Sikhs believe that God is within us all, no matter how weak or evil we may think or appear. We all can change for the better."

The meal was ending, and the community was dispersing. The heaters were burning out of coal. But Bir wanted to know more about Sikhism.

"Our scriptures contain nine hundred and seventy-four hymns composed by Guru Nanak. When inspiration came to him, he would sing these hymns, pouring out his soul's longing for the Lord. These constitute the *Guru Granth Sahib*, also called the Adi Granth. *Adi* means 'original.' This text is kept in all gurdwaras and shown the highest reverence."

"Do Sikhs have a holy city—like Banaras?"

"It's said that during the times of Guru Amar Das, Emperor Akbar, who, by the way, celebrated his entry into manhood at sixteen by beheading a Hindu, granted land in Amritsar where the Golden Temple was later built. It was inlaid with gold during the reign of Maharaja Ranjit Singh in the beginning of the nineteenth century. It's the most honored Sikh shrine, and as such, Amritsar is like Banaras."

Ispal looked at Bir and motioned to him not to ask further questions.

"Thank you for your temple's hospitality," he said and stood up. "Your village will see a lot of recruiting tomorrow. My friend Bir can always visit Amritsar. We will spend the night here and return to Delhi at dawn."

But the man with the large turban wasn't dissuaded. He had much to share.

"Of course your friend can always visit Amritsar, but does he know why the peace-loving Sikhs became martial?"

"Why?" Bir wanted to learn all that he could.

"In 1606, during the reign of Emperor Jahangir, Guru Arjan Dev was roasted alive on a griddle because he incurred the emperor's displeasure. His son Guru Hargobind succeeded him. He immediately instructed his followers to bear arms to defend themselves against the Mughals and prevent forced conversion to Islam. He also led them in fighting Mughal troops.

"In 1675, Emperor Aurangzeb beheaded the ninth guru, Tegh Bahadar, because he tried to intercede when a group of Kashmiri Brahmins was forced to convert to Islam. A few of his followers were sawed in half while others were roasted alive."

"Sawed in half! Roasted alive! Beheaded!" Bir muttered as he stared at the dwindling blue flame of the heater. He then blotted his eyes with his sleeve. "I . . . I . . ." He blew his nose.

The old man put his hand on his shoulder. "I didn't mean to upset you. I'm sorry."

Bir composed himself. "I want to scream. I want to tell Aurangzeb to stop his insanity. But he's dead! He won't hear! He won't hear."

"That's all history now," Ispal said calmly. "All we can do is remember and learn from it."

"Guru Gobind Singh, the son of Guru Tegh Bahadar, studied warfare and led his troops in battle," the old man continued. "His four sons were killed in 1705, two of them for refusing to convert to Islam. Gobind was himself killed in 1708 in fighting Afghan invaders."

After completing the history of his people, he carefully uncrossed his legs, rose slowly to an upright position, and straightened his back. He then stretched his arms above his head, took a deep breath as his iron bracelet slipped to his elbow. He looked at Bir and nodded slightly.

"How does one become wise—like you?" Bir asked.

"Wisdom comes from the heart, knowledge from the intellect. Know your heart," he said.

The temple square was now quiet and deserted.

"I wonder how Guru Nanak would feel if he were to be here today."

"He would be proud of his followers," Ispal replied as he laid his body on a visitor's cot close to the heaters. "He would be proud of their devotion and their fearlessness. He would be proud of them for realizing that only the strong can make and maintain peace."

War Years

"What can I do if the sahibs don't send me money?" the quarry overseer bellowed when Bir asked him to pay his stonecutters. They were not paid for days. They were frustrated and angry. A few already returned to their villages and prayed for early rain.

Rumors were that the war wasn't going well for the British against the Germans. They heard stories of flying machines fighting in the sky. Food and medicine were scarce and rationed everywhere. The British Raj ordered their tax collectors to coerce subjects to pay more and more—either in cash or in kind. Those who failed were beaten. Others lost their property.

Construction of the new capital was no longer of high priority. Bir and Ispal were two of many who lost their jobs. Ispal returned to his village while Bir considered returning home, but this would end his learning about the modern world.

One day at a tea shop Bir heard that in a village to the west of Delhi, the priests were asking villagers to offer animal sacrifices—preferably their goats—to Goddess Kali. If she is pleased with the sacrifices, the priests said, the monsoons would arrive early, and good fortune would return to the villagers.

"You know this isn't true," Bir said to the shopkeeper. "God or gods don't look for sacrifices of blood or meat."

"Of course it is true," a customer said. "We have been making such sacrifices to please Kali for ages. In fact, a few villages have offered human sacrifices."

"Human sacrifices? Disgusting! That's utter nonsense!"

"You must be a stranger to these parts. I know it's disgusting, but it's true," he replied while others watched and listened indifferently. A few sipped their steaming tea loudly.

"Last week, they sacrificed a young girl," another added. "They needed a virgin. So they kidnapped a three-year-old from the village of the untouchables. They bathed her, fed her, dressed her in colorful clothes, and adorned her with flowers. Then they purified her with prayers. The following morning, as the sun rose, they brought her to the front of the idol and made her sit. She must have been drugged for she was sleepy. Then they proceeded to first cut off her tongue with a sharp knife and offered it to Kali. As the child twisted and struggled in pain and horror, unable to cry or shout, they cut off her ears. Then they stabbed her with another knife and offered her bloody, beating heart to the goddess."

"You witnessed it?"

"Yes. I vomited and closed my eyes. I turned and ran—as quickly as my old legs could carry me."

"Did anyone report this to the police?"

"The police? What will they do? They keep away from the priests. Tradition says not to hurt priests. Otherwise they will curse and damn us. The priests know secret Vedic mantras. Mantras make them very powerful."

"This is ridiculous! This is murder!" Bir shouted, unable to control his disgust.

No one said anything. They looked at one another, their faces gloomy and glum.

"This is madness. I'll go to the police."

"That won't do any good," someone said indifferently.

"Then I will go to the newspapers. I'll tell them what happened here. I'll tell them that the country and the whole world need to know about such horrific crimes committed in the guise of religion." Bir smashed his earthenware teacup with the heels of his shoes and rushed away.

American Reporter

America joined the Allies in the war against the Central Powers in December 1917. Large numbers of American troops arrived in Europe during the summer of 1918. Earlier that year, the Germans launched their Spring Offensive. American war correspondents were everywhere. Guy Phillips of the *New York Daily* was in Delhi to report on the morale of Indian troops fighting in Mesopotamia under British command.

During his years in Calcutta, Bir learned that speaking English fluently gives you an advantage in dealing with British-Indian protocol. Somehow, most Indians felt that speaking English makes them the elite, entitling them to special privileges. The British agreed.

"The subeditor is away. Come back tomorrow," the Hindi-speaking office receptionist of the *Delhi Times* said without looking up from the paper he was reading.

"If I can't see an Indian reporter now, then I'm willing to meet with a foreign correspondent," Bir replied in English. "I know many of them are here covering the war. I'm sure other countries would like to know what is happening in the villages where most of the Indian troops hail from."

Startled by his articulation, the receptionist stood up quickly and then sat just as quickly. He looked around to see if anyone else heard Bir.

"Has Phillips sahib arrived yet?" he leaned toward the man sitting beside him. "Go and find out. Let me know." Looking up at Bir, he said, "Mr. Guy Phillips is a reporter from America. This is his first visit. He is interested in Indian culture also. Perhaps you would like to meet him."

"Howdy," Phillips said, touching his palms in front of his heart and bowing slightly, mimicking the Indian greeting. "I'm trying to be Indian."

"And I'm trying to be American," Bir smiled, extending his hand.

Guy laughed. Bir noticed his sunburned face and cigarette-stained teeth. "It must be hot where you come from in America."

"Yeah, New Mexico, have a ranch there," he said unassumingly. "Hot and dry—just like here. They tell me the monsoons will soon arrive to cool things off. But that doesn't matter. Right now I have a job to do. So what can you tell me about the fighting men of India? Why do they fight for the British? They sound like the Loyalists in America during the American Revolution."

Bir told him why he came.

"Hell, Bir! I'm not your man! I'm a war correspondent. I'm here to interview a few *DT* reporters and Indian soldiers. I know nothing about Hindu gods or goddess like Kali. They are too many of them anyway for me to write about during my short visit."

"But don't you think more Americans will buy your paper to read about Eastern mysticism, about traditional Indo-European human and animal sacrifice, about a holy gift to a god in feminine form, about—"

"Yeah, yeah. But I'm not here for that. I'm here to write about where these fighting men come from, about their lives and values, why hundreds of thousands of them fight and die for a foreign power that colonizes them. You see, Bir, more than a hundred years ago, America too was a British colony. But things are different now. America has entered the war to end militarism, to end aristocratic systems of government, and to end imperialism."

Bir became quiet. He wasn't getting anywhere with this American.

"Mr. Phillips, suppose you hire me to—"

"Call me Guy," he said, fumbling for a cigarette in his pockets.

"Right. Yes. Suppose you hire me to write articles about the worship of Kali in the villages where the soldiers are recruited."

"Have you written before?"

"Not for newspapers. But I can write. I have translated Sanskrit to English at Calcutta University."

Guy looked at him with more interest. "You know, that's a great idea. Tell you what: you write articles in less than five hundred words, and I'll submit them to both *NYD* and *DT*. What *DT* pays will be yours."

"Why in less than five hundred words?"

"Because Americans don't have time! They are always in a hurry. Long articles may not interest them. They like them succinct. So five hundred words—max."

His first article about the worship of goddess Durga, in the form of the Black or Dark Mother, destroying everything on her path until Lord Shiva interceded by throwing himself under her feet, awakened the minds of many readers to the plight of the illiterate and downtrodden. He stressed that superstitious sacrifices and primitive beliefs will end only if people have correct information and that reason must temper traditional beliefs.

"This responsibility lies not in the hands of the government alone but in the hands of every royal subject with any civic sense," he wrote, emphasizing self-reliance. His readers agreed and wrote to the paper, demanding immediate action to end such butchery.

Guy introduced him to American readers as a "Westernized Indian guru."

The Rising Sun, a weekly published from Boston, offered Bir a regular column to write on "Eastern Thought for the Western Mind."

"Do you know what impact your articles are having on American youths?" Guy asked during his next visit.

"Good, I hope."

"Your articles on Indian rural life have inspired schoolchildren in Michigan to compassionate acts. They collect nickels and dimes to help unfortunate and mistreated children in India. The very fact that you stress awareness, understanding, goodwill, and civic responsibility is good for all children. Let's hope that they will build a future free of wars."

After the war ended in November 1918, Bir emerged as a spokesperson for the disillusioned and the deprived. Schools and colleges in Delhi invited him to speak to their students about developing faith, self-reliance, and instilling the sense of civic responsibility in all, irrespective of age or learning. His fame spread to other large cities as a nonconformist, stressing truth and questioning suppressive traditional values.

"Good Heavens!" Bir wrote Guy in 1921, realizing that recognition is easier to attain at home if you first obtain it abroad. "You changed my life. You gave me new directions. You taught me that 'if a man is given a fish, he will eat for a day, but if he is taught to fish, he will eat for a lifetime.' You taught me the power of the pen."

After the establishment of the new university in Delhi in 1922, Bir became a frequent visitor to its campus. Because of his knowledge of Sanskrit and theology, he became a special lecturer at the university the following year.

West Meets East

"Even the visit of the Prince of Wales was boycotted by the Indians," the viceroy's chief secretary thumped the commissioner's table. "Is Gandhi's civil disobedience movement making the Britain Lion weak? Are we becoming lame? We must do something!" He shook his clenched fist.

"But what can we do, sir?" Mumford said meekly. "Hartals are everywhere."

"Quite right, Mumford, quite right," Commissioner Gait said thoughtfully. "We have to do something to maintain order. We need new ways to deal with this situation. Gandhi's idea of deliberate law violations and the courting of arrests by the thousands took us by surprise. His political activities in South Africa should have forewarned us. I tend to agree with Caesar when he said, 'Know thy enemy.'"

"Yes, sir."

"We must understand the people we govern. We must understand them politically, culturally, intellectually, and above all—spiritually. Yes, spiritually. Gandhi's movement has spiritual undertones." He became quiet for a while. "By the way, is the new ICS batch ready for orientation? Please find out. Then invite the Sanskrit scholar from Delhi to conduct the seminars."

"And which subjects do we request—"

"When I was at Cambridge, the lectures on reincarnation and karma interested many," Gait said, aware of his privileged upbringing.

On the day of the lectures, the neatly suited officers, with their well-scrubbed sunburned faces, sat and looked vacantly at the casually attired dark-complexioned Bir seated in front of the auditorium. Commissioner Gait, standing at the lectern in his starched blue suit, white shirt, and stripped Cambridge tie, looked every bit the officer in charge. He introduced Bir Dharma as a dynamic, self-educated king's loyal subject who succeeded in attracting Western attention to Eastern culture. "What you share with us today will assist us to appreciate Indian culture more, promote goodwill and understanding, and maintain peace in the empire."

Bir greeted them with the usual Indian gesture. "Namaste," he said, with a slight bow of his head. "Do you know what this means?"

Blond-haired Gait came to their rescue. "It means the spirit within me greets the spirit within you," he said and smiled, proud of his cosmopolitanism.

Bir nodded and looked at the expressionless faces. "I know a discussion is sometimes more interesting than a formal presentation, particularly with young people. So let's discuss Hinduism's core beliefs today. Please feel free to interrupt when you have questions."

They just sat and wondered what mumbo jumbo he was going to share.

"The term 'Hindu' can be a misnomer. It's a term used by ancient Persians to refer to the people who lived east of the river Sindhu, the present-day Indus. The Persians changed the *S* to an *H*. This is the origin of the term 'Hindu.'"

He then paused. He wanted participation, but as there was none, he continued. "With time, 'Hinduism' became a collective term for various beliefs, philosophies, ideas, customs, rituals, and sects. It accepts all forms of worship—as long as they develop the eternal soul."

"The soul? Develop the eternal soul?" one asked.

"Yes. Develop the eternal human soul or Atman."

"But how can soul be eternal when God first breathed life into man after making him out of clay? Wasn't the breath the soul? Wasn't that the beginning of the soul?"

"To a Hindu, Atman always existed. Lord Krishna said in the *Bhagavad-Gita* that 'there was never a time when he or we didn't exist, nor is there any future in which we shall cease to be.'"

"Lord Krishna?"

"Yes, a divine incarnate—like Jesus Christ. The *Bhagavad-Gita* tells us that when goodness grows weak, when evil increases, God returns 'to destroy sin of the sinner, to establish righteousness.'"

"Like the Second Coming?"

"Yes."

They looked at one another.

"My soul always existed?" an officer said, pointing at his heart.

"Yes. Your soul not only exists now, in this world, in this universe, but it existed in other universes, where there were other suns and moons."

"What happens when I die?" another asked.

"At death, when the body dies, the changeless Atman passes into another kind of body."

"What happens when one doesn't die but gets killed?"

"Lord Krishna said that the Atman can't be wounded by weapons, burned by fire, dried by the wind, or wetted by water. It is deathless eternal."

"If the soul doesn't change, what does?"

"Gross matter and mind change."

"What is eternity?"

"Eternity is the absence of time."

"How does one know? Did sons of God or angels reveal such beliefs?"

"These spiritual discoveries were realized by ancient sages through introspection. They lived around 1500 to 500 BC. These discoveries are infinite and eternal. They always existed. Sages who developed knowledge of God realized them. They were first transmitted orally and then committed to writing."

The officers became quiet until Gambino, who was attending the seminars along with Angelo and Julius, asked why truths differ from culture to culture, from nation to nation.

"Eternal truths are the same. Only sages call them by different names," Bir replied.

"Why do some declare their faith to be the only true faith?" Gambino asked.

"This is due to egoism that originates in ignorance. If God is unknowable to our limited and fallible minds, how can we claim ours to be the only, the absolute? If we are to be humble in the face of God, how can we impose our faith on others as it being the only?"

Bir studied the faces of the young officers. "What will happen if every religion claims to be the only true religion? Won't there be fanaticism, extremism, unrest, and wars?"

"Tell us about another eternal truth," Gait requested, anxious to prevent any unpleasant arguments.

"Another eternal truth is that the universe comes from the Unborn, and unto it, the universe periodically returns, to manifest again, at another period. The gross matter of this universe goes back to the finer state, remains there, and then manifests. This wavelike motion is eternal. Creation, or energy, is eternal—without beginning, without end."

"So God, soul, and creation are without beginning and without end?" Gambino asked. During the past years, he had learned enough of Eastern philosophy to dispel his conviction that Hindus are idol-worshipping pagans.

"Yes," Bir replied. "Eternal soul takes on a body and begins its spiritual journey towards salvation."

"Why does the soul manifest?" Gambino asked.

"It manifests due to ignorance. Ignorance here means the soul seeking identity as a separate self."

Mumford looked toward Gait and pointed to his watch. Gait nodded.

"Perhaps Professor Dharma would like to talk about the belief of karma and rebirth. After all, according to Matthew, Jesus did tell his three closest disciples that John the Baptist is actually an incarnation of the prophet Elijah."

Karma and Rebirth

"What Jesus said about the prophet Elijah makes the eternal and profound law of karma and rebirth more fascinating to us," Bir began. "I'm glad we can respectfully point to the commonalities between the teachings of Krishna, Buddha, and Jesus."

Commonalities? Gambino thought. *Why must we always talk about commonalities? Why can't Christ's teachings be treated as exceptional?*

"*Karma* is a Sanskrit word," Bir said. "It means 'to do' or 'to make.' Karma and rebirth is cause and effect. Karma is latent rebirth. You and I create causes. We are the result of what we think and do. According to Apostle Matthew, Jesus taught us that a 'good tree bringeth forth good fruit, but a corrupt tree bringeth forth evil fruit.' Here I equate 'good tree' with 'good thought and deed.' We, through our own karma, make our own future."

"It's similar to what Apostle Paul preached: 'Whosoever a man soweth that shall he reap,'" Gait interjected.

"Yes, yes," Gambino agreed excitedly.

"I would like to add that an English scientist discovered that every action has a reaction that is equal and opposite," Gait said lightheartedly.

Bir looked at Gait and thought for a while. "The law of karma is neither Hindu nor Buddhist. Universal laws don't belong to a particular culture or religion. They belong to humanity. We can understand this law best from the spiritual point of view. Spiritually, it's the law of moral retribution. One who acts experiences the effects."

"That which ye sow ye reap," Angelo added.

"The law of retribution?" the officer seated in the front asked.

"Yes, and to prove this law, we must understand that consciousness evolves through effort. It climbs from plane to plane. Beyond the intellect is intuition. Intuition is knowledge that originates from mind's reflection on itself."

"I have been told that I don't have intuition," an officer muttered and crossed his legs.

"We all have intuition," Bir said. "It may be dormant in most of us, but we can awaken it with the right effort. 'Seek and ye shall find, knock and it shall be opened to you,' Jesus said. At first, it will illuminate the seeker's intellect with flashes of understanding. Our consciousness will evolve and make us realize that this law is true."

"What does 'right effort' mean?" the officer without intuition asked.

"Here 'right effort' means quiet meditation, deep study, and constant, daily awareness and application of the law. Please remember that no one will prove to us that this law is true. We have to do it ourselves."

They listened, and their interest grew.

"If I speak with evil thoughts, pain will result," Bir said. "If I speak with pure thoughts, happiness will result. These results—good or bad—will follow me."

"So karma rewards good and punishes bad," Gambino said. *Karma*

"No. Karma doesn't reward or punish. We do, with our own thoughts and acts. Once a Christian missionary told me at Calcutta University that God doesn't send us to hell, we go to hell and burn ourselves because of our unworthiness."

"What separates the cause from the effect?" Gait wanted to know.

"Time separates cause from effect."

Gambino glanced at the attentive faces around him. He wondered what else Bir had learned from Christians. "Please go on," he urged.

"Since we are what we think and do, we are the result of our thoughts. We are thus karmic units. Karmic imprints collectively attain self-consciousness. This consciousness creates body or form, meaning and sense. Sense creates contact. Contact causes feeling. Feeling causes desire. Unfulfilled desire for earthly existence produces rebirth."

"Good God! This chap makes sense!" someone cried in disbelief.

Bir paused. He wondered how they would react to what he would say next. He continued, "At rebirth, the returning Atman chooses its own parents and body that it has earned or deserves. It does this to work out its unfulfilled desires. Mark my words: we choose our own parents."

"Does rebirth imply predestination or fatalism . . . 'whatever will be, will be'?" Gait asked.

"No. Since we can control our thoughts, we can control our own future. We may be slaves of our past, but we are masters of our future. What other spiritual law can be more optimistic? What other law gives us the power to shape our own future?"

"Where does the soul go after it leaves the human body?" asked one.

Bir looked at him and smiled. "This very question was posed to Lord Buddha. He answered it by blowing out a candle as if to ask, 'Where did the flame go?'"

"What is destiny?" someone asked.

"Destiny is decided in the past, before you are born. You can't control or influence that. For instance, you destiny is to be English. You can't change that. But you can use your free will to decide your present actions and, thus, your future. Karma is controllable."

"Does rebirth ever end?" Gambino asked.

"Yes. Rebirth ends when earthly desires end. The illusion that had caused separation of the individual self from the Ultimate Self also ends."

Gait looked toward the priests. "Didn't Christ say that only he who gives away his very life shall find it?"

They nodded.

"I can appreciate the law of karma. But the concept of rebirth is very foreign to me," another officer said.

"Then look around you. The law of rebirth is self-evident in nature. You can observe it in the law of cycles or in the law of periodicity. Witness the rhythmic ocean tide flowing in and out or the cyclical seasons of the year. Note that night follows day, rest follows activity," Bir said.

They looked at him and listened. He felt their energy, their intensity, and their inquisitiveness. After all, they were the best of Great Britain, sent to administer India.

"The adventure of death and rebirth continues, each life teaching us lessons. Finally, after countless experiences of life, with the right effort and understanding, we reach enlightenment—the realization that the individual self and the Ultimate Self are the same."

"What happens when one takes wrong turns and doesn't evolve spiritually?" Gambino asked.

"Spiritual progress may not be consistent, of course. Yes, it is possible for a character to undo his accumulated merit of good actions in one lifetime. If this happens, the spiritual journey begins again, for eternity is at its disposal."

"Is it possible for the soul to manifest in animal form?" Julius asked.

"Spiritual progress is achieved spirally. Descend is also spiral. But once consciousness attains human level, there is no return to animal forms."

"Why can't we remember our past lives?" Angelo asked.

"We don't remember past lives because memory is a faculty of the mind and not of the brain. Each new body has its own temporal brain. However, there have been many in recorded history who, due to their developed spirituality, have recalled past lives." Bir paused, expecting questions about recent newspaper reports of past life recollections in the Punjab.

"Forgetting past lives is actually merciful," he said. "For instance, even today, we would prefer not to remember our bad acts of yesterday. As civil service officers, wouldn't you like to remember only the good that you did in India as you grow old in England someday trout fishing?"

There was laughter in the auditorium at Bir's concluding remarks. The three priests approached him to introduce themselves. "Perhaps you would like to visit Mission Ikonpur," Gambino said. "Your lectures today have convinced me that we have much to discuss about the commonalities between different faiths."

Bir agreed.

Yoga

"How long have you experienced wheezing and shortness of breath, Father?" Dr. Donley of Bombay Civil Hospital asked Julius.

"I'm sorry, but I don't remember."

"Was it before or after King Edward VIII abdicated the throne?"

"I think it was before Christmas, just after the monsoons."

"Yes, of course. I reached India on October 12, 1936, two months before the abdication. So you had breathing difficulty for the last six months. Were you prescribed asthma medication?"

Julius shook his head. He appeared tired, even confused. Besides, he didn't sleep well the previous nights. He missed his old friend Prakash who died of pneumonia during the rainy season. He, however, was thankful that he saw the market school develop into the mission school—as he had hoped.

"We have so much to be grateful for," Gambino wrote in his journal. "I witnessed the unconditional love and support of a Hindu who demonstrated Christian virtue. Due to Prakash's charity, we have twenty-four students enrolled in the school."

Julius now relied more and more on Gambino though he kept some duties—like holding Mass and Baptism for himself. For reasons he knew best, he often urged Gambino to translate a few more Bible stories. Christ's calling to "make disciples of all nations" appeared to weigh heavily on him.

Twelve years after their first meeting, Gambino received an invitation from Bir to attend a seminar on "truth is the offspring of meditation" at Bombay University. Over the years, their pen pal relationship developed into a close friendship.

After Bir's presentation, Gambino spoke with him about Julius. "He suffers from asthma and allergies. The anti-inflammatory medications haven't helped. I wonder if emotions are the cause."

"Doctors may misdiagnose a stuffy nose or wheezing to be symptoms of cold or flu," Bir said. "I remember wheezing in Calcutta years ago. A yogi told me to examine my breathing and learn to breathe correctly. And when I did that regularly for three months, my wheezing stopped."

"Breathe correctly?"

"If you learn to breathe correctly, the life force that is in the air, or *prana*, will give all the energy you need. A yogi uses *prana* to improve his health, mind, and emotions. You see, very powerful forces remain dormant within us. We are unaware of them. But many of our physical ailments or imbalances can be cured by awakening these forces with yoga exercises."

"What types of illnesses can yoga cure?"

"Poor circulation, nervousness, tiredness, irritability, shortness of breath, and wheezing are the ones I'm most familiar with. Daily yoga exercises can also improve health and increase peace of mind. I'm proof of that."

At day's end, Bir accompanied Gambino to Mission Ikonpur.

"Yoga my way to better health without medication? Isn't yoga a Hindu folklore?" Julius asked.

"Is gravity a Christian folklore because Newton discovered it?" Bir joked. "You yourself said that faith is within all of us and that all we need to do is stir it. No, yoga isn't a Hindu folklore."

"What is it then?"

"It's a process or means to attain power and control over body and mind. It helps the brain and makes it more alert. Energy is produced by intense physical and mental effort. You can master your body through physical postures and increase the ability to concentrate through mental techniques. As I told Father Gambino, you can learn to control breath though breathing techniques."

"He thinks your asthma and wheezing can be controlled through yoga breathing," Gambino said.

"Well, I guess I have tried everything else," Julius said. "Go ahead, Professor, tell me what to do then."

"When you awake in the morning, remain in bed in the sleeping position that you find yourself. Observe how you are breathing for a minute or two. Concentrate with eyes closed. Don't let other thoughts enter your mind. They can wait for a few minutes. Most people take ten to fifteen breaths per minute while in a lying position. Then rise slowly. Don't jump out of bed. Keep wearing the same loose sleeping attire. And before shaving or any other activity, do the following exercises:

"Stand straight and relaxed on a rug or soft piece of cloth. Keep the rug for future use. Don't use it for anything else. Face east, towards the rising sun. Inhale a sharp, quick, forceful, and deep breath through the nostril, while pushing out your abdomen with your abdominal muscles. Hold for a second. Then exhale forcefully, through the nostril, contracting the abdomen quickly. Repeat ten times. Then pause. These forceful inhaling and exhaling may be noisy in the beginning. Don't let it worry you.

"Now do the same inhaling and exhaling, but do them very slowly and gently. As you inhale slowly, pushing out your abdomen, start expending your chest. You will notice your stomach contracting automatically. Slowly raise your arms simultaneously above your head as you inhale gently until your palms touch each other. Hold your breath for five seconds. Then exhale very slowly, lowering your arms to your sides at the same time. Control the exhalation and don't let the air rush out. Pause for a moment and then begin the sharp, forceful inhalation-exhalation exercise. After repeating ten times, do the slower one again. Repeat the whole exercise five times.

"Father Julius, if you do this exercise for a few months, your wheezing will gradually lessen."

Cyclones

"God cursed this province again," the exhausted volunteer said as he sat on the edge of a cot in a refugee shelter late that evening. He puffed on a cigarette to lessen the stench of the rotting dead animals around him. He was grateful when the breeze gradually changed directions and blew toward the sea.

For the previous three days, relief workers visited shelter after shelter, distributing food and medicine. Nearly a week ago, a cyclone destroyed the lives of hundreds of villagers on the shores of Bay of Bengal in Orrisa province.

It hit the region when Bir was visiting the Bhubaneswar temples. Just before he left Delhi on his pilgrimage, secrecy was engulfing the new capital. No one seemed to know when it would happen. But many were certain that if Germany invaded Poland, Great Britain and France would come to her defense. And India will be affected.

"I have never seen such misery, such destruction," Gambino said. He joined the Catholic Relief Mission to do his part to alleviate the suffering. "Dozens of corpses washed ashore, still lying there, bloating and decaying! In my dreams, I hear them cry for proper burial."

"We had a similar storm three years ago," the cigarette smoker said. "Even then the temple priests refused to help in gathering the dead for cremation. They just sat on the temple steps with their sleeked parted hair and watched, indifferent, aloof. Why don't they help?"

"I don't know why these disasters occur, but I know they are not God's punishment," Bir said. He was sitting on a three-legged wooden stool that a relief worker found half buried in the sandy beach with other household articles. "I just can't find satisfaction in explaining anything that we don't understand to be God's doing. But I know why the temple priests don't help."

"Why?"

"Because these corpses are those of low-caste fishermen. They think they don't have to get involved. They believe they are superior."

"But dead bodies are just corpses! They are neither Brahmins nor Sudras," the smoker said and coughed as he lit another cigarette.

"Of course they are. And the temple priests must understand this," Bir said. "We must convince people like them to volunteer and get involved in their community. Only then will our society change for the better. People must see civic duty as moral duty."

"And this is what Hindus can learn from Christian missionaries," Gambino blurted out, moved by what he saw. "We are all children of God. We are all equal before him."

He paused, looked down, and drew a circle in the sand with his toe. "Don't misunderstand me. I know charity is ingrained in Hinduism, but during the past twenty years I have been in India, I haven't met many who are willing to discuss solutions to this type of indifference."

"I agree," another volunteer said. "Many Hindus justify the caste system. They claim that castes are in every religion, in every society, and they say this with so much conviction that others follow."

"I find Hinduism to be introspective and profound, but I think its essence is too complicated for the common man," Gambino said. "Once a Hindu told me that old age, sickness, and death are caused by birth and that birth lies in the process of becoming, set in motion by desire. His friend said that self-awareness means becoming one with the universe. Becoming one with the universe? Can ordinary people understand such esoteric aphorisms? Can they apply them in daily life?"

"Yes," the volunteer said and nodded his head. "Hinduism can be confusing. I had a similar experience when a man told me that creation is *Lila*—the divine, rhythmic, and endless play in which Brahman transforms into the world. Such concepts are very interesting, but how do they help us to live good, practical lives and cremate bloating corpses?"

There were no answers in the refugee shelter. They were tired.

"Where will you go from here, Padre?" a relief worker said.

"My superiors have asked me to show these homeless how to frame houses and build septic systems. Then, if the bishop permits, I'll visit the orphanages in Calcutta and meet Father Kenny. But if war breaks out, my plans may change. I may be asked to perform other duties."

"Everything your church does is so well planned and organized!" Bir exclaimed. "This is your strength."

"Yes, and with organization, there can be unified and meaningful effort to deal with catastrophes. It can also generate order, purpose, and direction. This is why the faraway Roman Catholic Church can be here today."

Bishop's Orphanage

"The Indian Congress Party is disassociating itself from the war," Father Kenny informed Gambino. "When the war began in September 1939, the Indian government joined the British in declaring war without the consent of Congress. So Congress won't support the war efforts. But it will if India is promised independence when victory is gained."

"What will happen if Germany overruns Western Europe?" Gambino asked. "I'm sure Congress will cooperate." He was visiting Calcutta after the cyclone to assist Kenny build an orphanage in the Himalayan foothills.

"Congress said it would. But my main concern now is Japanese advances. They may enter Malaya and then turn west towards Mandalay and Rangoon. They may next try to cross the Indo-Burmese border and grab the oil-rich Brahmaputra valley."

They looked at each other, uncertain of their next step to spread Christianity to the remote and thinly populated frontier of northeast India.

"Bishop Le Mans has informed me that our mission work should continue even if the Japanese invade Assam. Many separate and independent tribes live in this region. They speak different dialects. Christianity has found them at last, and I'm happy to say that they have opened their hearts to Jesus."

Gambino listened. A slight smile crossed his bearded face. His eyes sparkled. *Soon I'll be an important instrument in spreading Christ's love to this new frontier,* he thought.

"Since you expressed interest in working in the mountainous regions, Le Mans suggests you visit the Gauhati Mission and work with Father Nongrim Hilly. He is a son of the soil and knows the region very well. Then you proceed northeast towards Tinsukia and Ledo to build Catholic orphanages. This region has large tea plantations, and most of their illiterate laborers need spiritual guidance."

"Le Mans, Le Mans, I have heard that name before. Is he the one who served with Monsignor Christopher Becker?"

"Yes."

"Did he once save him from drowning in a river during the monsoons?"

"Yes. He is the one. In fact, there are many interesting stories about his youth. Abandoned in Dijon as a child, he survived on his own, first in the streets and then in the orphanages. Once he was hit on his head that almost killed him. He claims that when he was unconscious, he saw bright lights and felt no pain. But when he became conscious, he experienced severe pain. A priest told him that the bright lights were callings from Christ. This changed his life. Priesthood became his mission. He came to India more than forty years ago and been here ever since, completely dedicated to Christ's work."

"I respect such faith and dedication."

"I do too. Because of ones like him, Christianity will continue to spread in this region. And you, Father Gambino, you will play an important part. I see that in you. You will leave your mark for future generations to admire and follow."

Father Nongrim Hilly

Gambino stood in front of the Gauhati Mission building with its white walls and corrugated iron roof. He then walked toward the nearby shores of the Brahmaputra and marveled at its width.

"This waterway will make it possible for us to go northeast and spread the Bible, even in the remote, unadministered areas," Father Hilly said, joining him.

"And we will be the few of the very first, very first missionaries in this region, wouldn't we, Father Hilly?" Gambino said, remembering Father Kenny's prediction.

"Father Gambino, did you know that in the 1830s, early British explorers like Major Jankins invited American Baptist missionaries to these hills? But until the 1870s, there weren't any significant growth in missionary activities. In the early years, relationship between the American Baptist Mission and the British authorities wasn't the best. By the 1920s, the missionaries became so influential that the British were unable to expel them."

"Why expel missionaries?"

"Because they felt Christianity would destroy traditional, native culture."

"Destroy native culture?"

"Well, you see, Father, native culture did get targeted. The Baptists, for instance, prohibited rice beer. They forbade singing and dancing. They encouraged Western dress and adoption of English. They banned everything traditional. In fact, they went so far as to demand that the converts renounce and despise their heathen neighbors."

Gambino became silent. He was sure Jesus didn't teach hatred or arrogance. "Jesus taught us to love our neighbor and—"

"Yes, yes." Hilly led him nearer to the edge of the steep bank. "See, the water is flowing west, but we will be going east," he said excitedly. They listened to the soothing sound of the ripples. "Isn't this a beautiful view, Father? But when the rains begin, this view will be different." Hilly stepped closer to the edge. "Anyway, when Catholic missionaries arrived later, they took a more relaxed approach. They didn't condemn traditional songs or beer."

"Where were the Hindus all this time? Didn't they try to draw these people into the mainstream of Hindu life?"

"Don't you know? Hindus don't try to convert anyone by approaching them as we Christians do. They wait for non-Hindus to come to them. And if they accept anyone as converts, they offer them low-caste status. Besides, converts are not considered equal to the ones who are born into Hindu families."

"This then creates opportunities for us to spread the mission?"

"Yes, it does. We offer converts equality and security in Christ's love, forgiveness, and salvation in place of tribal religious beliefs in spirits who can be impulsive and punitive," he said. "We also offer them education and modernity. We offer them freedom from other traditional obligations."

"Traditional obligations?"

"These are communal tasks—like farming and gathering crops—which every villager performs. If such an obligation falls on the Sabbath, they are asked not to perform them. Missionaries have taught converts to question the traditional authority of elders or chiefs."

"How else have we helped them?"

"With modern medicine. In fact, painkillers like morphine are associated with the new Christian God. So the village shamans are no longer needed and are losing their importance and influence. Very soon this whole region will be Christian."

"And Christ's work will be done. But how did Christianity establish such a strong foothold?"

Hilly thought for a while and grinned. "I give credit to the clever translation of the scriptures to native tongues. The translators first found commonalities between the teachings of the Bible and traditional native beliefs to include in the sermons. This had great impact. For instance, there is a tribal belief in a great fire ending the world. It's similar to the biblical Day of Judgment. Another tribal belief is that good and bad lives receive different rewards in the next life, similar to our heaven-hell belief."

Gambino's mind flashed back to his days of translating Bible stories. He now appreciated the importance of translating simply the complex theological concepts for the common people.

"Our mission builds schools and provides teachers. These in turn supply the British with needed clerical functionaries. The conversion to Christianity also gave birth to a strong pan-tribal identity to solidarity. Of course, solidarity existed before due to frequent contacts between different villages."

Lord, this is wonderful! I'm finally in the new frontier, Gambino thought.

"The schools train hundreds of tribal youths from different communities. The use of English as a common language also gave impetus to the pan-tribal concept."

"Is it easier to build mission schools and orphanages in these parts of India?" Gambino asked, thinking about St. Paul establishing more than twenty churches before his martyrdom.

"We will soon find out. All I can say now is that many Christian meeting places have been established in the last twenty years."

By the summer of 1942, the Japanese advanced as far as the Indo-Burmese border, but life continued uninterrupted in the misty hills and green valleys of Assam.

Father Gambino soon came to be known as "Bicycle Padre" for his tireless work. In this region of few roads, he rode his bicycle from village to village, from plantation to plantation. He raised funds from tea planters to buy *Bible Story* books for the orphans who had never seen books before. He taught them personal hygiene and that a white-skinned stranger is no one to hide from.

Gradually, the people of the region accepted him and looked to him to cure their illnesses.

At the end of the war in 1945, the *Delhi Times* published an article on Christian missionaries in Assam and about Father Gambino in particular. "Our mission is to spread Christ's love. This means caring and helping all to develop faith and strengthen hope," he was quoted as saying at his benediction during the dedication of the war memorial in Kohima.

British Raj

"Halt! Who goes there? Friend or foe?" Constable Aga Khan thundered.

He was standing guard at the main gate to the dimly lit police compound. His starched khaki uniform and steel helmet symbolized the discipline, strength, and power of the British Raj. He held a high-power Springfield rifle with fixed bayonet close to his wide chest, ready to spring into action. This drilled, booming command of a police sentry, particularly at a place where locals dared not to tread after dark, was enough to startle anyone.

Gambino, however, was used to it. He has been in this subdivision for four years now. "Friend," he shouted back as he dismounted from his creaky bicycle with its barely luminous kerosene headlamp. The moon was peeping through the dark monsoon clouds as the trilling crickets announced possible showers. The soft moonlight illuminated the manicured parade grounds of the station with rows of whitewashed barracks.

A bright beam of light from a battery-powered torch fell on his face and body. It revealed the white-robed intruder riding a rusty bicycle without a mudguard in the dark hours of a late humid evening not to be an enemy of the empire.

"Oh, it's you, Padre. Come in. Join me for a glass of lemonade," a voice welcomed him.

Deputy Superintendent of Police Bob Swanson was sitting comfortably on a chair near the heavy wooden door of the reinforced concrete station. He had his feet resting on a table and was holding a flashlight in one hand and a cigarette in the other. A bottle and a glass were on the table. Constable Prem Bahadur, wearing a red turban, was standing behind him, fanning the sahib to keep away mosquitoes, moths, and other bothersome insects.

"Prem Bahadur, get a chair for Padre Sahib." Gambino accepted but sat on the edge of the chair so that Swanson would notice that he was in a hurry.

"I'm in a hurry too, Padre. I'm almost done for the day. Just waiting for Inspector Komoleswar Dattani to arrive and take charge for the night," Swanson said while thinking about his regular evening shots of old Scotch whiskey—distilled, blended, and bottled in Scotland before being shipped to the colonies—a drink much coveted by British officers in India serving the king and empire.

Scotch whiskey was believed to be medicinal. Besides calming the nerves after a long day in His Majesty's service under the unforgiving Indian sun, it also fought off dysentery—or so they say.

"Bob, I want to report another death due to smallpox. This time it occurred on Ledo Road. The body is in the hospital morgue waiting doctor's confirmation," Gambino reported. Swanson listened but didn't say a word. He continued puffing his cigarette and sipping his lemonade.

"The dead man leaves behind a young son. He has no known kin. With the subdivisional officer's approval, we can admit the youngster to the orphanage."

"One more beggar to feed, one more," he said finally as he unsteadily got up to leave. "Add him to your flock, Padre, and save the bugger's soul also. Fill out the necessary forms with the inspector. He is a fine officer. You know, he has just been awarded the prestigious Indian Police Medal by Viceroy Lord Wavell for apprehending Welcott, a murderous American GI at the risk of his own life. Justly deserved, I say, justly deserved. Besides, he knows the local customs. He will take care of you. As for me, I'm done for the day. Oh, if you would like to join me later for a drink, please do. I'll be at my quarters."

"Thank you, Bob. But I don't have much time this evening."

"That's right! You chaps don't drink whiskey. You missionaries like wine, particularly Italian. Sorry, old boy, but I don't have anything from Milan."

Dattani helped Gambino fill out the forms. Manu became a ward of the mission until he comes of age. Then the title of the plot of land will be transferred to him.

"Thank you, Inspector. I have one more request: would you please post a constable to guard the boy's hut so that the villagers don't torch it when they find out that the old man died?"

The monsoon clouds displayed their magnificence and majesty with lightning and thunder as Gambino paddled his way through the storm to the mission church with its white steeple and statues to pray with his orphans.

PART G

Papaya

MANU'S QUIET WAIT that late afternoon came to an end, not because of the arrival of the bearded man, but because of Gopal. At a distance, he could see his friend racing toward him, wearing his usual short pants and white sleeveless vest. He had with him a small bundle wrapped in a piece of cloth.

"Is it true? Is it true?" he heard him cry.

"Yes, it is," Manu replied calmly as if he had become more mature than he was the last time they met.

"Why? When? Were you going to tell me before you left?" He was out of breath.

"Of course I was. You are my friend. But tell me, how did you know? I haven't told anyone nor have I left the yard. Only Bicycle Padre and a policeman were here."

"So it's true!" Gopal was disappointed. "You are going away with the sahib."

There was an awkward moment as they stared at each other. Emotions overcame them—youthful emotions that they couldn't verbalize. Suddenly they embraced each other and held on so tightly that they could feel the pounding of the other's heart.

When they finally loosened themselves, Gopal handed him the papaya he was carrying.

"My mother picked it today. It's the largest of the bunch and the most ripened."

Manu looked at the golden papaya. "This is nice. You know, Gopal, of all the gifts my father gave me, the best one is his hope that I would know more than he did." His friend made no reply.

"Say, Manu, aren't you afraid to go away with him? I would be if I was you."

"I was very afraid when my father was dying. I was so afraid that I couldn't even put water in his dry mouth. I wished Rumi was here." He dried his eyes with the back of his left hand. "Then something happened. A bearded stranger came to my house to help my father. He told me not to be afraid. And when my father died, he said I could go and live in his school for boys—if I wanted to. So now I'm not as afraid." After a pause, he murmured, "What else can I do?"

"Yesterday, the policeman told my father that your house will be used as a storehouse by Agarwala—the rice merchant," Gopal said.

Manu said nothing. He tried to stop sobbing.

"Weren't you afraid to sleep alone in the room where your father died?" Gopal went on. "Didn't you see his ghost? Didn't he scare you? Many in our village say it won't leave for twenty-one days, for it's confused and doesn't know when to leave."

"No, I didn't see his ghost. But every time I woke feeling cold and hungry, I heard sounds coming from the darker parts of the house. On the first night, I kept my eyes closed and my head covered. But as I got used to the sounds, I peeped often. I didn't see a ghost. By the way, what does it look like? How will I know if I see one?"

"I don't know," Gopal said.

"Bicycle Padre said my father went to heaven to be with God Jesus. I don't know what it means when he said that Jesus is our only savior for eternal life. Will you ask your father what it means?"

"If I ask my father, and if he doesn't know, he will be embarrassed. Then he will get angry. Every time he drinks that smelly rice beer, he gets angry. We have to be very quiet then. Otherwise he beats my brother and me. Last week, when I wanted to come and see you, he slapped my face so hard that my nose bled. I couldn't see properly with my left eye for a long time. Even my mother is afraid of him."

After listening to his friend, he went inside his hut and returned with a small rusty metallic container. In it were two blue glass marbles. "You keep them," he said. "I don't want them anymore."

"Aren't these the ones you won from me the last time we played?"

The two friends sat close to each other, their shoulders touching and wondered what they should discuss next. They were so engrossed in thoughts that they hardly noticed Father Gambino enter the yard.

Manu at the Orphanage

"The first few weeks may be difficult, Manu. You will see many new things, but slowly you will adjust and learn. You will be fine," Gambino assured him.

For the first time in his life, Manu saw bunk beds, books, tables, chairs, and bookshelves. He saw boys studying and playing in groups. He noticed that no one ate meals on banana leaves or slept on floors. They rose at the same time every morning and prayed together like one large family. He too wanted to be a member of the family but soon realized that he was trading his simple and free life for one of discipline and purpose.

The boys between six and nine slept near the entrance to the large dormitory while the older ones slept at the rear. There were three classes in the school. Mrs. Simpson taught the boys from six to nine. Mrs. Pinto who recently joined the mission taught the ones between ten to thirteen years. Father Fresno taught the older boys, while Father Hilly did church work. Father Gambino taught gardening and carpentry and appeared to be everywhere at the same time.

There was only one orphan above sixteen, and he was learning to be a carpenter. Every time anything wooden needed fixing, Tubull Thomas was there to fix it. Gambino introduced Manu to him and said that he was now approaching the age when he was almost ready to support himself. Besides, he could read, write, and do arithmetic—the skills very necessary in life. He knew how to measure and calculate how much wood he would need to fix the broken fence around the mission, which was about three miles from the tributary.

"Mending the fence is very important," Tubull told Manu. "It keeps the boys within the compound and prevents wandering cows and goats from eating the vegetables we grow."

There was a very old teak in the mission yard. Underneath that tree was the grave of Father Balawan, the founder of the orphanage.

"Father Balawan was a Benedictine monk," Father Fresno once told Tubull. "He loved the simple people of India. He studied *Vedanta* and the *Upanishads* and meditated with two Hindu ascetics under this teak. No one can recall when he first arrived, but some say that he followed the footsteps of Apostle Thomas who brought Christianity to India nearly nineteen hundred years ago. He was always happy and contented. He followed his own bliss. He understood the true meaning of Christ's sayings: 'Blessed are you poor, blessed are you that mourn, blessed are you that are hungry,' and 'Come unto me, all ye that labor and are heavy laden, and I will give you rest.'"

Initially, Manu was placed with the ten—to thirteen-year-olds, but when Mrs. Pinto realized that he needed much individual attention and tutoring, he was moved to Mrs. Simpson's class that had fewer students. Manu did what he was told to do, for he didn't know anything about placements.

Mrs. Simpson gave him a lot of attention. She understood his situation and challenges of the new environment. More than twenty years ago, she herself was in a similar situation when she married Colonial Officer Henry Simpson who chose India for His Majesty's civil service.

Manu paid attention in class and worked diligently, though his mind wondered sometimes when he thought of his father, his sister, and Gopal. But he wanted to please Mrs. Simpson who was kind and patient. He was always the first to volunteer when the blackboard needed wiping or when the potted rose plants needed watering.

Mrs. Simpson loved growing roses in her classroom to teach her students about the three seasons of the year. Besides, it became a hobby for her after her husband disappeared mysteriously about twelve years ago while on a hunting trip to the Himalayas. She decided to live and teach in India. She was one of those Britons who loved India deeply. She and Mrs. Pinto had their rooms next to the dormitory.

Once when he carried a rose plant to her room, he saw and heard something that he had never seen or heard before. Pleasant but strange music came out of a wooden box that had the picture of a big white dog glued to it. As his eyes were fixed on the box, Mrs. Simpson came close to him, placed her hand on his shoulder, and said, "That's a gramophone." Manu smiled. He didn't say anything, but long into that night, he wondered how music and singing could come out of a wooden box.

On another occasion when he was in her room, he noticed a large book on a small square table. It had a red cross on its hard black cover. The book appeared to be a hundred times thicker than his books.

"Go ahead, Manu, open it. Turn the pages," she urged. As he did, his eyes widened with amazement. For the first time in his life, he saw diagrams of the human anatomy.

"What is this book? Why so big and heavy?"

"It's a first aid reference book. It tells you what to do when you are hurt, injured, or sick. You see, I was a nurse during the big war. I was young then, full of energy and ideals," she said, pointing to her framed picture as a young nurse on the wall. "I wanted to help others." Noticing the puzzlement on his face, she added, "That was a long time ago. I was in England then."

As he left her room, he thought, *Mrs. Simpson knows so much. Wouldn't it have been wonderful if she were to be my mother? I could have learnt so much more.*

Within a short period, he surprised his teacher by being able to read and write simple words. He could also do addition and subtraction and soon became one of the better students in arithmetic. He often remembered his father laboriously keeping count of his money with a system of small dots and circles he devised that only he could decipher. He asked himself why his father didn't know how to count and write numbers. Didn't he have anyone to teach him?

Gandhi's Truth

The euphoria that accompanied India's independence in August 1947 dampened when millions lost their homes and became refugees for partitioning Bengal and Punjab to create Pakistan out of British India. Hundreds of thousands were massacred for religious hatred and intolerance. On January 30, 1948, Mahatma Gandhi was assassinated while leading a prayer meeting.

The editor of *Delhi Times*, Reena Lynn, sat in her third-story office with wide glass windows. She tapped her long manicured fingers nervously on her table. Her eyes were red and swollen. She, like millions of others, still wept, although the cremation was a week ago.

"So this is how we treat the father of Indian nationalism," she said to freelancer Bir Dharma. "This is how we thank our leader who led us to freedom. Our Bapu, our light, our soul, is no more. I miss the love and confidence he inspired in all of us. With him, we could have achieved anything." She wiped her tears with her white silken handkerchief. "I agree with the prime minister: there is darkness everywhere. What have we done, Bir? What are we to do now?"

He felt her emotions but didn't know how to comfort her although they were close friends for many years. He rose from his chair and walked slowly toward the windows facing south. He stared vacantly at the row of commercial buildings.

"He will always be with us," he said softly, massaging his forehead. "All we have to do is keep him in our hearts and thoughts. We must never forget him. And we will continue with his work. This will be our tribute, our gratitude to the prince of nonviolence."

She got up from her chair and stood beside him. They looked out together as if searching for something. Across the quiet street, they saw a large green banner partially draping the second floor of a building. "Long Live Gandhiji," the banner read.

"Hundreds of articles have been published about his political philosophy," she said. "But what I want for our readers is something they don't know much about. For instance, why did he become a champion for the untouchables?"

"Then we should research his lawyer's life in South Africa. After all, circumstances make the man," Bir said.

"I remember his close friend Charles Freer Andrews," Reena said. "He was a missionary. Gandhi called him 'Charlie.' He wrote one of his earliest biographies. Of course, there are other sources besides him. For instance, you can interview Mrs. Millie Polak's niece. She is currently visiting India from England. She plans to write Gandhi's biography. Millie and her husband, Henry Polak, and the Gandhi family lived together with several other families in a community farm near Johannesburg."

"Johannesburg?"

"Yes. In fact, he met many Christians in South Africa. They liked his sharp intellect and wanted him to accept Christianity. One by the name of Baker, a lawyer and an evangelical preacher, took him to their prayer meetings. And you, Bir, because of your interest in religions, you would be perfect for this assignment."

After reading Andrews's biography, Bir met Polak's niece Emily Jones.

"I'm very lucky indeed," Jones said. "I had the good fortune to meet and know him. I was twenty then and lived in a farm with Aunt Millie. He was an intellectual giant, and my aunt always wanted to convert him."

"Convert him? Why?"

"Because she believed Christianity teaches mankind's most important lesson—love. Gandhi, of course, reminded her that Hinduism also teaches the same great truth, just like Islam and Zoroastrianism."

Bir scribbled on his pad. He didn't want to miss anything of this interview.

"To me, he was greater than the greatest. He was always open to the truth, the universal truth, irrespective of source. He believed this eternal truth to be greater than the capacity of one person, one tradition, or one church to contain."

"How did he arrive at this belief?"

"He believed that though Truth is changeless, our understanding of it doesn't remain unchanged."

"Besides being described as God, what is Truth?"

"Truth is the realization of self."

"What did he say of Jesus Christ?"

"He believed that the true message of Jesus Christ is the message of love as preached in the Sermon on the Mount. This love means the absolute rejection of all forms of violence. He had no difficulty in embracing this of Jesus. In fact, many feel Christ's teaching of love operated through his practice of nonviolence."

"Love through nonviolence?"

"To him, nonviolence is a way of life based on unconditional love, respect, understanding, acceptance, and appreciation, similar to Lord Buddha's compassion."

"Did he ever think of converting?"

"He lived in South Africa from 1893 to 1915. During these years, he had extensive contact with many Christian denominations. He appreciated their goodwill and enjoyed the discussions with them. Some say that once he even contemplated embracing Christianity."

"That's interesting. Why?"

"Because Jesus Christ impressed him as a beautiful example of a perfect man. He was touched by his gentleness, his patience, his kindness, his love and forgiveness. Jesus taught his followers not to strike back when struck but to turn the other cheek. To Gandhi, this was divine."

Bir remembered his meetings with Donovan and Curren in Calcutta. They too impressed him as gentle and loving. He thought about his own feelings toward Christ's teachings.

"Is there any other reason why he didn't accept Christianity?"

"He didn't convert because he realized that Christianity didn't offer anything new that his own Hindu scriptures didn't have. So there was no need to convert. To him, truth is God, and God is not the exclusive property of one religion. Believing one to be an exclusive religion encourages arrogance, intolerance, conflicts, and torture of heretics. This is why he criticized the dogmatic claims of orthodoxy."

"Then what did he believe in?"

"He believed in the equality of all good religions. He said that God wills the salvation of all people, and as such, salvation is available in all religions. He said that Jesus called all human beings to a new life. He didn't call them to a new religion. He believed that all religions are paths to the same Truth and that nonviolence is the way to the Truth."

"Did he try to convert others to his own Hindu faith?"

"Gandhi didn't try to convert anyone to his own faith. His sincere hope was that his example would help Christians to become better Christians and Muslims to become better Muslims. He believed that a person should demonstrate his faith in deeds rather than in words. He said that when a faith is lived well, it is self-propagating. He gave the example of a rose not needing an army of missionaries to proclaim or spread its fragrance."

"Did you become a better Christian because of Gandhi?"

"Yes. I did. Many did. He pointed out what Jesus emphasized in the Gospels: 'Verily, verily, I say unto you, not every one that sayeth unto me Lord, Lord shall enter the Kingdom of Heaven, but he that doeth the will of my Father which is in Heaven shall enter the Kingdom.'"

"Was he influenced by Christ's teaching the Kingdom of Heaven?"

"Yes, but in his mind, Christ's Kingdom message suffered distortion in the West. In fact, he was the first to point out the distinction between the teachings of Christ and Western culture and civilization. He reminded us that Christ didn't preach Christianity the way we know it to be today. He often asked why Christianity is presented only from the Western point of view."

"Western point of view?"

"If Christianity is a universal religion, why is it presented in Western language and in terms of Western history and culture?"

Bir didn't attempt to answer. He continued with his interview. "What did he think would lead us to salvation?"

Jones thought for a while. "I think Gandhi believed that a life committed to serving others and changing society for the better is the way to salvation and enlightenment. He believed that service to man is service to God."

"What did he say about Hindus being converted to Christianity by missionaries?"

"He said that missionaries represent the religion of the conquerors. Conversion is a form of spiritual imperialism. Poor natives in Asia, Africa, and Latin America have been persuaded to convert to Christianity as a path of upward mobility. These people have been taught that the only path to salvation lies in the Christian religion. This form of proselytizing will only lead to unrest in the world."

"How does conversion lead to unrest?"

"Gandhi said that he heard of a Hindu who was converted to Christianity. After baptism, this man had to eat beef and drink liquor, change his clothes to European clothes, and even wear a Western hat. He then started abusing his ancestral religion and customs—even his country."

"What should a missionary do then?"

"A good missionary will realize that all religions are fundamentally equal. A good missionary, therefore, should be involved in promoting peace, justice, and values of the Kingdom, keeping in mind that such values are not exclusively Christian. A missionary should help unhappy Hindus find happiness in their own faith rather than in converting to another faith. This can be done by pointing out the best in Hinduism and asking them to live accordingly."

"What should conversion mean to me if I seek another path?"

"Gandhi said that conversion should mean you giving up the evil of old and adopting all the good of new—leading to greater self-purification."

"If he were to be alive today, what do you think he would have said to us?"

"He probably would have said that the lives of followers of all faiths would be incomplete without studying the teachings of great teachers like the Buddha and Jesus. He would have asked us to broaden our minds by their teachings instead of narrowing our hearts. He would have encouraged inner discipline through spiritual awareness."

"What did he say of women's rights?"

Emily became thoughtful. She remembered 1920 when American women were first granted suffrage by an amendment to their constitution.

"In Eastern cultures, as in other cultures, many myths were created to dominate women. Gandhi realized that as long as half the Indian population is subjugated, when their intelligence and potential are unrecognized and underutilized due to traditions, then political freedom would mean nothing to them. He, therefore, urged them to empower and unshackle themselves. He encouraged them to participate in the freedom struggle and even face imprisonment when necessary."

"What did he say about the untouchables?"

"He couldn't tolerate the inhumane treatment they suffered at the hands of the upper castes. He emphasized the dignity of menial labor. He, therefore, made all members of the Johannesburg community, including his wife, perform latrine duties. Then in India, in the late 1930s, he called for the boycott of all temples that didn't permit untouchables to worship."

"And these are the reasons why he is called the 'Mahatma'?"

"Yes. These are some of the reasons why he is called the 'Great Soul.'"

A week passed but the publication of the article didn't produce the level of interest Bir wanted. On the third week, however, he received a letter from Gambino:

"Father Kenny of Calcutta sent me a newspaper clipping of your recent article. We don't get the *Delhi Times* in upper Assam. Tinsukia and Ledo are small towns with neighboring oil fields, refineries, and tea plantations.

"Our mission has opened two orphanages in the last five years. This region thirsts for Christ's love. Of course, much remains to be done.

"If you haven't been to these beautiful Himalayan foothills, please visit us next winter so that you can see for yourself what the Gauhati Mission is doing. Besides, we have much to discuss."

"Yes, of course. *Delhi Times* will cover your expenses," the editor said. "Your article will be on this strategic border region that played an important part during the war. American and British armed forces had their outposts, armories, and airfields there. Across the border, in Burma, many Allies' soldiers perished fighting the invading Japanese."

Bir thought for a while. "I'm sure Father Gambino wants to discuss conversions and Gandhi's expectations of missionaries."

"Wonderful! And that would be an interesting article."

Land of Rhinos and Elephants

Traveling by train to upper Assam from Gauhati was in itself an adventure for Bir. He had heard of the greenery and wildlife in this province before. He, therefore, constantly looked out of the glass window and examined the long sharp-edged elephant grass, expecting to see wild animals in their habitat. But all he saw that afternoon were jungles and a few hawks gliding the rising columns of warm air. This narrow-gauge train was the main means of transporting tea grown in the region to the auction centers of Calcutta. Soon the coal-fed steam engine reached its maximum speed of 20 mph.

"At this speed, we will reach Tinsukia in less than twenty-four hours," Isa Rahman, the other passenger in Bir's first-class compartment said. "I'm assuming, of course, that rogue elephants and rhinos don't block the tracks when we pass the sanctuary. Without delays, we will be home on time to celebrate our first Republic Day."

Bir remained quiet as he untied his bedroll on his berth and made himself comfortable.

"Rogue elephants and rhinos?" he said finally after wiping his spectacles.

"Didn't you know? Herds of elephants come from the Bhutan hills at this time of the year. They like the ripening paddy. The rhinos and water buffalos of course stick to the swamps while the tigers and deer are elusive. If you don't mind me asking, is this your first trip to Assam?"

"Yes, first trip. I have seen elephants before but never a rhino in the wild."

Working in the tea business made Rahman outgoing and inquisitive. "If you don't mind me asking, where are you from? Where are you going?"

"I'm from Delhi, and I'm visiting the Christian missions."

"I see," he said and nodded his head. He looked closely at his face. It was almost all covered with a woolen scarf. "Yes. People like you are doing a lot to educate children here," he said, assuming Bir to be a Christian missionary because he introduced himself with his first name only.

"I know people take Christian surnames upon conversion. So it's easy to know who is a Christian. In fact, I have a friend who changed his first name from 'Anil' to 'O'Neal' when he converted. He even wore a tie that day," he said and laughed loudly at his own wit.

Bir remained quiet. He didn't laugh. He just kept looking out of the window.

"Of course the same religion-recognition rule applies to many Muslim and Hindu names also," he went on. "For example, my grandfather's name was Rahman. Anyone would know it's a Muslim name. He was born in Chittagong on the mouth of the Ganges. He took a second wife when he came to Assam, a Hindu girl from Sibsagar. My father was born in Jorhat, I in Dibrugarh. The descendants of my grandfather's first wife still live in Chittagong. They are jute merchants. I visit them sometimes." He was full of energy and very talkative. "Am I boring you?"

"No, you are not," Bir said, looking at him. "Yes, the missionaries are doing good work. In these days we have to learn from different cultures and religions to create our own lifestyles."

Rahman nodded his head.

"Your grandmother was Hindu then?" Bir asked after a brief pause.

"Yes, just like Emperor Shah Jahan's mother. She was a Rajput princess, you know," he said and tried not to laugh.

"Are you of royal blood also?" Bir asked with a smile.

"No! No! Not even of Arabian, Afghan, or Turkish," the young man laughed. "I'm a son of the soil of Assam, just like my grandfather who was a son of the deltas. Do you know anything about the people of East Pakistan?"

Rahman didn't wait for an answer. "Many think that Hindus were forcefully converted to Islam during Muslim rule. But this is not entirely correct. Yes, it is true some were, but the majority wasn't."

"Really?"

"Yes. In fact, historians say that the main body of Muslims were Hindus and Buddhists who themselves chose to convert. Some upper-class Hindus converted to gain reward and status. Many chose Islam for the freedom that came with it. For instance, many of the Buddhists, who were mostly peasants, were treated as low castes by the upper-caste Hindus, causing resentment. So they converted in large groups. Village after village converted as a result of communal decisions."

"So Indian Muslims are not all descendants of Afghans, Turks, or Mongols?"

"Another significant and appealing factor is the preaching of the Muslim Sufis. They appeal to the heart through inner devotion to Allah. They teach brotherhood. They are open and inviting to the ones who are dissatisfied with life."

"I like the concept of brotherhood and simplicity in beliefs," Bir said. "How can I learn about the Sufis?"

"You can visit their shrines and places of pilgrimage in Ajmir and Delhi. Even Hindus go there to pray. But I haven't heard of people like you visiting these places."

"People like me?"

"Christians!"

"But I'm a Hindu. Why did you think I'm a Christian?"

"Because you said you are visiting the Christian missions!"

Rahman felt uncomfortable. He forgot that when he was a boy, his father advised him not to assume anything.

"I feel silly," he said awkwardly. "But since you are a modern, educated Hindu, may I ask you a question? With respect, why don't most Hindus eat meat?"

"Meat-eating inflames passions, like anger and rage, which Hindus try to discipline. Besides, meat-eating involves killing."

"That's interesting. I didn't look at it that way. Please tell me why is the cow holy and why is the bull worshipped."

"The cow and the bull are used as symbols. All religions use symbols. For instance, during the crusades to the Holy Lands during the eleventh, twelfth, and thirteenth centuries, crusaders used the Christian cross as a symbol on their shields and armor. They believed that this symbol would make them invincible against Muslim armies. The Muslims used the crescent moon as their symbol. In India, the cow is the symbol of many beliefs. To Gandhi, it's the symbol of nonviolence. To others, cow is a mother, it gives milk. It's also a symbol of abundance. And in Hindu mythology, the bull is 'Nandi,' or Siva's carrier."

"Since Lord Siva is an omnipresent god, why does he need carrying from one place to another?"

Bir smiled and nodded his head. "I see your logic, but remember beliefs aren't based on logic or rationality. Logic can't prove that God speaks to us through angels. Nor can it prove that Christ walked on water or that God's name is Allah or Brahman. But we need beliefs to give meaning and value to our lives, to make sense of—" Before he could complete his sentence, the train came to a screeching halt. The compartment lights started blinking. They heard screams and sound of metal utensils falling in adjoining compartments. Rahman remained calm. He opened the window, popped out his head into the darkness, and looked ahead. "There must be a rough elephant exercising his territorial rights!" he said.

"As long as it isn't Goddess Laksmi's elephant," Bir laughed, trying to conceal his apprehension. After all, he was now sixty-seven and susceptible to cool, humid air. He was glad when Rahman finally closed the window.

Common Enemy

A large flock of snow-white cranes, the size of seagulls, flew over the Tinsukia Catholic Orphanage to feed in the neighboring wetlands that dewy January morning. Bir, Gambino, and Father Fresno were basking in the sun, trying to keep warm, while Father Hilly prepared for the Sunday Mass in the compound's church built long ago by Father Balawan.

Bir looked up at the brightening cloudless blue sky and admired the cranes' aerodynamic flying formation. "How can they fly so close without collisions?" he asked.

"Due to God's omnipresence," Gambino said. "The older I get, the more I appreciate his wonders. Now I see what the poet sees: morning dew crowning blades of grass with sparkling gems. Life is good. I feel closer to Christ." He crossed himself and looked at Bir. "Do you know what I mean?"

Before Bir answered, they heard a man calling from the main gate, "Is Bicycle Padre there?"

Gambino waved him in. "You are a bit early for Mass today, Butu Fishcot. What do you have in your hands?" he asked, noticing something wrapped in gunny.

"A carp, we caught it in the river last night. We want to give it to you and the boys. We couldn't donate anything last month."

"Thank you, Butu. Take it to the kitchen. Lily is there."

"Is Fishcot one of your new converts?" Bir whispered.

"Yes," Gambino said with a smile. "I suppose you would like to know why."

"Why?"

"His name was Butu Bora. He converted to experience Christ's boundless love. He chose Jesus because fishermen were his original disciples." He paused to observe Bir's face. "Upper-caste Hindus treat fishermen as low caste. They say that their souls haven't developed spiritually. Butu wouldn't accept such beliefs. Gandhi taught untouchables their rights. So he came to Christ, and the church accepted him and his family."

"My assignment is to write about missionary work, similar to the one published after World War II. You were quoted in that article, remember? So tell me about the Ledo Catholic Orphanage."

"Ledo took us nearly two years to build. We bought most of the building materials, like bamboo and hay, from the locals. The cement was donated by two tea planters. The Tinsukia parishioners provided free labor."

Bir took out a pad from his pocket and started taking notes.

"And the number of new converts?" he asked without looking up.

"It's difficult to give exact numbers of new converts," Gambino said. "But if you ask me what we need right now, I would say we need money to feed, clothe, and house the growing number of orphans. During the war, a few American soldiers donated blankets and canned food. The boys liked canned fish and oatmeal." He paused for a while and strained his neck to watch a straggly crane in the sky. "I remember a Captain Gary Rowland," he said. "The boys loved him. He always gave them chewing gum and chocolate bars."

"But you must also receive funds from elsewhere to build churches and orphanages."

"That's correct," Gambino said. "Overseas Catholic churches send donations through the archbishop's office for our mission work."

"Do you know what happened in Bengal in 1579?" Bir said, recalling Gandhi's comments on conversion.

"I don't. What happened?"

"Well, that year, during Mughal rule, the Portuguese settled in Hooghly to conduct trade. But they soon became very oppressive and got involved in the slave trade. They captured Hindu and Muslim orphans and converted them to Christianity. Naturally, Emperor Shah Jahan had to deal with the situation. So in 1632, the Portuguese settlements were completely destroyed by his forces. Four thousand Portuguese were taken prisoners."

Gregory's relaxed facial expressions suddenly changed. He felt provoked. He frowned. The veins on his forehead bulged. "Naturally?" He raised his voice. "Are you implying that we use coercion to convert?" He looked at Father Fresno who shifted uncomfortably on his chair. "What we do is according to the legal rights of the citizens. India is a sovereign, democratic republic! Its citizens are free. Yes, free to choose. In fact, the new constitution of India, framing such rights, came into effect on Republic Day."

"Constitution of India?" Bir said and removed the scarf from his head and ears. "Where can I get a copy? I spent Republic Day in the train, you know."

"The *Assam Sun* published an outline of the constitution in its magazine section," Fresno said. "Besides, the archbishop of Calcutta had informed us before that India doesn't have an official state religion and that every person has the right to preach, practice, and propagate any religion."

"Is India a secular country then?" Bir asked in disbelief.

"Well, the word 'secular' doesn't appear in the constitution per se," Fresno said. "But Bishop Le Mans in his recent communiqué from Gauhati stated that many features of the constitution have been adapted from other constitutions, like United States, Canadian, Australian, French, Soviet, and so on."

Bir didn't say anything. He just coughed a few times.

They just sat there quietly. Fresno examined the moist grass with his toes. Finally, the graying priest broke the silence. "Are you thinking of Gandhi's vision where foreign missionaries would come and help Hindus to become better Hindus? Sweet Jesus! The Catholic Church has a two-thousand-year-old mission to proselytize and to save lost souls through the power of the Bible and the risen savior in Christ."

Bir coughed again and clear his throat. The high humidity of the valley bothered him. "Proselytize to save lost souls!" he said and shook his head disapprovingly.

"Why don't the Hindus proselytize?" Gambino asked. "Why do they stay aloof when their brethren suffer? Why don't they accept a non-Hindu into their society when she marries a Hindu? Why must one be born in a Hindu family to be a Hindu?" Gambino was out of breath. "You will do well to look into your own practices first!"

Gambino soon regained his composure. He nervously fingered the beads of the rosary hung around his neck. When he found the crucifix with his thumb and forefinger, he said the Hail Mary prayer inaudibly.

"Would you like to see the results of our work?" Gambino asked. "Would you like to meet a young man who recently accepted Jesus as his savior?"

When Bir didn't reply, Gambino continued, "My friend, I have read *The Discovery of India* by the prime minister. In it he says that 'to call a starving man free is to mock him.' I say that to deny a soul of its right to seek salvation is to deny its very existence."

Bir fumbled with his woolen scarf but finally managed to wrap it around his neck. "Nor must we deny our history to teach us," he said. "Otherwise, we will repeat our follies. Our future must be free of repressions, and we must use the lessons of our past to build our future."

"History is full of mistakes and repressions," Gambino said. "What the Portuguese did was more than three hundred years ago. Muslims subjugated Hindus for six hundred to seven hundred years. Hindus have ostracized Buddhists for more than twelve hundred years. They still practice the thousand-year caste system. But let's live in the present and remember that good religions teach respect. They don't convert by coercion. Only zealots and misled followers do."

"So there is no coercion now as in the past?" Bir wanted a clear statement from the priest.

"A people's progress stems more from social and religious reformation and opportunity to learn," Gambino continued. "Therefore, we must not discourage people when they try to change for the better. Do you remember Noah of the Genesis facing ridicule when he tried to save lives by building the ark?"

Bir nodded his head.

"We must eradicate traditions that are nothing but roadblocks, ones that don't contribute towards liberation," Gambino continued. "My dear Bir, there is more than enough work here for all of us to dispel ignorance. Come, let's share this work, this unique opportunity to love and serve a few souls before our common enemies vanquish them."

Bir turned the pages on his pad and scribbled faster and faster.

"Our common enemies are poverty and ignorance. If you enter a mud hut of an ordinary family, what would you find? Practically nothing! There may be a few pots and utensils, a few bundles of clothes, but there is nothing else. No light, no book, no furniture, no sanitation."

By now Gambino was on the edge of his wooden armchair, leaning closer to Bir. His confidence and inspiration came from his conviction of the justness of his mission.

Bir looked depressed. The weight of his forefathers' sins was too heavy to bear. "Yes," he said meekly. "Yes. You are right. When can I meet this young man you mentioned?"

"Perhaps this afternoon when he comes to tend his godmother's grave."

Manu Thomas

"For two more annas, I'll let you off right in front of Bicycle Padre's house," the lorry driver of the Kajan Tea Estate said while the Digboi Oil pump attendant filled his large tank with forty-eight imperial gallons of petrol. "You know I'm not allowed to pick up riders. I'm to carry tea, plywood containers, and plantation laborers only. But I'm a nice man. I like to help." He smiled, pleased with his own wit as he jingled the coins in his pocket.

"All right, I'll give you one more anna, but that's all," Manu asserted as he climbed the lorry's rear wooden platform and sat beside four other passengers.

"Why are you going to Bicycle Padre's house?" one asked.

"Because that's my home. I grew up there."

"You are a Christian then?"

Manu nodded.

"Really? Why did you become a Christian?"

Manu ignored the question.

The driver rumbled through the potholes and accelerated, jolting the huddled passengers. He had to be back at the plantation before noon.

"Is it true?" asked another.

"What is true?"

The man pointed at Manu's genitals. "You know what I mean."

"No, I don't know what you mean."

"He wants to know if they cut off a piece of it when you became Christian," the third said.

"No! No!" Manu said with disgust as he moved his wiry body to the other side of the platform and sat alone. The four laughed.

"You shouldn't laugh at things you don't understand," Manu said. The four looked at one another and became quiet. One pulled out a half-smoked cigarette from his breast pocket, lit it, and started puffing. Then he shared it with his companions.

As the lorry bumped its way, he remembered worrying about his Baptism the previous year. Gambino had comforted him, "You have nothing to fear, Manu. Jesus was himself baptized by John the Baptist in the Jordan before he began his mission. Baptism is necessary for salvation. Through it, Catholics become members of the church and share in its mission."

Manu thought of his godparents. He thought of Mrs. Simpson, of Tubull Thomas. Though Tubull wasn't much older than him, he wanted to help Manu grow in the faith. Mrs. Simpson made him very happy when she agreed to be his godmother. From the time he came to the orphanage, he always imagined her to be his mother. He remembered asking Gambino what happens when he is immersed in water.

"Baptism is one of the seven sacraments. The immersion is symbolic of death and rebirth. You as the baptized person die in the water, and you are then reborn in Christ. It's like Jesus dying on the cross and then resurrecting."

Manu had asked him if he would be given a Christian surname like Tubull's. He said he liked the name "Thomas." This name made him feel closer to the church and to Tubull—his friend and adopted brother.

Five months after his baptism, Mrs. Simpson died. Tubull, the three priests, and he were at her bedside while the other orphans waited and prayed in the yard. As he knelt beside her bed to pay his last respects to the woman he loved as his mother, he promised secretly that as long as he can, he will tend her grave for the love she showed him when he was a helpless orphan.

Football

Manu got off the lorry and entered the orphanage. In front of the church with its plastered walls painted white with lime, he saw a group of boisterous boys playing football with a fist-size rubber ball. When they saw him, they stopped playing. Two little boys, one with a runny nose, rushed toward him and grabbed his hands. "Are you going to play with us?" one asked. "Did you bring the leather football? Did you?" the other asked excitedly.

"No, I didn't. But I'll—I promise."

"You said the same thing last week," a gangly barefooted boy in a torn vest and a scar on his left cheek said. "Have you spoken with Tubull yet? He said both of you would put your money together and buy us a cricket bat."

"I went to the bazaar, Dhon," he said. "I priced the balls and bats. They are very expensive, but as soon as I save enough, I'll get them for you, the football first and the bat second." He kept walking toward Mrs. Simpson's grave. It was next to Father Balawan's under the old teak.

He picked two large white dahlias from the bunch that bloomed near the three-foot tall statue of the Blessed Virgin Mary near the entrance to the church. As he looked at the rosary in her right hand and smelt the flowers, he heard Bicycle Padre calling him. "After you are done, come and meet someone here who is waiting for you."

Manu could think of no one who would come to meet him. He already paid the Digboi Oil Refinery maintenance contractor for the sleeping space he rented from him. He liked working for him as an assistant carpenter. Singh was a master carpenter and bricklayer before he got the senior position of contractor. Howard Witt, the British general manager himself, hired him, or so he claimed. Singh always paid him on time. Once he asked him why he became a carpenter. "Because Jesus was a carpenter," Manu replied, to which Singh didn't say anything.

After picking the few weeds that had grown with his rusted trowel that he kept near the grave, he knelt beside the tombstone that read, "Sharon Simpson 1898-1949." He then placed the dahlias gently on the headstone and said a prayer. "I don't have roses for you today, Mrs. Simpson, but I know you like all types of flowers. I know you are in heaven now because you were good and kind. I'm doing well as a carpenter. I'll come back next Sunday, and I'll have a few roses for you. May Christ bless you." The seventeen-year-old then stood up and wiped his tears with the back of his soiled hands.

Bir and Gambino were waiting for him in Mrs. Simpson's old room. It was now used as a multipurpose room and looked very different to Manu. Her bookcase was gone. There were no signs of her potted rose plants he used to water or the anatomic pictures on the walls. He tried not to remember them, but somehow he couldn't help feeling that the room still belonged to her.

"Manu Thomas, this is Bir Dharma. He is a reporter from a Delhi paper. He's visiting us to write an article about life in a Catholic orphanage. Since you are here today, I thought he should meet you."

Bir smiled and greeted him. "How are you?" But Manu avoided his eyes. He looked away. "Where are Mrs. Simpson's things? Where is her picture as a young nurse?"

"We stored them for now. But they will be used by Mother Rita when she arrives after the monsoons."

"Mother Rita?"

"Yes. She is from Madras. The bishop said she could teach Mrs. Simpson's class. Besides, she is also a seamstress. Someday, she may open a girls' orphanage."

Manu looked for the table where Mrs. Simpson kept her first aid book. He didn't seem to be interested in looking at Bir.

"How are you, Manu?" Bir tried again.

"It's difficult for me to think that Mrs. Simpson is no more," his voice quivered. "Why must good people always die?"

Gambino got up from his chair and placed his right hand on Manu's shoulder. "Only through death we can be with Christ, Manu. She is in heaven now. Someday we will meet her again."

The thought of meeting her again comforted him. He looked at Bir. "I'm fine, sir."

When Manu appeared reassured, Gambino left the room.

Charity of the Poor

It didn't take long for Manu to tell his life's story. He talked about why he became a carpenter, about his dreams and plans to donate storybooks to orphans and build brick houses for the poor. He talked about how his father died of smallpox when no one at the village could help him, how Bicycle Padre gave him a bag of rice and brought him to the orphanage where Mrs. Simpson taught him to read and write and do arithmetic.

"Are you still angry with the villagers who wanted to burn your house after your father died?"

"Not anymore."

"Why not?"

"Bicycle Padre taught me that to be able to see God, I have to be pure at heart. To be pure, I must not judge, be angry, or kill. Then in heaven, I'll see my sister, my father, and Mrs. Simpson."

"You didn't mention your mother?"

"I told you she died giving birth to me!" Manu raised his voice. "I didn't even know her!"

"Yes, you are right. I'm sorry. Tell me which Bible story you like the most?"

"When I was young, I liked the story of David slaying Goliath, like the story of Rama slaying Ravana that my father told me."

"How old are you now?"

"Bicycle Padre thinks I'm sixteen or seventeen. I must have been around nine or ten when he found me."

"I remember when I was seventeen. I began a pilgrimage with two friends. Those were good days."

"Where were you seven years ago?"

"I was in Delhi, writing for the papers."

"Seven years ago I was alone and starving," he said with resentment. "If the missionaries weren't to find me, I could have died."

For some reason, Bir felt uneasy. In fact, he felt guilty. "Besides Jesus Christ and carpentry, what else did they teach that really changed you and made you a better person?"

"In Digboi, I watch rich people play cricket. They wear clean white shirts, pants, and boots. When they hit the ball over the fence into the thorny bushes, they often ask me to find the ball for them. I do. Sometimes I think of hiding the ball and then bring it here for the boys. But Christ tells us not to steal."

"That's very good. Tell me what more you know of Jesus Christ."

"He is the Son of God, and he loves us. He said that if we just believe in him, he will save us." Manu paused abruptly and stared at Bir with his unwavering dark brown eyes. "Why do you ask such difficult questions? Before I say more of Jesus, tell me how your newspaper story will help us?"

"Readers will know about your orphanage."

"What will happen then? Will they know how much loneliness and rejection hurt? Will they know how hunger hurts? Will they know that a single piece of gold ornament that a rich lady wears around her neck in Digboi can change the lives of the thirty-three boys in this orphanage? Will they have more food because you write?"

Bir felt Manu's long-suppressed emotions about to erupt. He had to think fast. To save the moment, he tried a reward. "What will you do if the newspaper gives you fifty rupees for talking with me?"

His eyes widened. His mouth fell open. "Fifty rupees? That's a lot of money! I'm paid less than that in a month!"

Bir smiled and remained quiet. He cleared his throat as he scribbled some notes.

"It will be best if you give the money to Bicycle Padre. Give it to him and ask him to buy a football and a cricket bat for the boys. Dhon needs a shirt also."

"Why, don't you want the money?"

"Of course I want the money, but the boys need it more," he said as he ended the session and hurried toward the door. He then stopped, turned, and faced Bir.

"Go ahead, go ahead and ask. Why don't you ask what you wanted to ask all this time?"

"Ask what?"

"Ask why I became Christian—just like many of you do with your eyes."

Surprised at Manu's sudden change in behavior, Bir could only comply. "We all need to change to become what we want to become. You have shown your ability to change your mind, to adapt to new situations, and to grow. This is wonderful."

Manu glanced at the four corners of the cluttered room as if searching for Mrs. Simpson's ghost to help him. "I changed because no one loved or cared. But Bicycle Padre did." After a slight pause, he said, "Will you, after you leave Tinsukia?" Before Bir could answer, Manu left the room.

Volunteer

The day before Bir returned to Delhi, he asked Gambino for directions to the telegraph and post office. He wanted to send a telegram to his editor.

"It's opposite the police station," Gambino said. "If I were you, I would take a rickshaw."

At the telegraph office, Bir saw a long line of people waiting patiently for the service window to open.

"When will it open?" Bir asked the man standing last in line.

"It should have opened long ago," he answered without looking at him.

Bir checked his watch and stood behind him. When the line didn't move, he went to the front and knocked on the wooden window bolted to an iron frame with vertical rods. No one opened it. He tried again to no avail. He then went to the closed door that showed the office hours and banged on it with his fist.

"Coming, coming," he heard a voice.

A man with puffed rice crumbs stuck on his lips opened the door slightly and peeped out. "Yes?" he said calmly as if unaware of the long line of waiting customers.

"Why isn't the window open?" Bir demanded. "Don't you know your own office hours?" Bir went back to the end of the line.

"No, no, sahib," a grateful man in line said. "You deserve to be in front. You got them to open the window."

Bir stood where he was and waited his turn. As the line crawled forward, a man accompanied by a woman wearing silver ornaments around her neck and wrists approached him.

"We saw, sahib. We saw what you did," he said haltingly. "Will you write this for us? We don't know writing."

Bir got out of line and filled out the money order form to transmit thirty-two rupees to an addressee in Bihar province. He used the counter of the adjoining window to rest the form. As soon as he was done, two other men standing in line approached him.

"If I weren't here today, who would fill out your forms?"

They looked at each other and shrugged their shoulders.

"If I come here every Saturday morning to write forms, will it help people who don't know writing?"

They fidgeted and laughed nervously. They weren't sure if they understood him.

"Well, will it help?"

"Why will you do that? We are ordinary people. We don't make enough to pay someone like you."

"But if I do it free—as a volunteer—will it help?"

They looked at the long line and whispered to each other. "If that's your pleasure, sahib, we will be grateful," one said. "But why volunteer?"

"Because if you help others by volunteering, you help yourself," Bir said. "Gandhiji told us that service to man is service to God."

"So helping others is like a prayer then?"

"Yes."

"Ah, I see," the man said. He smiled and nodded his head. "Can I volunteer?"

"No, no, you can't," his friend said without hesitation. "You are just a gardener. You don't know writing."

His friend's smile faded quickly. He looked away.

"Of course you can volunteer," Bir said. "Anyone can volunteer. A good *mali* can grow both vegetables and flowers. What do you grow best?"

"Orchids. I also graft them and grow different varieties. The flowers are of many colors. My employer-sahib sends my potted orchids to his country in planes," he said proudly while his friend remained quiet and looked at his own dust-covered bare feet.

"See, all of us know something important to share with others," Bir said.

The orchid grower grinned and looked at his friend. "So can you, Naman."

PART H

Proposal to Empower

"IT'S TRUE, REENA," Bir said at her office after his return from the Himalayan foothills. "The Kingdom of God is within us, just like the source of our strength is in us. Manu Thomas convinced me that love, faith, and hope are the basis for empowering."

She looked at his tired, wrinkled face as he sat across her glass-topped table, checking his notes.

"We develop self-esteem when we think well of ourselves," he said. "Look at what Father Gambino did: he taught Manu to have faith in Christ's love and hope. This empowered him."

She listened to the self-educated man whom she had grown to love and respect.

"If we can help our mistreated and neglected people to develop self-worth, many societal abuses will end. So instead of writing an article on missionary activities, I want to write a proposal to encourage the strong among us to give and empower the weak."

"Give and empower the weak?" Reena tried to understand.

"The concept of giving and empowering is nothing new. Let's look at history. When Emperor Constantine I closed pagan temples in the fourth century, the church began giving to the destitute and created hope for them. Previously, they depended on the largesse of wealthy pagan temples. This giving was the beginning of organized Christian charity that still exists today.

"Seven hundred years before Constantine, Asoka of India built hospitals throughout his empire to treat and give hope to the sick and injured. In fact, he was the first emperor in the world to promote veterinary medicine and build animal care centers."

"But how will empowering help the mistreated?"

"If you empower yourself through introspection and realistic reasoning, you'll assume the responsibility to make yourself strong and worthy. You'll then stand up for your rights and those of others."

"How will you promote such a culture?"

"I'll appeal to the socially conscious and create opportunities for them to organize and take ownership of the ways and means of empowering. A community will give for such a cause."

"Why should a community give?"

"Because all of us strive for happiness in life and helping others generates happiness. We all want to do something good to make the world a bit better before we die. Besides, involvement generates feelings of belonging and confidence."

Bir looked sure of himself. He sipped the steaming tea that Reena poured for him.

"For fifty years I traveled the width and breadth of India, exploring beliefs, meeting many good and wise people, seeking their wisdom, becoming 'educated' and 'modern.' Yet I don't remember meeting someone like Manu—a young lost orphan raised by Christian missionaries who is now an icon of charity, hope, and volunteerism."

Bir coughed again. "He asked me where I was seven years ago when his father died and he was alone and hungry. All I could do was hang my head in shame. People like me failed him. But Father Gambino didn't. He was there for him."

"He was there," Reena said gently, "because he is a missionary and because his Catholic Church is the oldest and largest organization on earth. It's like a global corporation with structure, resources, and mission. It supports Gambino's work."

She refilled his teacup as he looked out of the window.

"He establishes orphanages and churches in remote places," Bir went on. "He devotes his entire life to help others. Look at Mother Teresa. She heard her call to missionary work at seventeen! And two years ago, the Vatican permitted her to leave the Sisters of Loreto to work in the slums."

Bir began speaking faster and faster as if he was running out of time.

"Why can't we?" His voice was hoarse. "I'm sure we have caring and practical people who will get involved as they did during the freedom struggle. Instead of churches, mosques, temples, or other places of worship, let's establish secular centers to empower ordinary people. Let's offer guidance and counseling on self-development, human rights, and constitutional guarantees. Let's promote understanding and respect amongst ourselves to eliminate ignorance and zealotry abuses. After all, reform takes place only if the ordinary people can understand and live with it."

She was impressed by what she heard. "Please go on," she said.

"Let's call them 'Empowering and Counseling Centers.' The empowering segment would offer seminars and workshops for self-improvement, self-transformation, and self-esteem. The counseling segment would offer group and individual sessions to fill the voids and hopelessness we sometimes experience in life. The intent would be to discuss, reexamine, rethink, and understand anew old customs to eradicate ignorance, poverty, superstition, and hopelessness.

"Those who attend must be taught that they are capable of being responsible for their own decisions, actions, and lives, that they are somebody worthy who can make a difference, and that they have rights to question misused authority and exploitative, suppressive traditions.

"In my life," Bir continued, "I discovered that all good religions encourage love, mercy, and hope. We also see God the way we want to believe. Some believe in an authoritarian God who can be angry and punitive. Some believe in a benevolent God involved in our daily lives. Others believe it to be aloof, uninvolved, and not personal but a cosmic force with natural laws for us to discover and live by, while some believe it to be beyond our comprehension. But they are all beliefs—beliefs to better ourselves and give meaning to our lives.

"In diverse and secular India, beliefs are many, paths are many. Our mission won't be to proselytize or promote one faith over another. Our mission will be to defeat our common enemy: ignorance. Keep in mind that ignorance is a kin of poverty. Therefore, I propose establishing community centers where mature and skilled volunteers will invest their resources—like knowledge, time, money—to offer counseling on life's challenges."

She listened attentively. "Where will we find these counselors?"

"From ourselves. The community centers will select their own knowledgeable people as counselors."

"How can ones like me become members?"

"By sharing your knowledge or giving money to rent or build centers like the small churches and orphanages I saw.

"When necessary, a highly skilled volunteer of one center will train counselors from other centers also. A counselor will be mature, like a wise retiree, who has experienced life's turpitudes and strongly believes that ordinary people can do extraordinary things—if given the chance. Of course, we will work out details later. Besides, we can always learn about volunteerism and how to organize charitable work from the Catholic Church."

"Learn from Catholics?" She was amused.

"We should always learn compassion and goodness from all, irrespective of the source, just like Christianity did from Judaism and Buddhism from Hinduism. And why shouldn't we? If we can accept Western science, systems of administration, education, health, and trade to develop our living standard, if we can accept constitutional directives of other nations to guide our rulers, why can't we adopt voluntarism from the Catholic Church or others for the betterment of our people?"

"What does 'goodness from all' mean?"

"'Goodness from all' means duty and pluralism as taught by Lord Krishna, commandments and community responsibility as taught by Hebrew prophets, compassion and ego conquest as taught by the Buddha, mercy and love as taught by Jesus Christ, charity and surrender to God as taught by the Sufis, brotherhood and equality as taught by Prophet Muhammad, and courage and discipline as taught by Guru Nanak."

"And what will be the essence of these empowerment centers?"

"Understanding, respect, and hope."

"You didn't mention faith."

"I didn't mention faith because faith alone, by itself, doesn't always offer guidance on modern education, wealth generation and distribution, poverty eradication, human rights, women and children rights, constitutional guarantees, parliamentary democracy, or law and justice. Besides, we already have many worshipping places."

"And what will we do after the proposal is published?"

"Depending on readers' responses, I'll initially visit colleges and universities throughout the country and appeal to their social sciences faculty and students for their involvement and leadership. With faculty guidance, students will have opportunities to establish and serve these centers. They will also receive hands-on, career-related work experience that may lead them to future political leadership."

She looked at him, smiled, and nodded. "You know, this may work."

We Are What We Think and Do

Within a month after Bir's publication, the *Delhi Times* editor received nearly three hundred letters expressing need for such community centers. Some wrote neatly in script on white lined paper, others in a feverish scrawl on tattered scraps of parchment. Most signed their letters, while a few didn't.

A retired military officer volunteered to teach self-discipline and team effort. A dentist offered to speak on dental health. A law professor and her students offered legal advice. A banker wanted to speak about how to use a bank. An unwed mother wrote a heartbreaking letter seeking advice as to how to make the baby's father marry her. Another needed information on starting a small business. A student wanted to find ways to deal with the unrealistic expectations of his parents. A young bride wrote about contemplating suicide because her whiskey-loving husband didn't want anything to do with her. An unsigned letter wanted relief from incest.

"They are from all segments of society," Reena said. "They are clamoring for self-transformation and self-empowerment. So let's begin. Let's invite community elders and the local academics to our auditorium for the first seminar."

"I'll invite Professors Islam Malik and Ram Singh to chair the seminar," Bir said excitedly. "Yes, we will empower ourselves and become enlightened and worthy. I know we can," he reassured himself as he remembered the old ascetic saying "We are neither good nor bad but we become what we think and do."

—END—

reincarnation?
caste system